THE EISENSTEIN READER

THE EISENSTEIN READER

Edited by Richard Taylor

Translated by Richard Taylor and
William Powell

 Publishing

First published in 1998 by the
British Film Institute
21 Stephen Street
London W1P 2LN

This collection copyright © British Film Institute 1998
Introduction and notes
copyright © Richard Taylor 1998
Translations © Richard Taylor and William Powell

The British Film Institute is the UK national agency with responsibility for encouraging the arts of
film and television and conserving them in the national interest.

Cover design: Swerlybird Art & Design
Cover image: (front) Sergei Eisenstein and *The Battleship Potemkin*; (back) Sergei Eisenstein,
Mexico, 1929 – 'Speaks for itself and makes people jealous!'

Set in 10/12pt Minion by Fakenham Photosetting Limited, Fakenham, Norfolk, Norfolk NR21 8NL
Printed in Great Britain by St Edmunsbury Press, Bury St Edmunds

British Library Cataloguing-in-Publication Data
A catalogue record for this book is available from the British Library
ISBN 0–85170–675–4 hbk
ISBN 0–85170–676–2 pbk

Contents

Note on Transliteration and Translation   vi

Eisenstein: A Soviet Artist   1
Richard Taylor

  1 The Montage of Attractions (1923)   29

  2 The Montage of Film Attractions (1924)   35

  3 The Problem of the Materialist Approach to Form (1925)   53

  4 Constanța (Whither *The Battleship Potemkin*) (1926)   60

  5 Eisenstein on Eisenstein, the Director of *Potemkin* (1926)   64

  6 Béla Forgets the Scissors (1926)   67

  7 Our *October*. Beyond the Played and the Non-Played (1928)   73

  8 Statement on Sound (1928): Eisenstein, Pudovkin and Alexandrov   80

  9 Beyond the Shot (1929)   82

10 The Dramaturgy of Film Form (The Dialectical Approach to Film Form) (1929)   93

11 The Fourth Dimension in Cinema (1929)   111

12 'Eh!' On the Purity of Film Language (1934)   124

13 The Mistakes of *Bezhin Meadow* (1937)   134

14 Alexander Nevsky and the Rout of the Germans (1938)   140

15 The Problems of the Soviet Historical Film (1940)   145

16 Stalin, Molotov and Zhdanov on *Ivan the Terrible, Part Two* (1947)   160

17 From Lectures on Music and Colour in *Ivan the Terrible* (1947)   167

Notes   187

Index   209

Note on Transliteration and Translation

Transliteration from the Cyrillic to the Latin alphabet presents many problems and no system will resolve them all. Perhaps the most important is the difficulty of reconciling the two principal requirements of transliteration: on the one hand the need to convey to the non-Russian-speaking reader a reasonable approximation of the original Russian pronunciation, and on the other the necessity of rendering for the specialist an accurate representation of the original Russian spelling. There is a further complication in that some Russian names have a non-Russian origin or an accepted English spelling that takes little heed of the two requirements just mentioned. We have therefore used two systems of transliteration in this edition. In the main text and in the index we have used the generally accepted spellings of proper names (such as Alexander Nevsky) or the spellings that reflect their linguistic origins (such as Meyerhold, Strauch and, indeed, Eisenstein), whereas in the endnotes we have attempted to cater for the needs of the Russian-speaking specialist. There the names listed above will be found as Aleksandr Nevskii, Meierkhol'd, Shtraukh and Eizenshtein. There are inevitably some inconsistencies in this practice but we hope that the system we have adopted will clarify rather than confuse the issue.

Eisenstein was unfortunately not always consistent in his use of key terms and the reader should bear this in mind. In this and other volumes the editor and translator have offered a particular version of a particular term but some degree of ambiguity, if not downright confusion, must always remain. When talking about 'plot' Eisenstein, like other Russian writers of the time, distinguishes between *fabula* and *syuzhet*, which we have normally rendered as 'story' and 'plot' respectively. Naum Kleiman, consultant editor on this edition, has offered the following distinction:

> *fabula*: a Formalist concept, the structure of events, what actually happened, the facts.
> *syuzhet*: everything connected with the characters, all the associations, motivations, etc. Formalist critics also used the term to include technical aspects of film-making, such as lighting, camera angle, shot composition and montage.

Other problematic words include the following, and the reader is strongly advised to bear the alternatives constantly in mind:

> *kadr*: shot or frame
> *kusok*: piece or fragment or sequence of montage

material: material or raw material

montazh: montage or editing, the arrangement of the shots, frames or sequences through cutting. In Eisenstein's view, as in the view of others, it was *montazh* that distinguished the specificity of cinema as opposed to related art forms such as theatre, literature or painting.

To minimise the risk of confusion, the original Russian word is occasionally given in square brackets thus, [...], in the text.

Lastly, Russian does not have either an indefinite or a definite article and it is a moot point whether one sometimes needs to be supplied in the English translation. We have preferred *The Strike* to *Strike* as a translation of the title of Eisenstein's film *Stachka*, *The Battleship Potemkin* to *Battleship Potemkin* for *Bronenosets Potemkin*, and so on. We have done this in the hope of clarifying the meaning of the original Russian title for the English-speaking reader.

Documents 1–12 were translated by Richard Taylor, 13–17 by William Powell. Minor alterations have been made to some of the previously published versions. Eisenstein's own comments are rendered as footnotes with editorial comments as endnotes.

Eisenstein: A Soviet Artist
Richard Taylor

The master

'I lived, I contemplated, I admired.'
Eisenstein, 1944[1]

Eisenstein has become a myth. He has been acclaimed as a genius, as the greatest film-maker of all time, as the maker of the greatest film of all time (*The Battleship Potemkin*), and as one of the great philosophers of art of our century. More has been written about him than about any other film director and he himself wrote more than any other film director both about his own work and about cinema as a medium and as an art form.[2] It is the purpose of this collection to bring together in a single affordable volume the key shorter film-related writings that illuminate the background to his films. For reasons of space the longer writings on montage contained in the second volume of the BFI Eisenstein edition, *Towards A Theory of Montage*, including those relating specifically to his later films, have had to be omitted.

Because of his prominence, if not his eminence, Eisenstein has also been virulently attacked: most notoriously as a formalist and dilettante in the Soviet Union of the 1930s,[3] and as a Party hack or 'red dog' introducing the bacillus of the Bolshevik plague into the United States of the 1930s[4] – a fear that was obviously rather widespread at that time, because Eisenstein must have been expelled from more countries than any other European artist of the 20th century.

But he has also been attacked on artistic grounds for the perceived 'totalitarianism' of his montage theory, most notably by Andrey Tarkovsky, who in *Sculpting in Time* remarks:

> I reject the principles of 'montage cinema' because they do not allow the film to continue beyond the edges of the screen: they do not allow the audience to bring personal experience to bear on what is in front of them on film ... Eisenstein makes thought into a despot: it leaves no 'air', nothing of that unspoken elusiveness which is perhaps the most captivating quality of all art, and which makes it possible for an individual to relate to a film.[5]

In this Introduction I want to try to rescue Eisenstein from both his most fervent hagiographers and his most virulent detractors by tracing, as far as I can, the developing relationship between his writings, his films and his life as a leading Soviet artist, widely acknowledged by his colleagues through the epithet 'the Master'.

The little boy from Riga

Sergei Mikhailovich Eisenstein was born in Riga, then part of the Russian Empire and now capital of independent Latvia, on 23 January 1898.[6] His father was the city

1

architect and engineer Mikhail Osipovich Eisenstein, of German-Jewish descent. Eisenstein came to associate his father with all forms of repression. None the less it was from his library that he discovered Victor Hugo, Alexandre Dumas, Emile Zola and Honoré Daumier. His mother, Yulia Ivanovna Konetskaya, came from an established St Petersburg merchant family who felt that she had married beneath her. When they divorced in 1909,[7] she returned to St Petersburg and it was there that Eisenstein discovered her unusual taste in other authors – the Marquis de Sade, Octave Mirbeau and Leopold Sacher-Masoch[8] – who were to help to liberate his own imagination and eventually to free him from the dominance of his father.

As a child, Eisenstein attended the German *Realschule* in Riga, which was at that time a predominantly German-speaking port. He spoke German before he spoke Russian, and he never spoke more than a few words of Latvian, which was then scarcely recognised as an official language. In some senses he was a child of the colonial class, an outsider in an outpost of German culture in a Russian state. As the only child of a broken home, his sense of isolation was intensified. His escape route lay in books,[9] above all those that he had discovered in his parents' respective libraries, which opened up the world to him so that, while he may have been then, and remained later, in many ways an isolated outsider in his own country in his own time, he also became an intellectual citizen of the world, drawing his inspiration now from Freud or G. K. Chesterton, now from Chinese theatre *en travestie* or Japanese watercolours, now from so-called primitive images of the deity or Mexican notions of religious ecstasy, both Christian and pre-Christian.

In 1915 Eisenstein graduated from school with his best marks in religious studies. Making use of his childhood talent for drawing,[10] and still following in his father's footsteps, he enrolled as a student at the Petrograd Institute of Civil Engineering, while at the same time living with his mother in her apartment. This 'double life' continued for two years, and it was only the October Revolution of 1917, with the final overthrow of the *ancien régime* and the subsequent closure of the Institute,[11] that gave him the decisive opportunity to escape from what he perceived as the oppressive influence of his father, 'a pillar of the Church and the autocracy':[12] some of his drawings at the time depict Saturn devouring his own children. As his father volunteered for the Whites, so his now no longer so 'obedient child'[13] enrolled in the Red Army, devouring, as it were, the memory of his own father.[14] It was during this military service in the ensuing Civil War of 1918–21 that Eisenstein first began to work regularly on stage, largely as a designer of sets and costumes.[15] It was also then that he jotted down a note in his diary asking himself why he always felt it necessary to 'wear a mask'.[16]

He never forgot this debt to the Revolution, even during the time of troubles that overshadowed the last decade and a half of his life. These and many other influences informed his films and his writings, and indeed his approach to both, from his first published article in 1922 to the very moment of his death twenty-six years later.[17]

From stage to screen

The draughtsmanship that took Eisenstein into set design in the Red Army also enabled him to find similar employment in the newly established Proletkult

Theatre in Moscow when he was demobilised in 1920.[18] His first design for Proletkult was for a stage adaptation of Jack London's *The Mexican*: the costumes were Cubist and for one scene the theatre space was converted into a boxing ring.[19] During this production Eisenstein was studying with the innovative theatre director Vsevolod Meyerhold, whom he was later to describe as his 'spiritual father'.[20] He took Meyerhold to see *The Mexican* and 'teacher' approved. For a time Meyerhold's studio occupied the same building as the workshop grouped around Lev Kuleshov and this proximity helped to expose Eisenstein for the first time to Kuleshov's pioneering work on montage as the element defining cinema's specificity and its autonomy from theatre. It also exposed him to the 'films without film' methods of the workshop and to the notion of the *naturshchik* or 'model actor'.[21]

Eisenstein was part of a general influx of young people into post-Revolutionary Soviet cultural life: the October Revolution not only broke down the old social, economic and political order, it also overthrew the traditional notions of art and of the arts. The torch was passed to a new generation who took new revolutionary content for granted and were therefore primarily concerned to seek out new forms with which to express that revolutionary content: it was the primacy of this concern that was later to lay them open to the charge of 'Formalism', of being more interested in form rather than the revolutionary content that they took for granted.

If one thing characterises the avant-garde Soviet artists of the 1920s it is the relative ease with which they moved from one art form to another, from literature to scriptwriting, from painting to set design – in Eisenstein's case from sketching through set design and stage direction eventually to film-making – and this in turn helps to explain the ease with which they drew upon the techniques of those various art forms to enhance the effectiveness of their own activity in one particular art form. It was Eisenstein's association with the Petrograd-based Factory of the Eccentric Actor (FEKS) that convinced him of the utility of circus forms.[22] In the FEKS manifesto of 1922 Grigori Kozintsev demanded 'art without a capital letter, a pedestal or a fig-leaf',[23] while Leonid Trauberg denounced 'serious people in galoshes' and argued:

> The slogan of their time is: 'Revolution brings tasteful art out of the palaces and on to the streets!' ... From the streets into the palaces with the revolution! The streets bring revolution to art. Our street mud is now circus, cinema, music-hall, Pinkerton.[24]

These preoccupations are reflected in Eisenstein's first published article, written in November 1922 with Sergei Yutkevich.[25] They held up the techniques of the circus (Eccentrism), of the detective story (Pinkerton), and of Chaplin as models for emulation: indeed, it was Chaplin who was credited with having given cinema 'the eighth seat in the Council of the Muses', of having, in other words, 'moved from the streets into the palaces with the revolution'. The streets had indeed brought revolution to art.

The influence of Eccentrism was just as strong in 'The Montage of Attractions', Eisenstein's first major theoretical work, published in 1923 while he was working on *The Wise Man*, his stage adaptation of the classic Russian drama which included his first film, the short parody *Glumov's Diary*.[26] Although Eisenstein's concern here was with the methods by which *theatre* could be made more effective, many of the arguments deployed were later to be applied to *cinema*, when theatre's limitations had proved all too apparent. He argued that 'the moulding of the audience in a desired direction (or mood) is the task of every utilitarian theatre'. Hence Tarkovsky's critique mentioned earlier. But, whereas in the FEKS manifesto Kozintsev proposed a hegemony of the new 'low' art forms to the exclusion of the traditional 'high' forms, encapsulated in the slogan, 'We prefer Charlie's arse to Eleonore Duse's hand's,'[27] Eisenstein was prepared to use whatever was most *effective*, and this flexibility helps to explain the continuing development of his montage theory over the next two decades:

> all the parts that constitute the apparatus of theatre (Ostuzhev's 'chatter' no more than the colour of the prima donna's tights, a roll on the drums just as much as Romeo's soliloquy, the cricket on the hearth no less than a salvo under the seats of the auditorium) because, despite their differences, they all lead to one thing – which their presence legitimates – to their common quality of *attraction*.

The concept of attractions was central to Eisenstein's early montage theory and was to recur in different guises throughout his later career. The ends justified the means and for Eisenstein the end was always *ultimately* ideological (in the broadest sense of conveying an idea), even if it was frequently expressed in aesthetic terms:

> An attraction . . . is any aggressive moment in theatre, i.e. any element of it that subjects the audience to emotional or psychological influence, verified by experience and mathematically calculated to produce specific emotional shocks in the spectator in their proper order within the whole. These shocks provide the only opportunity of perceiving the ideological aspect of what is being shown, the final ideological conclusion.

The attraction was 'an independent and primary element in structuring the show': it derived its coherence from the perception of the 'final ideological conclusion' that it facilitated. He was later to describe the 'attraction' as 'the mathematical calculation of . . . effect', reflecting the influence of his training with Meyerhold and the notion of 'biomechanics'.[28]

Eisenstein, like his FEKS colleagues, was, however, becoming increasingly frustrated with the limitations of theatre: his final drama production, of Sergei Tretyakov's *Gas Masks* in the Moscow gas works during working hours, has been described by Yon Barna:

> . . . the final scene was timed to coincide with the entry of actual night-shift workers, who took over from the actors and set about lighting their fires as a grand finale to the show. The pitfalls soon became all too evident, however: not only was the work of the gasworks being seriously disrupted, but the audience did not take kindly to the effects of the evil-smelling gas.[29]

Eisenstein himself later recalled this transition from theatre to cinema, which he described as 'the next dimension of means of expression':

> The broadening of the palette, the inclusion of real objects, of genuine elements of reality, was one of the key tendencies of the time. Setting a play in a gasworks was

naturally to move across to a means of expression such as a gasworks, and not just a gasworks but also its surroundings, and the street, the town and the country in our [theatricalised] spectacle. [Hence] it provided a perfectly natural exit to another means of expression – to cinema, which could seize the gasworks by the scruff of the neck and shove it wherever it was needed, without any stink of gas.[30]

Eisenstein therefore 'crawled out of the whole mess of potage and on to the screen'.[31] From then on 'The Montage of Attractions' became essentially 'The Montage of Film Attractions'.

The montage of film attractions

Eisenstein's first full-length film was *The Strike*, made for Proletkult in the course of 1924. A dispute over the authorship of the screenplay led to an acrimonious divorce.[32] While the film was in production, Eisenstein reiterated the purpose of the attraction in the second document in this collection, 'The Montage of Film Attractions', which was not published until after his death:

> An attraction ... is in our understanding any demonstrable fact (an action, an object, a phenomenon, a conscious combination, and so on) that is known and proven to exercise a definite effect on the attention and emotions of the audience and that, combined with others, possesses the characteristic of concentrating the audience's emotions in any direction dictated by the production's purpose.

Without this overarching purpose, the independent and primary elements would fall apart, as Eisenstein felt they did in the work of Dziga Vertov and the Cine-Eyes, which he characterised at this stage as a mere 'montage of separate sequences'.[33] Each montage element, each attraction had to contribute towards the total effect of the work. These attractions worked on the audience's psyche through their associations and through chains of such associations: the effect of each attraction depended to a great extent on its montage context, on the relationship between each individual shot and its internal associations and between those and the associations of the shots that surrounded it. Eisenstein chose the slaughter sequence from *The Strike* to illustrate his point.

In 'The Montage of Film Attractions' Eisenstein also broached the problem of the role of the script in film-making. Given his experiences in making *The Strike* and those he was shortly to have with *The Battleship Potemkin*, it is perhaps hardly surprising to find him describing the script as 'a "prescription" that summarises the general projected emotional effect on the audience and the pressure that will inevitably be exerted on the audience's psyche' and arguing:

> More often than not, given our scriptwriters' utterly feeble approach to the construction of a script, this task falls entirely to the director. The transposition of the theme into a chain of attractions with a previously determined end effect is the definition we have given of a director's work. The presence or absence of a written script is by no means all that important. (p. 41)

The script was justified only if it performed a useful function in furthering the effectiveness of the film, in facilitating the communication of its ideological purpose.

This too was the actor's role and Eisenstein judged the concept of the *natur-shchik* or model actor associated with Kuleshov accordingly. In so far as the model actor succeeded in exposing the underlying motivation of a character through the expressiveness of his external movements, his technique was justified. Eisenstein discerned a productive conflict in the model actor between the desires of the actor and the inertia of his body: this notion of conflict contained the germ of the idea of the centrality of conflict to art that Eisenstein was to develop later. It also presaged the perception of montage as a means of resolving such conflict through the Marxist notion of the dialectic (even if it had come down to Eisenstein in a rather functional, perhaps even mechanistic, version through Engels and Lenin): thesis – antithesis – synthesis. The test for all the various elements employed in cinema was then, as it was to be later, its efficiency in communicating the purpose of a film:

> An idea expressed in its completeness is photogenic; that is, an object is photogenic when it corresponds most closely to the idea that it embodies. (A car is more photogenic than a cart because its whole structure corresponds more closely to its purpose of transportation and so on.)[34] (p. 51)

The montage of attractions in cinema was justified by its utility, just as it had previously been justified in theatre as long as it had been effective in that medium.

Eisenstein had completed *The Strike* by the time that he wrote 'The Problem of the Materialist Approach to Form'. He claimed that this film represented 'an ideological victory in the field of form' because of its

> discovery of the manufacturing logic and the exposition of the technique of the methods of struggle as of a 'living' current process that knows no inviolable rules other than its final aim and the methods that are varied and devised at a particular moment according to the conditions and the balance of forces at that particular phase of the struggle. (p. 53)

Here again, the *purpose* was the overriding consideration. Before *The Strike*, he argued, cinema had absorbed 'the external characteristics of "neighbouring arts"' but the 'revolutionary quality' of *The Strike* lay in the fact that its 'renewing principle' was a 'directly utilitarian' one and, more specifically, an *industrial* one. Eisenstein denied a conflict of interest between form and content but argued instead that revolutionary form would derive from revolutionary ideology, just as the locomotive had derived from the discovery of steam as a motive power:

> It is not by 'revolutionising' the forms of the stage-coach that the locomotive is created but through a proper technical calculation of the practical emergence of a *new and previously non-existent kind of energy* – steam. It is not the 'research' for forms that correspond to the new content but the logical *realisation of all the phases of the technical production of a work of art consonant with* the 'new *kind* of energy' – the *ruling ideology* – that will produce the forms of revolutionary art.

The decisive factor 'for art in general and revolutionary art in particular' was 'the maximum intensification of the emotional seizure of the audience' and 'a formal approach that is *correctly* conducted in Marxist terms [and that] results in an ideologically valuable and socially useful product'. Eisenstein argued that formal effectiveness was impotent if it was not thematically effective and in this context he renewed his attack on the work of Vertov and the Cine-Eyes as 'primitive Impressionism'. He compared art, a 'tractor ploughing over the audience's psyche', with Vertov's position, the '*reductio ad absurdum* of the technical methods that are valid for newsreel', and noted the different effect of 'the abattoir that is *recorded* in *Cine-Eyes* and *gorily effective* in *The Strike*'. He attributed the difference to the method by which in *The Strike* he had snatched '*fragments from our surroundings according to a conscious and predetermined plan calculated to launch them at the audience in the appropriate combination, to subjugate it to the appropriate association with the obvious final ideological motivation*' (p. 57).

Eisenstein accused the Cine-Eyes, with their view of cinema as 'life caught unawares', of 'passionless representation', of 'the fixing of phenomena that goes no further than fixing the audience's attention' rather than 'ploughing the audience's psyche'. By implication he was here engaging in the same kind of critique of the Cine-Eyes as those who were later to accuse them of empty Formalism. Their work certainly had form, but it lacked ideological direction: 'It is not a "Cine-Eye" that we need but a "Cine-Fist." '

The pride of Soviet cinema

In January 1926 Eisenstein's second feature-length film, *The Battleship Potemkin*, was given its premiere. *Potemkin* is one of the most important films in the history of cinema and it was the film that brought Eisenstein international acclaim. It was not popular with Soviet audiences who had been reared on the same diet of popular and unchallenging Hollywood films as their counterparts in the West, despite an advertising campaign describing the film as 'the pride of Soviet cinema'. But, when it reached the West it created a sensation amongst the intelligentsia and a *succès de scandale* in the press because of attempts to censor or suppress it altogether.[35] Eisenstein became an international celebrity and the principal ambassador abroad of Soviet culture. He went to Berlin, his first visit abroad as an adult, to promote the film and it was there that he first tasted the delights of the Western way of life. His comparisons between film-making in the Soviet Union and in Germany were conveyed in an interview with the *Berliner Tageblatt* entitled 'Eisenstein on Eisenstein, the Director of *Potemkin*', where he reiterated his view that 'by "film" I understand tendentiousness and nothing else'.[36]

Why was *Potemkin* so much more popular in Berlin than in Moscow, where paying audiences preferred to see Douglas Fairbanks and Mary Pickford in *Robin Hood*?[37] The censorship scandal was only part of the reason. Germany had a highly developed network of workers' cinemas and cultural organisations affiliated to a powerful and growing Communist Party and sympathetic to the Soviet model as an alternative to the 'bourgeois' realities of the Weimar Republic. For them, and for left-inclined intellectuals, *Potemkin* came from the Soviet Union like a message from an unknown, exotic and hopeful world, in which everything seemed possible – this was the cultural milieu of Bertolt Brecht, George Grosz and John Heartfield, among others. But there was also a more down-to-earth reason for the success and that was the remarkably powerful score composed by Edmund Meisel, the Austrian-born first violinist of the Berlin Philharmonic Orchestra.

Eisenstein saw his film performed with this score in Berlin and the impression was instrumental in the formulation of his views on the contrapuntal use of sound expressed in later articles.[38] As a result of this encounter Meisel also composed a score for *October*.[39]

It was *Potemkin* that introduced Soviet cinema to the world's screens and *Potemkin* that gave Eisenstein a reputation and raised expectations that he perhaps never subsequently fulfilled, nor could have fulfilled. 'Constanţa (Whither *The Battleship Potemkin*)' was his first attempt to explain its significance and the intentions that lay behind it. He argued that *Potemkin* marked an advance on *The Strike* because '*The Strike* is a treatise; *Potemkin* is a hymn.' Citing the roaring lions as his example, he suggested that in his latest work 'the object is not just an illustration acting as an object (an accordion, a toilet); the object is psychologised both by way of its positioning and in its very presentation.' This represented a further distancing from the Vertov school and, indeed, from what Eisenstein now called 'the Cine-Eye qualities of *The Strike*'. He explained the refinement of his methods by arguing:

> There is one thing we have no right to do and that is to *make generalisations*. The current phase of audience reaction determines our methods of influence: what it reacts to. Without this *there can be no influential art and certainly no art with maximum influence.* (p. 62)

It was once again a matter of the end justifying the means: 'Art admits *all* methods except those that fail to achieve their end.' The aim of art, at least of Soviet art, was not to lull the audience in the way that bourgeois art did (a point that he also made in his interview with the *Berliner Tageblatt*) but to provoke and challenge it: 'art always exacerbates a current conflict rather than distracting audiences from it'. *Potemkin*, by 'psychologising' objects, marked a logical progression from the chains of associations that he had identified at an earlier stage in the development of his ideas:

> For those of us who take our stand on the basis of the montage of attractions, this change is neither an overturning of the foundations of cinema nor a change in course in understanding our cinema. For us it is the next consecutive stage of attraction – the next tactical manoeuvre in the attack on the audience under the slogan of October. (p. 63)

Eisenstein felt that his arguments, despite their refinement, retained an underlying coherence and consistency. A similar process was discernible in his attitude towards the role of the model actor and the relationship between theatre and cinema, both subjects that he re-visited in the course of 1926.[40]

Probably his most important article of that year was 'Béla Forgets the Scissors', a response to an article by Béla Balázs, the Hungarian-born critic working in Germany, in which he had argued that the role of the cameraman was central to the specificity of cinema. This was, of course, diametrically opposed to Eisenstein's own view of the 'authorship' of a film. From his own experience of German cinema, he regarded Balázs's view as a reflection of German conditions and characterised what he termed the Hungarian's 'starism' as the individualism of bourgeois countries in general. They do not think beyond this in the West. Someone has to be the 'star'. *One* person. Yesterday it was the actor. This time let's say it's the cameraman. Tomorrow it will be the lighting technician. (p. 68)

By contrast with the USSR, in the West 'the idea that a film is the result of *collective* efforts goes to the devil'. Balázs's individualism had led him to an erroneous belief in 'the shot itself as "star" '. Eisenstein, on the other hand, repeated his view that it was montage, which enabled the individual shot to be seen in the context of a particular sequence that gave it meaning through association (what he here called 'contextual confrontation'), that defined the specificity of cinema, above all in relation to theatre.

Towards intellectual cinema

In 'The Two Skulls of Alexander the Great', also written in 1926, Eisenstein re-examined the relationship between cinema and theatre. By now he was quite convinced that theatre was finished as an effective medium and that the past role of theatre would be fulfilled by cinema 'by-passing theatre':

> There's no point in perfecting the wooden plough. The tractor has been invented. Drawing attention to the success of tractorisation, i.e. to cinema, and organising life through clubs are the task of every serious theatre worker.[41]

The agricultural analogy was no accident because Eisenstein was already working on his next film, *The General Line*, which dealt with the collectivisation of the Soviet countryside, and was his first film on a contemporary subject. Although this film is still not nearly as well known as his much more controversial revolutionary anniversary film *October*, Eisenstein considered it much more important. In 'Give Us a State Plan' in 1927 he claimed that '*October* was an overtime job: our main job was and is *The General Line*, a film that we consider to be the next new stage in our film work.'[42] Pursuing his agricultural analogy further, he argued for centralised control of cinema: 'The tractors whose movements are not organised by a single will do not plough the fields.' If the fields were not ploughed, the audience's psyche would not be ploughed either. Planning was the only answer: 'When that happens, the freight trains will perhaps arrive at their destinations with a full and valuable load.' Here, at a crucial turning-point in Soviet cultural history, Eisenstein was indulging in extraordinary naivety, because centralised planning would inevitably mean centralised *political* planning and increasing interference from outside the immediate cultural sphere. In this sense Eisenstein was, at least in this article, fulfilling Boris Groys's stereotype of the Soviet artist almost blindly digging his own grave.[43]

By December 1927, when the article was published, neither of Eisenstein's own 'freight trains' – *The General Line* and *October* – had yet arrived at their destinations. The collectivisation film had been interrupted by the making of *October*, but *October*, although completed, still had to be re-edited for general release because some scenes were officially regarded as politically unsatisfactory. The public attacks launched on this anniversary film were to mark the beginning of a downward slide from the apparently unassailable position in which *Potemkin* had placed him at the age of 28. All his subsequent films were to encounter problems of one kind or another.

The year 1928 marked a turning-point in the history of Soviet cinema and in that of the Soviet Union as a whole, as the first of Stalin's Five-Year Plans got under way. The tenth anniversary of the October Revolution had focused attention on the continuing failure of the authorities to organise cinema as an effective ideological weapon, and on their failure to effect the kind of centralised control that Eisenstein had called for. Cinema audiences were still being fed a diet of the kind of fiction films that Eisenstein and other intellectual film-makers despised, the kind of films that imitated the commercial films produced in the West. In the words of one film journal, Soviet cinema had been 'allowed ... to drift on the Soviet sea "rudderless and without sails" '.[44] These remarks were part of the official campaign to prepare for the first Party Conference on Cinema which, after some delays, was eventually held in March 1928. Its purpose was to sort out the crisis that had created a perceived antithesis between commerce and ideology, 'cash' and 'class'.[45] Eisenstein made his own thoughts clear in 'What We Are Expecting from the Party Conference on Cinema',[46] the kind of statement of political identification that was itself already becoming expected of Soviet film-makers and that was to become *de rigueur* in the 1930s. He elaborated his critique of the existing policies of Sovkino, the state cinema organisation, in both 'For a Workers' Hit'[47] and 'The Twelfth Year'.[48] In this last article Eisenstein and his assistant, Grigori Alexandrov, reiterated once again the importance of a 'tendentious' cinema and argued the need for an improved training programme for young directors in order to overcome 'the unprincipled behaviour of our industry and its leadership' and ensure that 'we shall be able to meet the thirteenth October *with a fully armed Cinema October*'.[49]

None the less Eisenstein's principal concern remained the theory and practice of the film-making process. In a series of articles in 1928 he re-examined the central tenets of cinema, moved towards the notion of 'intellectual cinema' and confronted for the first time the problems associated with the advent of sound. In 'Our *October*: Beyond the Played and the Non-Played' he was defending his anniversary film against the thrust of the attacks made on it. Just as he had earlier argued that *Potemkin* should not be judged by the standards of *The Strike*, so now he argued that *October* should not be judged by the standards of his earlier works, but as a further stage on the path towards his next film. He compared *October* to the stage in life at which the male voice breaks:

> The voice has a habit of 'breaking' at a transitional age.
> At an age when you are growing. The transition to adulthood.
> *October* appears at a similar turning-point for cinema.
> *October* spans two epochs in cinema.

For Eisenstein the film represented the transition from the uttermost limits of the old forms to new forms that had 'by no means all yet been found'. *October* embodied the transition from the old antithesis between fiction and documentary film, between played and non-played, to a new and as yet unclearly defined stage 'beyond the played and the non-played' where 'cinema ... stands on its *own two* feet with its own, admittedly as yet undesignated terminology'. We are back to the dialectic: thesis – antithesis – synthesis. In this dialectical process:

> A theoretical novelty – the 'non-played' film – has in due course replaced plot by *fact*. Illusion by *raw material*.

But the new synthesis was characterised not by fact or raw material, but by what Eisenstein rather provocatively called 'CONTEMPT FOR RAW MATERIAL'. Using an analogy only slightly less dismissive of the Cine-Eyes than his earlier remarks, he observed:

> slaves of the machine are becoming exploiters of raw material.
> Slaves of raw material are becoming exploiters of raw material.
> If in the preceding period the material prevailed, the object replaced 'soul and mood', then the next stage will replace the presentation of a phenomenon (material, object) by a *conclusion* based on the phenomenon and a *judgment* on the material, given concrete form in finished concepts.

We are back here to the 'tendentiousness' of cinema, to its 'ruling ideology' and its 'final ideological motivation'. Attractions still worked through their chains of associations, objects were still 'psychologised', but what Eisenstein had on a previous occasion called 'the next tactical manoeuvre in the attack on the audience under the slogan of October' meant now that 'Cinema is ready to begin operating through the abstract word that leads to a concrete *concept*.' This was 'intellectual cinema' in all but name:

> The sphere of the new film language will, as it happens, not be the sphere of the presentation of phenomena, not even that of social interpretation, but the opportunity of *abstract social evaluation*.

The paradigm of this 'abstract social evaluation' was to be Eisenstein's projected film version of Marx's *Capital*, but that film was never made.

Those who had felt unduly constrained by the limitations of cinema as a *silent* medium welcomed the advent of sound as a liberating force, but to the majority it was a cause of considerable trepidation. Some feared the loss of their jobs, others worried about the destruction of cinema as an independent art form. These concerns were universal: it was not for nothing that Alexander Walker entitled his study of Hollywood at the same period *The Shattered Silents*.[50]

The significance of sound was examined by Eisenstein, Alexandrov and Vsevolod Pudovkin, in their famous 'Statement on Sound'. Their principal concern was that sound would be used merely as an accompaniment to images, creating the illusion of naturalism, destroying the 'culture of montage' and thus the specificity and autonomy of cinema as an art form by re-establishing the hegemony of outmoded theatrical methods (' "dramas of high culture" and other photographed representations of a theatrical order'). In other words, and to pursue one of Eisenstein's own analogies, this would be to replace the tractor with the horse-drawn plough. The writers argued that, in order to avoid this 'blind alley', film-makers should experiment first and foremost with '*the contrapuntal use of sound vis-à-vis* the visual fragment of montage' with a view to enhancing cinematic language by 'the creation of a new *orchestral counterpoint* of visual and sound images'. This idea developed the earlier notion of a visual montage collision between individual shots.

It is obvious from Eisenstein's earlier comments on *October*, and especially 'Our *October*. Beyond the Played and the Non-Played', that he regarded that film in particular and cinema in general as having reached the limits of its old cinematic language. The way out of this impasse lay through sound used imaginatively as part of a new audio-visual orchestral counterpoint:

> Sound, treated as a new element of montage (as an independent entity combined with the visual image) cannot fail to provide new and enormously powerful means of expressing and resolving the most complex problems, which have been depressing us with their insurmountability using the imperfect methods of a cinema operating only in visual images.

The joint 'Statement on Sound' left matters there, but the search for a montage theory that would embrace more than the relationship between an individual shot and its context in a sequence was to occupy Eisenstein for the rest of his life. But first he had to find a 'common denominator' to measure the equivalence between sound and image 'attractions'.

The visit to Moscow of the Kabuki theatre from Japan in 1928 provided Eisenstein with further food for thought:

> here we find an *unexpected juncture* between the Kabuki and those extreme experiments in theatre in which theatre has already ceased to exist and has become cinema. What is more, it has become cinema at the latest stage of its development: *sound* cinema.[51]

The Kabuki offered what he termed 'the *monistic ensemble*. Sound, movement, space and voice *do not accompany* (or even parallel) one another but are treated as *equivalent elements*.'[52] Each element was a 'single unit of theatre' in the same way that Eisenstein had defined the attraction in 1923. But the Kabuki had found a method for 'the transference of the basic affective intention from one material to another, from one category of "stimulant" to another', so that 'we actually "hear movement" and "see sound." ' The Japanese could treat sound and image as 'equivalent elements' because they had discovered the 'common denominator' between them.

Eisenstein developed these ideas further in his 1929 article 'Beyond the Shot'. He argued that Japanese script, with its use of ideograms – or, as he wrongly called them, hieroglyphs – had important lessons for cinema:

> The point is that ... the combination ... of two hieroglyphs of the simplest series is regarded not as their sum total but as their product, i.e. as a value of another dimension, another degree: each taken separately corresponds to an object but their combination corresponds to a *concept*. The combination of two 'representable' objects achieves the representation of something that cannot be graphically represented.

Thesis, antithesis, synthesis. This was precisely the aim that Eisenstein had set out in 'Our *October*. Beyond the Played and the Non-Played': 'the next stage will replace the presentation of a phenomenon (material, object) by a *conclusion* based on the phenomenon and a *judgement* on the material, given concrete form in finished concepts'. There was no better way to achieve the aim of 'operating through the abstract word that leads to the concrete *concept*' than to employ the 'hieroglyphic' method of Japanese script, which was, in turn, effectively a montage of associations:

> a dog and a mouth mean 'to bark'
> a mouth and a baby mean 'to scream'
> a knife and a heart mean 'sorrow', and so on.
> But – this is montage!!

This 'laconicism', as he called it, was also 'the starting point for "intellectual cinema" '. In Eisenstein's analysis, the hieroglyphic method of 'denotation through representation' involved 'splitting endlessly into two'. It was the interplay between the two elements (both of the method itself and of each splitting) that created 'something that cannot be graphically represented', something akin to 'abstract social evaluation'.

This led Eisenstein to challenge more directly the Kuleshovian notion of serial montage, with each shot as an 'element of montage' building up 'brick by brick' to the construction of a sequence. He regarded serial montage as 'merely one possible *particular* case', in the same way that he had considered the illustrative use of sound as just one, not very exciting, possibility:

> The shot is by no means a montage *element.*
> The shot is a montage cell. Beyond the dialectical jump in the *single* series: shot – montage.
> What then characterises montage and, consequently, its embryo, the shot?
> Collision. Conflict between the two neighbouring fragments. Conflict. Collision.

Eisenstein compared montage with 'the series of explosions of the internal combustion engine', separate 'fragments' combining into a 'dynamic'. But, if 'montage is conflict', then the shot, as a 'montage cell', had also to be 'examined from the point of view of *conflict*', in this instance of 'conflict within the shot'. He delineated the various types of conflict:

> the conflict of graphic directions (lines)
> the conflict of shot levels (between one another)
> the conflict of volumes
> the conflict of masses (of volumes filled with varying intensities of light)
> the conflict of spaces, etc.

He also isolated 'the conflict between an object and its spatial nature and the conflict between an event and its temporal nature'. This particular aspect of conflict within the shot owed much to Viktor Shklovsky's notion of 'impeded form' and his belief in *ostranenie* or 'de-familiarisation'.[53]

The range of different conflicts both within the shot and between one shot and another could all too easily cause a film 'to break up into antagonistic pairs of fragments'. This could be avoided by the discovery of 'a single system of methods of cinematic expression that will cover all its elements', by the identification and exposure of the 'single indicator' that lay at the basis of that mode of expression. Here he was returning to the 'common denominator' for visual and sound perceptions identified by the Kabuki. Now the discovery of conflict provided the necessary common denominator for cinema. In the instance of conflict within the shot this could be expressed as 'the principle of optical counterpoint'. But conflict was not a new discovery for Eisenstein. In his 1923 'The Montage of Attractions' he had implicitly recognised the significance of conflict in his assertion: 'These shocks [i.e. attractions] provide the only opportunity of perceiving the ideological aspect of what is being shown, the final ideological conclusion'.

Eisenstein's last concern in 'Beyond the Shot' was with the frame that actually surrounded the shot, and here too he argued that the West could and should learn from the tenets of Japanese culture. Whereas in the West, or so he claimed, the film-maker began with the frame and then composed the shot within the confines of the frame, 'the Japanese do it the other way round' so that the image dictates the shape of the frame. The West 'staged' the scene, the Japanese 'captured' it, using the camera to organise the raw material, 'Cutting out a fragment of reality by means of the lens'. Furthermore he described the acting method of the Kabuki theatre as 'decomposed acting' because 'the whole process of the death agony was decomposed into solo performances by each "party" separately: the legs, the arms, the head' (p. 91). It was quite simply 'decomposition into shot levels'. The analogy with cinematic montage was crystal clear: 'the most varied branches of Japanese culture are permeated by a purely cinematic element and by its basic nerve – montage'.

There were, however, other elements that resulted from this analysis: the use of the camera to organise the material recalls the Cine-Eyes' 1923 claim:

> I am the Cine-Eye. I create a man more perfect than Adam was created ... I take the strongest and most agile hands from one man, the fastest and best proportioned legs from another, the most handsome and expressive head from a third and through montage I create a new, perfect man.[54]

The notion of 'decomposed acting' also recalls both Meyerholdian biomechanics and Kuleshov's practical experiments with the *naturshchik* or model actor. This synthesis of different strands took cinema 'beyond the played and the non-played' into a new realm that he identified in another 1929 article, 'Perspectives', as 'Purely and solely intellectual cinema, the synthesis of emotional, documentary and absolute film':[55]

> Only *intellectual* cinema will be able to put an end to the conflict between the 'language of logic' and the 'language of images'. On the basis of the language of the cinema dialectic.[56]

This intellectual cinema had a specific ideological purpose: 'the task of irrevocably inculcating communist ideology into the millions'. It was, in Eisenstein's view, destined to play a central role in the coming age of communism.

In 1929 Eisenstein did not have to express himself publicly like this, although it was becoming increasingly necessary to do so. The notions of conflict and of the

14

dialectic remained central to his thinking and, although he continued to be at least nominally a convinced Marxist, it is difficult to believe that his understanding of Marxist theory and practice was particularly profound. In Stalinist Russia appearances were all-important and appearances can always be deceptive. Soviet cultural life was becoming very much a masque of masks and in order to survive Eisenstein, like his colleagues, had to learn to become a 'Soviet director'. Boris Barnet, who once described Eisenstein as 'a chemist ... who poisons slowly' shed a telling light on this phenomenon many years later in an exchange recalled by the Georgian director, Otar Ioseliani:

> He [Barnet] asked me [Ioseliani]: 'Who are you?' I [Ioseliani] said: 'A director'... 'Soviet,' he corrected, 'you must always say "Soviet director". It is a very special profession.' 'In what way?' I asked. 'Because if you ever manage to become honest, which would surprise me, you can remove the word "Soviet".'[57]

It is therefore not surprising that his next major article, 'The Dramaturgy of Film Form' should have been given the alternative title 'The Dialectical Approach to Film Form'. This piece can be seen largely as a schematisation of the ideas that Eisenstein had already expressed elsewhere. He reiterated his belief in the centrality of collision and conflict and repeated that 'both the whole and the minutest detail must be permeated by a *single principle*'. However, the synthesis that montage represented 'is not an idea composed of successive shots stuck together but an idea that DERIVES from the collision between two shots that are independent of one another'. The notion of synthesis and of montage as a kind of 'blending' was therefore a 'vulgar description of what happens'. One new element here was Eisenstein's analysis of the way in which 'each sequential element is arrayed, not *next* to the one it follows, but on *top* of it'. The retained impression of the first image (thesis) had, thanks to visual memory, a second image superimposed upon it (antithesis) and this produced a totality that was greater than the sum of its parts, 'a completely new higher dimension' (synthesis).

In 'The Dramaturgy of Film Form' Eisenstein also analysed the nature of pictorial dynamism and, for the first time, the use of colour. He concluded that the basis of dynamic effect lay once more with counterpoint or conflict. There were three 'different *phases in the formation of a homogeneous expressive task*': formulation, conflict and explosion – thesis, antithesis, synthesis.

In further analysing the different kinds of conflict that might arise in film form Eisenstein borrowed from music the idea of the dominant as the principal sign of each shot, although he did not at this stage develop the analogy. He proposed what he called a 'tentative film syntax', a series of examples of the ways in which the film director could realise the 'emotional dynamisation' of the raw material. The concept of emotional dynamisation was itself a development of Eisenstein's earlier notions of 'ploughing the audience's psyche' ('The Problem of the Materialist Approach to Form') and of 'psychologising objects' ('Constanţa'). Despite his view, expressed in opposition to the Kuleshov/Pudovkin concept of serial montage, that the shot/montage relationship was not analogous to the word/sentence relationship, he was now arguing that film should use language, rather than theatre or painting, as its model:

15

Why then should cinema in its forms follow theatre and painting rather than the methodology of language, which gives rise, through the combination of concrete descriptions and concrete objects, to quite new concepts and ideas?

Each montage fragment 'has in itself no reality at all'. It had associations and it was the accumulation of those associations through the compositional structure of the montage sequence as a whole that made it 'work emotionally'. The isolated word acquired meaning only in the context of the sentence: the isolated shot acquired meaning only in the context of the montage sequence. Intellectual cinema too depended on the montage of associations and the final ideological conclusion. Citing the sequence of images of various gods from *October*, Eisenstein suggested that:

> The conventional *descriptive* form of the film becomes a kind of reasoning (as a formal possibility).
> Whereas in the conventional film the film directs and develops the *emotions*, here we have a hint of the possibility of likewise developing and directing the entire *thought process*.

Intellectual cinema, while still 'embryonic', would 'construct a really quite new form of filmic expression', which

> will achieve forms for thoughts, systems and concepts without any transitions or paraphrases.
> And which can therefore become a
> SYNTHESIS OF ART AND SCIENCE.

Once again Eisenstein expressed his intention of experimenting with this synthesis in his projected film version of Marx's *Capital*.

In 'The Dramaturgy of Film Form' Eisenstein had for the first time suggested that a montage sequence derived its expressive effect from the conflict between the dominant sign of each shot within the sequence, in the same way that in music the dominant related to the scale. He developed this idea in 'The Fourth Dimension in Cinema'. This level of intensity of the conflict could range 'from a complete opposition between the dominants, i.e. a sharply contrasting construction, to a scarcely noticeable "modulation" from shot to shot'. What is more, this dominant could be 'more or less specifically defined, but never absolutely'. Each montage sequence took its general meaning from an indicator or signpost 'that immediately "christens" the whole series with a particular "sign" ': each combination of dominants had its own dominant. The rejection of the Kuleshov/Pudovkin analogy between shot/montage and word/phrase was now complete:

> The shot never becomes a letter but always remains an ambiguous hieroglyph.
> It can be read only in context, just like a hieroglyph, acquiring specific *meaning, sense* and even *pronunciation* (sometimes dramatically opposed to one another) only *in combination with* a separate reading or a small sign or reading indicator placed alongside it.

But the dominant was, after all, only the dominant: there were other signs contained within the shot as well. Eisenstein claimed that *The General Line* had been edited 'by the method of "democratic" equal rights for all the stimulants, viewed together as a complex'. In other words, in this film he had applied the Kabuki method of calculating the sum of equivalent elements in order to determine the overall effect. He applied the argument that 'a whole complex of secondary stimulants always accompanies the central stimulant' to both the acoustical and optical aspects of montage. These 'secondary resonances' furnished a whole complex of overtones and undertones to complement the dominant: 'This is the method on which the montage of *The General Line* is constructed. This montage is not constructed on the individual dominant but takes the sum of stimuli of all the stimulants as the dominant.' In a sense Eisenstein was now applying the methodology of the montage of attractions to the construction of the individual shot: thesis (tone/dominant), antithesis (overtone/undertone), synthesis (sum total/new dominant). Each shot was constructed on the basis of internal tension or conflict, in the same way that each phrase of montage was constructed. But each shot, like each note in a musical phrase, was meaningless in isolation:

> Both emerge as a real constant only in the dynamics of the musical or cinematic *process*.
> Overtonal conflicts, which are foreseen but not 'recorded' in the score, emerge only through dialectical formation when the film passes through the projector or the orchestra performs a symphony.

This then was the significance of the 'fourth dimension' – time – in cinema.

Eisenstein offered the overtone as the long-sought common denominator between sound and image in audiovisual counterpoint: 'Because, while a shot is a visual *perception* and a tone is a sound perception, *both visual and sound overtones are totally physiological sensations*'. It was the conflict between visual and sound overtones that, echoing the stipulation for 'orchestral counterpoint' in the 'Statement on Sound', 'will give rise to the composition of the Soviet sound film' and also provide the basic method for intellectual cinema:

> For the musical overtone (a beat) the term 'I hear' is no longer strictly appropriate.
> Nor 'I see' for the visual.
> For both we introduce a new uniform formula: '*I feel*'.

It was not until the 'Battle on the Ice' sequence in *Alexander Nevsky* that Eisenstein, in collaboration with the composer Sergei Prokofiev, was able to realise his ideas on audiovisual orchestral counterpoint and later also to analyse the experience in 'Vertical Montage'.[58]

In 'The Fourth Dimension in Cinema' Eisenstein went on to analyse the four different 'methods of montage' that cinema could utilise: metric, rhythmic, tonal and overtonal. He made it clear that he regarded overtonal montage as 'an advance on the other stages': it therefore followed that *The General Line* marked for him an advance on all his other films, just as *Potemkin* had earlier marked an advance on *The Strike*. 'Cinema,' he remarked, 'begins where the collision between different cinematic measures of movement and vibration begins.' This dialectic lay at the basis of what Lenin, in Eisenstein's paraphrase, had called 'an endless process of deepening the human cognition of objects, phenomena, processes, etc., from appearances to essence and from the less profound to the more profound essence'.

17

As the next stage in this process Eisenstein proposed the notion of 'intellectual montage'. Whereas overtonal montage depended on the stimulation of physiological reactions:

> Intellectual montage is montage not of primitively physiological overtonal resonances but of the resonances of overtones of an intellectual order.
>   i.e. the conflicting combination of accompanying intellectual effects with one another

Once more the justification for the means was the end: he had ended 'The Dramaturgy of Film Form' with a call for intellectual cinema as 'a synthesis of art and science', but he concluded 'The Fourth Dimension in Cinema' with a call for a synthesis of art, science and ideology:

> Intellectual cinema will be the cinema that resolves the conflicting combination of physiological overtones and intellectual overtones, creating an unheard-of form of cinema which inculcates the Revolution into the general history of culture, creating a synthesis of science, art and militant class-consciousness.

We are back yet again to the 'final ideological conclusion' that underpinned the montage of attractions in 1923.

There is thus a clear line of development from the essential components of the montage of attractions to those of the theory of intellectual montage that Eisenstein had evolved by the end of the 1920s. It would be fair to say that, with intellectual montage, he thought that he had found the common denominator of art that would enable him to construct a general theory of the centrality of montage in all forms of art. It was what he himself called 'the building to be built' and the building of it was to be his central theoretical concern for the remainder of his life in such major projects as his works on non-indifferent nature, montage and direction.[59] By 1929 the foundations for that edifice were in place.

But westward, look, the land is bright

A week before the publication of 'The Fourth Dimension in Cinema' and two months before the première of the revised version of *The General Line* under the less controversial title of *The Old and the New*, Eisenstein, Alexandrov and the cameraman Eduard Tisse left the Soviet Union for Western Europe, ostensibly to study the latest developments in sound film in the West. Eisenstein's reception was warmest in that other outcast country of the Europe of the 1920s, Germany: at least there his films were shown and his ideas treated with respect. After attending the Congress of Independent Film-Makers at La Sarraz, near Lausanne, he was expelled from Switzerland.[60] When he lectured at the Sorbonne, the Prefect of the Paris Police banned the planned showing of *The Old and the New* at very short notice.[61] When he came to Britain he was greeted with the news that *Potemkin* could still not be shown to the general public because, after the 1926 General Strike, it was regarded as being too inflammatory.[62]

When Eisenstein eventually arrived in the United States he was treated either as something of a curiosity or as a deadly danger. The contrast between the cultural attitudes implicit in the decision to introduce the 'red dog' to Rin-Tin-Tin[63] and the interviews that had been published in German newspapers and French and British journals provided eloquent testimony to the different cultural traditions that prevailed on opposite sides of the Atlantic and should have furnished a timely warning of the almost inevitable conflict between the collectivist approach of the Soviet system and the commercialism of the American. A number of film projects for Hollywood were aborted, in particular *Sutter's Gold* and *An American Tragedy*, and the collapse of his beloved Mexican project, *Que viva México!*, so near its completion was to haunt him for the rest of his life.[64] Eisenstein's time in North America was no more fruitful in terms of completed writings than it was in terms of finished films: his only major piece was a lecture delivered in Hollywood, which reiterated the points made in 'Beyond the Shot' about the relationship between shot and frame and almost certainly went right over the heads of the audience to whom it was addressed.[65] Having arrived in 1930 as a curiosity, Eisenstein was to leave the United States after the Mexican fiasco denounced as 'a sadist and a monster', as a 'Jewish Bolshevik', a degenerate and a pornographer. These last two accusations derived from the large number of erotic, often homoerotic, drawings that Eisenstein produced while in Mexico and which provide a clue to his increasing vulnerability in Stalin's Russia of the 1930s.

What a magnificent opportunity America must have seemed to offer in 1930: the chance of a lifetime for the boy from Riga to make a film in Hollywood, the film capital of the world, in the heart of the 'enemy camp'! And what a terrible blow the disappointment must have been when it all came eventually to naught. Needless to say, Eisenstein's absence abroad provoked jealousy, which may to some extent have been officially encouraged, so that on several occasions he had specifically to deny that he planned to defect to the West. Eisenstein returned to the Soviet Union in May 1932 as a frustrated artist and a bitterly disillusioned man.

A survivor in Moscow

Eisenstein also returned to a different Soviet Union from the one that he had left in 1929. Both the country and the cinema were in the throes of the cultural revolution that accompanied the first Five-Year Plan. Soviet cinema had been centralised in 1930 under the firm hand of Boris Shumyatsky, an Old Bolshevik whose first priority was to produce a 'cinema for the millions', one that would be both popular and ideologically effective, overcoming the antithesis between cash and class that was perceived to have dogged Soviet cinema in the 1920s.[66] Eisenstein had left as the undisputed 'master' but he had been abroad at a crucial period of transformation. There had been rumours, repeatedly denied, that he had intended to defect and in any case his absence at a critical time for Soviet cinema increased the resentment that resulted from the petty – and not so petty – jealousies of colleagues envious of his earlier elevated and apparently unassailable position in the iconostasis of Soviet art, and most probably also envious of his achievements and his talent. He came back to find that the criticisms of *October* and *The General Line* had now hardened into open accusations of Formalism.[67] He returned, not as the 'master', but as the man who had not made a film for three years and whose last two films had been 'unintelligible to the millions'. He returned in more than one sense as a foreigner to his own country.

Eisenstein had therefore to re-establish his credentials as a film-maker, as a film theorist and, above all from the official standpoint, as a loyal Soviet artist. In 'Help Yourself!', published in October 1932,[68] he argued that the purpose of cinema was 'to grip and not to amuse' the audience, the difference lying in the particular 'ideological premiss' that should underpin Soviet films but that was missing from Hollywood, citing his experience over *An American Tragedy* as symptomatic of the difference. He also argued for a collective approach to film-making: instead of 'pissoirs' students at the State Film School should be encouraged to work together to produce a 'cathedral'. In the same month Eisenstein was put in charge of the Faculty of Direction at the Film School, so that, even if for much of the time he was unable to put his ideas into practice in his own finished films, he could influence the thought and practice of the younger generation. Making films was only one of the activities expected of Soviet film-makers.

None the less the continuing failure to produce a completed film was being held against him. In the creation of a cinema that was 'intelligible to the millions' the Master had lost his foothold and, when asked to make a musical comedy – the genre that Shumyatsky was particularly keen to develop as part of his cinema for the millions – Eisenstein contemptuously rejected the suggestion, thus simultaneously incurring Shumyatsky's wrath and opening the door for Grigori Alexandrov, his assistant, to found the new Soviet genre and eventually (after *The Happy Guys* [1934], *The Circus* [1936] and *Volga-Volga* [1938]) to become Stalin's favourite film-maker, so much so that during the wartime alliance Stalin presented President Roosevelt with a copy of *Volga-Volga*. Eisenstein's will to experiment lay in other directions, fascinating though it is to speculate on how he would have married orchestral counterpoint with the musical comedy.

At this time a whole series of projects was mooted and abandoned, for all sorts of reasons. In 1934 Eisenstein launched an attack on Soviet films for their artistic conservatism and their theatricality in the use of both sound and actors in ' "Eh!" On the Purity of Film Language'. He argued that the poor quality of the montage had led to disjointed and meaningless films, which hardly represented progress:

> We must demand that the quality of montage, film syntax and film speech not only matches the quality of earlier works but exceeds and surpasses them. That is what the battle for the high quality of film culture requires of us.

However, while Eisenstein was arguing for the high quality of film culture, the authorities were arguing for a higher degree of accessibility and intelligibility. Boris Shumyatsky emphasised the need for plot and strong characters and Eisenstein now accepted that the plots that he had earlier rejected were now appropriate:[69]

> Now Soviet cinema is historically correct in joining battle for plot. There are still many obstacles along the path, many risks of a false understanding of the principles of plot. The most terrible of these is the underestimation of the opportunities that a temporary emancipation from the old traditions of plot has given us:

20

the opportunity to re-examine in principle and once more the bases and problems of film plot
and advance in a progressive cinematic movement not 'back to plot' but 'forward to plot'. (pp. 131–2)

Eisenstein held up one film as a model and that film was *Chapayev*, directed by the so-called Vasiliev 'brothers' who had been his pupils. The film was also held up as the official model film because of its 'intelligibility to the millions' but for Eisenstein its significance consisted in its synthesis of the achievements of the first (poetic) and second (prosaic) five-year periods in the history of Soviet cinema. 'It is not a return to the old plot forms that were filmed in the first stage of our cinema. It is not "back to plot". But "forward to a new kind of plot".' Forward to that final ideological conclusion, that he described in 'At Last!' as a

great synthesis, when all the achievements of the whole preceding era of Soviet cinema in their uncompromisingly high quality become at the same time the property of the many millions of the masses, infecting them with the new energy of heroism, struggle and creativity.

It may have seemed that a new synthesis was in fact emerging between Eisenstein and the official view of Soviet cinema, and it is this appearance that has exposed Eisenstein to the accusation of complicity with Stalinism. In reality, apart from a few brief interludes of harmony, Eisenstein was to be in conflict with the cultural commissars for the rest of his life. But Eisenstein was by no means the only film director whose work was interrupted in the 1930s: Dziga Vertov confided his depression to his diary,[70] while Abram Room (a director whose credits included *Bay of Death* [1926], *Bed and Sofa* [1927] and *The Ghost that Never Returns* [1930]) had one film stopped as was *Bezhin Meadow* (*Once One Summer* [1932]) – and one film banned after completion – (*A Stern Young Man* [1936]).[71] Eisenstein was not therefore alone: but he was peculiarly vulnerable for a variety of reasons. First of all – and this was only partly his fault – his own career pattern provoked the jealousy of some of his less talented contemporaries; second, he had been abroad at a crucial time and, in the increasing and officially encouraged paranoia of the 1930s about saboteurs, wreckers and 'enemies of the people', this aroused suspicion, again officially encouraged; third, he had not completed a film for eight years, since the 'flawed' *General Line*, which made him seem unreliable from the industrial and political point of view. In other words, the 'Master' himself was deemed to be flawed, because he had failed to set a good example to his lesser contemporaries.

But beyond this was another, more personal characteristic that made Eisenstein peculiarly vulnerable at that time: his sexual orientation. Although it is true that there is no document in the archives confessing, or declaring, his homosexuality, this is hardly surprising in the circumstances. In 1934, as part of the return to conservative family values under Stalin, homosexual activity had for the first time since the Revolution been criminalised in the Soviet Union, and it is no coincidence that it was shortly after this criminalisation that Eisenstein entered into his marriage of convenience with Pera Atasheva. In the atmosphere of the Great Terror that pervaded the middle and late 1930s very few people were going to be brave or foolhardy enough to incriminate themselves unnecessarily. Another, more complex and subtle masque of masks had to be acted out.

In a sense, both despite and because of the setbacks in his film-making, Eisenstein's real career continued as a teacher at the State Film Institute in Moscow. Most of his later film projects never matured to fruition, while his publications became increasingly focused on the promotion of particular films and the explanation of their production and content. His attempt to justify his theoretical position in the first of his two speeches to the January 1935 All-Union Creative Conference of Soviet Filmworkers (held partly to celebrate, albeit somewhat belatedly, the fifteenth anniversary of the nationalisation of Soviet cinema in August 1919, and partly to ratify the new doctrine of Socialist Realism promulgated at the first Writers' Congress in August 1934) demonstrated how out of touch with the everyday political and practical realities of Soviet cinema he had become during his time abroad.

This rather rambling and self-indulgent speech attracted widespread criticism from his colleagues. Only Kuleshov stood up for Eisenstein, pointing out that

> Very many comrades have talked about Sergei Mikhailovich as if he were dead ... Yutkevich said that knowledge exhausts people and that he is afraid that this is happening to you. Dear Sergei Mikhailovich, it is not knowledge that exhausts people, but envy.[72]

In his speech Leonid Trauberg, a former collaborator in FEKS and a genuine friend, dismissed the classic pantheon of Soviet cinema – Eisenstein, Kuleshov, Pudovkin, Vertov and Dovzhenko – as a 'museum of wax figures', distinguished not by their current work but by the 'fantastic illusions' of people who were living in the past. These people, remarked Trauberg, 'talk only about when they started work ... writing about what they were preaching in 1924 or later'. He rejected 'abstract genius worship' and argued instead for the 'study of reality, discussion with living people': 'Since 1929 we have seen in a sense the "twilight of the Gods", if you will forgive the joke.'[73]

Although Eisenstein claimed in an interjection that this joke had been his, the situation in which he now found himself was no joke at all. Two days before the conference opened, there had been an award ceremony also held to celebrate the anniversary. The Order of Lenin went to Shumyatsky, Pudovkin, Ermler, the Vasilievs, Kozintsev and Trauberg, Dovzhenko, and the Georgian director Chiaureli.[74] Vertov was awarded the Order of the Red Star, while Eisenstein was humiliated with the title of Honoured Artist, alongside his defender Kuleshov and the pre-Revolutionary director Protazanov,[75] and other relatively minor figures. As a result of all this, his second speech, which was the official closing speech of the conference, was virtually an *apologia pro vita sua*.[76] In an article published in the Party newspaper *Pravda* he made the necessary obeisance, which was becoming almost a commonplace for Soviet public figures, to Stalin:

> And today, when those who work in cinema are so favoured by the attentions of Stalin, our Party, our government and the whole country, we can sense that it is only thanks to the vital link with all these that our cinema can say that on its fifteenth birthday cinema has really become the most important of the arts, as Lenin had ordained.[77]

Having donned the mask of Soviet artist and paid the necessary tribute to Stalin, Eisenstein was allowed to begin making his next film, another treatment of the collectivisation of the Soviet countryside, *Bezhin Meadow*.

The film's central character was based on the true-life story of Pavlik Morozov, a Young Pioneer who organised a night watch over the harvest in order to frustrate the plans of his kulak father to sabotage it. Instead the father is so enraged that he kills his son: Eisenstein's old obsession with the tyrannical father returned. It was a sign of Eisenstein's continuing prestige and influence, despite the criticisms heaped upon him, that so many colleagues and friends came to view the shooting and give him moral support: these included Kuleshov, Trauberg, Ermler, Savchenko, Barnet, Esfir Shub and the Vasilievs.[78] The filming was however dogged by bad luck: with more than half the film completed on schedule, Eisenstein contracted smallpox in October 1935 and, after a long convalescence, he fell ill again with a virulent form of influenza. The delay in completing *Bezhin Meadow* meant that it could not be judged as a whole according to Eisenstein's original conception, and Shumyatsky did not like the fragments that he had seen and heard about. Eisenstein was forced to revise the script, with assistance from Isaak Babel, whose *Red Cavalry* stories had provided him with the raw material for an unrealised film project between *The Strike* and *Potemkin*. On 17 January 1937 he was made Professor of Direction at the State Film Institute: it seemed that the humiliation of the awards ceremony two years earlier had been reversed and that his status as Soviet artist was now officially endorsed. But in the same month the filming of this second version was interrupted by another bout of influenza and Eisenstein was unable to resume work until March 1937, by which time the die was cast. On 17 March 1937, precisely two months after Eisenstein's appointment to the professorship, Shumyatsky ordered that production be stopped, accusing the director in a *Pravda* article two days later of creating 'Biblical and mythological types rather than images of collective farm workers' and of indulging in a 'bacchanalia of destruction' which had 'promoted the pathos of destruction to first place'. What the Party state had given with one hand, it was now taking away with the other. Eisenstein, Shumyatsky claimed, 'was interested in producing *Bezhin Meadow* solely as a pretext for harmful Formalistic exercises'. Angered by Eisenstein's speech to a recent fiction-film conference, Shumyatsky announced that the Party Central Committee had 'declared the film anti-artistic and politically quite unsound'.[79]

Eisenstein was forced to issue a public apology, openly admitting to 'The Mistakes of *Bezhin Meadow*', first published in *Sovetskoe iskusstvo* on 17 April 1937 and to confess, whether he believed it or not, that:

> In recent years I have become self-absorbed. I have retreated into my shell. The country fulfilled its Five-Year Plans. Industrialisation took giant steps forward. I remained in my shell. My alienation from life was, it is true, not complete. It was in those years that I was intensively involved with the younger generation, devoting all my energies to my work at the Institute of Cinema. But this was also a retreat within the walls of an academic institute; there was no broad creative exit towards the masses, towards reality.
>
> The twentieth anniversary of Soviet cinema has given me a real shock. In 1935 I threw myself into my work. But the habit of self-absorption and alienation had already taken hold. I worked shut away with my film crew. I created the picture not out of the flesh and blood of socialist reality, but out of a tissue of associations and theoretical conceptions relating to that reality. The results are obvious.

Eisenstein paid tribute to his colleagues at Mosfilm for helping him to understand the error of his own ways: 'Why am I so firm and calm? I understand my own mistakes.' In fact we now know that Eisenstein threatened to commit suicide if he was not allowed to make another film.[80] The day before the publication of his abjectly self-critical article he also wrote to Shumyatsky seeking permission for a film based on Vsevolod Vishnevsky's script *We, the Russian People*. Shumyatsky sent the proposal to Stalin with a covering letter opposing the request. The correspondence was referred to the Central Committee's Cultural Education Section which reported that

> Comrade Shumyatsky's view is wrong because the director Eisenstein, despite all his Formalist errors, is a talented artist and, with guidance, can make a good Soviet film. The Central Committee's decision on *Bezhin Meadow* and the sharp criticisms of Comrade Eisenstein's errors have taught him a serious lesson. He has admitted his errors and asks to be given the chance to make a new film that will prove that he is worthy of the name Soviet artist.[81]

The Central Committee decided in favour of Eisenstein, with Vishnevsky and later another scriptwriter, Pyotr Pavlenko, acting as his minders, an arrangement that almost certainly saved his life.

The *Bezhin Meadow* affair was a traumatic episode for Eisenstein, coming so soon after the débâcle over the Mexican film. It seemed, eleven years after the triumph of *Potemkin* and eight years after the final release of *The Old and the New* that he could not complete a film in either the West or the Soviet Union. But, fortunately for Eisenstein, the episode was also to prove fatal for Shumyatsky, who had to take the official blame for wasting approximately two million roubles on the project. In the course of the rest of the year the film press contained increasingly open and strident attacks on the head of Soviet cinema until on 8 January 1938 he was arrested and denounced as a 'captive of the saboteurs' and a 'fascist cur' and shot in July.[82] But yet again what the Party state gave with one hand, it took away with the other: on the very same day the theatre run by Vsevolod Meyerhold, Eisenstein's 'spiritual father', was closed down. Meyerhold was protected by his old adversary at the Moscow Art Theatre, Konstantin Stanislavsky, who employed him as assistant director at the Opera Theatre until his own death later that year. Meyerhold was arrested in June 1939 and shot in prison in February 1940. Eighteen months afterwards Eisenstein saved Meyerhold's personal papers for posterity during the German advance in 1941.[83] In 1936 Meyerhold had sent Eisenstein a photograph of himself inscribed on the collar: 'I am proud of my pupil who has now become a master. I love the master who has now founded a school. I bow to this pupil and master.'[84] Meyerhold never knew the real debt that he was to owe to Eisenstein and the real pride that he would have felt in his pupil's actions. This was all part of the price that had to be paid in the Stalin period as a Soviet artist. Eisenstein survived; Meyerhold did not.

Shumyatsky's removal opened the door for Eisenstein to make, not *We, the Russian People*, but another historical epic, *Alexander Nevsky*. He chose the story of the thirteenth-century struggle against the Teutonic knights because there was little documentary evidence available and he could give full range to the imagination whose overuse Shumyatsky had so decried, and because there was a clear contemporary message in Alexander's ultimate defeat of the Teutonic invaders. It was a film in which he had to prove himself to be, for the first time since *Potemkin*, a loyal Soviet artist, and it was completed in five months, by deliberate contrast with the two years spent on filming *Bezhin Meadow*. The most famous scene in the film is the Battle on the Ice, where Eisenstein and the composer Sergei Prokofiev were able to apply the concept of audiovisual counterpoint in a way that Eisenstein analysed later in 'Vertical Montage'.[85] The film's plot is clear and simple and the atmosphere one of folkloristic staginess. *Alexander Nevsky* marks a distinct stylistic rupture from Eisenstein's silent films and is closer to *Ivan the Terrible* than to anything else. Perhaps because of this the film was both a popular and critical success and gained the approval of the authorities: Stalin liked it. In other words, it fulfilled its task in terms of Eisenstein's rehabilitation as a Soviet artist, as well as performing an important and, as it transpired, an international propaganda function as the shadows of impending war lengthened across Europe. His best known account of the rationale behind the film, 'My Subject is Patriotism', was first published in English in 1939 and not in fact published in the USSR until 1956.[86] But the propaganda message of *Alexander Nevsky* was clearly brought out in 'Alexander Nevsky and the Rout of the Germans', published in the government newspaper *Izvestiya* in July 1938 before the film was completed:

> For if the might of our national soul was able to punish the enemy in this way, when the country lay exhausted in the grip of the Tatar yoke, then nothing will be strong enough to destroy this country which has broken the last chains of its oppression; a country which has become a socialist motherland; a country which is being led to unprecedented victories by the greatest strategist in world history – Stalin.

These sentiments are echoed in Alexander's speech whose text rolls up at the very end of the film: 'He who comes by the sword shall perish by the sword. On this Rus stands and will stand forever!'

Alexander Nevsky not surprisingly brought Eisenstein unprecedented official recognition. On 1 February 1939 he was awarded the Order of Lenin that had been denied him four years earlier by the now executed Shumyatsky. On 15 March 1941 he was awarded the Stalin Prize, First Class, even though the film had been withdrawn from distribution immediately after the Nazi–Soviet Pact had been signed in August 1939. It was released again after the German invasion of June 1941 and the Soviet government instituted a new battle honour, the Order of Alexander Nevsky.[87]

In January 1940 Eisenstein addressed a conference of film-makers on the subject of the Soviet historical film. He made it clear that historical film had both contemporary relevance and purpose:

> I should like to reiterate that our fundamental, chief and general aim is the depiction of the present, of contemporary man, elevated to a broad historical generalisation. The historical film is of great use in this, and I am certain that we will succeed in showing our great epoch thus.

Death and transfiguration

In the wake of the Nazi–Soviet Pact Eisenstein had also been asked to stage a new production of Wagner's *Die Walküre* at the Bolshoi Theatre, where *Potemkin* had been premiered fifteen years previously.[88] It remains to this day a matter of conjecture whether this invitation came because of his international renown as a Soviet artist, more specifically because he had directed such a successful anti-Nazi film, or whether Eisenstein's own German-Jewish descent may well have made the invitation to direct an opera by Hitler's favourite 'Germanic' composer, a man known for his virulent antisemitism, a particular and deliberate humiliation.[89] His international prominence undoubtedly made him vulnerable to pressure, as well perhaps as enabling him subtly to resist, or at least subvert it: there is anecdotal evidence that two German officers invited to the première were overheard remarking during the interval that Eisenstein's production was '*reiner Kulturbolschewismus*' [pure cultural Bolshevism].[90]

The last years of Eisenstein's life were devoted to making his historical epic *Ivan the Terrible* and to writing his fragmented memoirs, published in English as *Beyond the Stars*. The memoirs were, like Goebbels' diaries, designed for posterity and provide us almost entirely with Eisenstein's public mask.[91] It is in the film that the mask began to slip. His thoughts on the incorporation of music and colour into the montage framework of the film were delivered in a series of lectures in March 1947. Leonid Kozlov has argued convincingly that Eisenstein was genuinely horrified to discover not only that Stalin approved of *Ivan the Terrible, Part One*, for which he and others involved (Prokofiev, Nikolai Cherkasov, Serafima Birman, Andrei Moskvin and Eduard Tisse) won the Stalin Prize, First Class – rather like making a clean sweep of the Oscars.[92] Perhaps Eisenstein's realisation of his own 'complicity' came too late: at any rate he suffered his first heart attack at the dinner celebrating the award on 2 February 1946, which really marked his final acceptance as a 'Soviet director' by none other than the 'Kremlin censor' himself. But Eisenstein was almost certainly more horrified to realise that his film was capable of a Stalinist interpretation. It was for this reason that he altered Part Two to illustrate the loneliness and isolation of power, to 'undo' the message that had been read into Part One. In this he was certainly successful, and at great risk to his own livelihood and, indeed, to his life itself. Yet again the Party state was to take away with one hand what it had given with the other: on 26 January 1946 the Stalin Prize for Part One had been announced; on 4 September 1946 another decree 'On the Film *A Great Life*' severely criticised Part Two:

> The director Sergei Eisenstein, in Part Two of *Ivan the Terrible*, has revealed his ignorance in his portrayal of historical facts, by representing the progressive army of Ivan the Terrible's *oprichniki** as a gang of degenerates akin to the American Ku-Klux-Klan; and Ivan the Terrible, a strong-willed man of character, as a man of weak will and character, not unlike Hamlet.[93]

If you substitute 'Stalin' for Ivan the Terrible, and 'the NKVD' for the *oprichniki*

---

* The *oprichniki* were a standing army raised by Ivan and owing direct personal allegiance to him. Their political function was to undermine the influence of the boyar or gentry class.

you will see what high stakes were being played for. That is why Eisenstein took such copious notes when summoned to the Kremlin with Cherkasov on 25 February 1947 to hear Stalin's criticisms of the film (pp. 160–6). That meeting was also attended by Andrei Zhdanov, who by then had become Stalin's ideological and cultural commissar and the instigator of several decrees in the immediate postwar years restricting Soviet cultural activities, and Vyacheslav Molotov, whose role as People's Commissar for Foreign Affairs apparently provided him with the qualifications necessary to be an authoritative film critic. In context the final note is rather ominous:

> When the conversation came round to submitting the script for approval, Comrade Molotov said, 'There is no need to submit it for approval, especially as I expect Comrade Eisenstein will have thought out all the details about Ivan the Terrible by then.'
> Stalin enquired after Eisenstein's heart and [said he] thought that he looked very well. (pp. 165–6)

Eisenstein subsequently remarked, 'Went to see Stalin yesterday. We didn't like one another.'[94] Stalin, however, did like Nikolai Cherkasov and on the day after the interview, the day on which Eisenstein made the remark just quoted, Cherkasov was made a People's Artist of the USSR.[95] In a final gesture of defiance, Eisenstein told his friends that he was not going to re-work the film: 'What re-shooting? ... Don't you realise that I'd die at the very first shot? I can't think of *Ivan* without feeling a pain in my heart!'[96]

Eisenstein did not re-shoot Part Two: the re-working had been planned for 1948 after the period of thought mentioned by Molotov. But Eisenstein had long expected to die at the age of 50 and this expectation had been the principal motor force behind the writing of his memoirs, especially after that first heart attack in February 1946. His second heart attack killed him on 11 February 1948, with both *Ivan the Terrible* and the memoirs unfinished except in fragmented form.

Eisenstein's premature death deprived a generation of film-makers of his direct influence as a teacher and by the time that Part Two was released in 1958, ten years after Eisenstein's death and five years after Stalin's, Soviet culture had moved on to the Thaw period and much of Eisenstein's work looked dated and compromised, while his montage cinema seemed to many outmoded and irrelevant. But times change: there is some truth in Vitaly Yerenkov's remark that 'The technique of montage has now become commonplace and totally demystified, most notably by advertisements and MTV.'[97] While it may be true that Eisenstein's theory of 'intellectual cinema' has not had a consistent impact on mainstream commercial cinema (to its detriment), it cannot be denied that, a century after his birth and fifty years after his death, Eisenstein remains a crucial figure in the history, theory and practice of cinema *as an art form*. Another Soviet artist, the poet Vladimir Mayakovsky, once remarked that 'Politicians come and go, but art remains.' Eisenstein's art has outlived its immediate ideological context, and that of course raises awkward questions about the relationship between art and ideology.

That is one of the many reasons why Eisenstein was a quintessentially 'Soviet artist', a man who felt that he had to wear a mask in public so that he could survive as an artist. But we do not have to wear the masks that Soviet artists had to wear: the masks that we wear are different ones. Perhaps greater exposure to

Eisenstein's writings and a re-examination of his films will persuade new generations that what cinema needs is 'not a Cine-Eye but a Cine-Fist!' If this *Reader* helps to bring Eisenstein to a wider audience, it will have achieved its purpose.

Swansea, St David's Day, 1998

1   The Montage of Attractions[1]

(On the production of A. N. Ostrovsky's *Enough Simplicity for Every Wise Man* at the Moscow Proletkult Theatre[2])

I.   Proletkult's[3] theatrical line

In a few words: Proletkult's theatrical programme consists not in 'using the treasures of the past' or in 'discovering new forms of theatre' but in abolishing the very institution of theatre as such and replacing it by a showplace for achievements in the field at the *level of the everyday skills of the masses*. The organisation of workshops and the elaboration of a scientific system to raise this level are the immediate tasks of the Scientific Department of Proletkult in the theatrical field.

The rest we are doing under the rubric 'interim', carrying out the subsidiary, but not the fundamental tasks of Proletkult. This 'interim' has two meanings under the general rubric of revolutionary content:

1. The *figurative-narrative theatre* (static, domestic – the right wing: *The Dawns of Proletkult*,[4] *Lena*[5] and a series of unfinished productions of a similar type. It is the line taken by the former Workers' Theatre of the Proletkult Central Committee).
2. The *agitational theatre of attractions* (dynamic and Eccentric – the left wing). It is the line devised in principle for the Touring Troupe of the Moscow Proletkult Theatre by Boris Arvatov[6] and myself.

This path has already been traced – in outline, but with sufficient precision – in *The Mexican*,[7] a production by the author of the present article and V. S Smyshlyayev[8] (in the First Studio of the Moscow Art Theatre). Later, in our next collaboration (V. Pletnyov's *On the Abyss*[9]) we had a complete disagreement on principle that led to a split and subsequently to our working separately, as you can see by *Wise Man* and *The Taming of the Shrew*, not to mention Smyshlyayev's *Theory of Construction of the Stage Show*, which overlooked all the worthwhile achievements of *The Mexican*.

I feel that I must digress because any review of *Wise Man* that tries to establish a common link with other productions completely ignores *The Mexican* (January–March 1921), whereas *Wise Man* and the whole theory of attractions are a further elaboration and a logical development of my contribution to that production.
3. *Wise Man* was begun in the Touring Troupe (and finished when the two troupes combined) as the first work of agitation based on a new method of structuring a show.

II. The montage of attractions

This term is being used for the first time. It requires explanation.

Theatre's basic material derives from the audience: the moulding of the audience in a desired direction (or mood) is the task of every utilitarian theatre (agitation, advertising, health education, etc.). The instrument of this process consists of all the parts that constitute the apparatus of theatre (Ostuzhev's[10] 'chatter' no more than the colour of the prima donna's tights, a roll on the drums just as much as Romeo's soliloquy, the cricket on the hearth[11] no less than a salvo under the seats of the auditorium[12]) because, despite their differences, they all lead to one thing – which their presence legitimates – to their common quality of *attraction*.

An attraction (in our diagnosis of theatre) is any aggressive moment in theatre, i.e. any element of it that subjects the audience to emotional or psychological influence, verified by experience and mathematically calculated to produce specific emotional shocks in the spectator in their proper order within the whole. These shocks provide the only opportunity of perceiving the ideological aspect of what is being shown, the final ideological conclusion. (The path to knowledge encapsulated in the phrase, 'through the living play of the passions', is specific to theatre.)

Emotional and psychological, of course, in the sense of direct reality as employed, for instance, in the Grand Guignol, where eyes are gouged out or arms and legs amputated on stage, or the direct reality of an actor on stage involved through the telephone with a nightmarish event taking place dozens of miles away, or the situation of a drunkard who, sensing his approaching end, pleads for protection and whose pleas are taken as a sign of madness. In this sense and not in the sense of the unravelling of psychological problems where the attraction is the theme itself, existing and taking effect *outside* the particular action, but topical enough. (Most agit-theatres make the mistake of being satisfied with attractions solely of that sort in their productions.)

I regard the attraction as being in normal conditions an independent and primary element in structuring the show, a molecular (i.e. compound) unity of the *effectiveness* of theatre and of *theatre as a whole*. It is completely analogous to Grosz's[13] 'rough sketches', or the elements of Rodchenko's[14] photo-illustrations.

'Compound'? It is difficult to distinguish where the fascination of the hero's nobility ends (the psychological moment) and where the moment of his personal charm (i.e. his erotic effect) begins. The lyrical effect of a whole series of Chaplin scenes is inseparable from the attractional quality of the specific mechanics of his movements. Similarly, it is difficult to distinguish where religious pathos gives way to sadistic satisfaction in the torture scenes of the mystery plays, and so on.

The attraction has nothing in common with the stunt. The stunt or, more accurately, the trick (it is high time that this much abused term was returned to its rightful place) is a finished achievement of a particular kind of mastery (acrobatics, for the most part) and it is only one kind of attraction that is suitable for presentation (or, as they say in the circus, 'sale'). In so far as the trick is absolute and complete *within itself* it means the direct opposite of the attraction, which is based exclusively on something relative, the reactions of the audience.

Our present approach radically alters our opportunities in the principles of creating an 'effective structure' (the show as a whole) instead of a static 'reflection' of a particular event dictated by the theme, and our opportunities for resolving it through an effect that is logically implicit in that event, and this gives rise to a new concept: a free montage with arbitrarily chosen independent (of both the PARTICULAR composition and any thematic connection with the actors) effects (attractions) but with the precise aim of a specific final thematic effect – montage of attractions.

The path that will liberate theatre completely from the yoke of the 'illusory depictions' and 'representations' that have hitherto been the decisive, unavoidable and only possible approach lies through a move to the montage of 'realistic artificialities', at the same time admitting to the weave of this montage whole 'illusory sequences', and a plot integral to the subject, not something self-contained or all-determining but something consciously and specifically determined for a particular purpose, and an attraction chosen purely for its powerful effect.

Since it is not a matter of 'revealing the playwright's purpose', 'correctly interpreting the author' or 'faithfully reflecting an epoch', etc., the attraction and a system of attractions provide the only basis for an effective show. In the hands of every skilled director the attraction has been used intuitively in one way or another, not, of course, on the level of montage or structure but at least in a 'harmonic composition' (from which a whole new vocabulary derives: an 'effective curtain', a 'rich exit', 'a good stunt', etc.) but essentially this has been done only within the framework of the logical plausibility of the subject (it has been 'justified' by the play) and in the main unconsciously and in pursuit of something entirely different (something that had been enumerated at the 'start' of the proceedings). What remains to us in reorganising the system we use to structure a show is merely to shift the focus of attention to the essential (what was earlier regarded as attendant decoration but is in fact the principal messenger of the abnormal intentions of a production and is not logically connected with the run-of-the-mill reverence of literary tradition), *to establish this particular approach as a production method* (which, since the autumn of 1922, has been the work of the Proletkult Workshops).

The school for the montageur[15] is cinema and, principally, music-hall and circus because (from the point of view of form) putting on a good show means constructing a strong music-hall/circus programme that derives from the situations found in the play that is taken as a basis.

As an example here is a list of the sections of numbers in the epilogue to *Wise Man:*

1. The hero's explanatory monologue. 2. A fragment from a detective film. (A classification of 1., the theft of the diary.) 3. An Eccentric[16] music-hall entrée (the bride and her three rejected suitors – all one person in the play – in the role of best men): a melancholy scene reminiscent of the song 'Your hands smell of incense' and 'May I be punished by the grave' (we intended that the bride would have a xylophone and this would be played on six rows of bells, the officers' buttons). 4.5.6. Three parallel two-phrased clowning entrées (the theme: payment for organising the wedding). 7. An entrée with a star (the aunt) and three officers (the theme: the restraint of the rejected suitors), punning (by reference to a horse) on a triple volte number on a saddled horse (on the impossibility of bringing it into

the room, traditionally, in 'triple harness'). 8. Good agit-songs ('The priest had a dog' accompanied by a rubber priest like a dog. The theme: the start of the wedding ceremony). 9. A break in the action (a paper-boy's voice announcing that the hero is leaving). 10. The villain appears in a mask. A fragment from a comedy film. (A résumé of five acts of the play. The theme: the publication of the diary.) 11. The continuation of the (interrupted) action in another grouping (a simultaneous wedding with the three rejected suitors). 12. Anti-religious songs ('Allah-Verdi'[17] – a punning theme tune on the need to bring in a mullah because of the large number of suitors that one bride is marrying) from the choir and a new character used only in this scene, a soloist dressed as a mullah. 13. General dancing. Some play with a poster inscribed: 'Religion is the opium of the people.' 14. A farcical scene. (The bride and her three suitors are packed into a box and pots are smashed against the lid.) 15. The marital trio – a parody of life. (The song: 'Who here is young?') 16. A precipice. The hero's return. 17. The hero's winged flight beneath the big top (the theme: suicide in despair). 18. A break. The villain's return. The suicide is held up. 19. A sword fight (the theme: enmity). 20. An agit-entrée involving the hero and the villain on the theme of NEP.[18] 21. An act on a sloping wire (crossing from the arena to the balcony over the audience's heads. The theme: 'leaving for Russia'). 22. A clowning parody of this number (with the hero). Descent from the wire. 23. A clown descends the same wire from the balcony, holding on by his teeth. 24. The final entrée with two clowns throwing water over one another (as per tradition), finishing with the announcement: 'The End'. 25. A volley of shots beneath the seats of the auditorium as a finale. The connecting features of the numbers, if there is no direct transition, are used as linking elements: they are handled with different arrangements of equipment, musical interludes, dancing, pantomime, carpet-clowns.

Editor's Note

The final section of Eisenstein's 'The Montage of Attractions', where he characterises the Epilogue to *Enough Simplicity for Every Wise Man,* makes little sense to the reader who is not acquainted with the production or with the Ostrovsky play upon which it is very loosely based. The editors of the six-volume Eisenstein *Selected Works* in Russian have included a reconstruction of the Epilogue provided by the surviving members of the production led by Maxim Strauch. It is reproduced here:

1. On stage (in the arena) we see Glumov who, in an ['explanatory'] monologue, recounts how his diary has been stolen and he has been threatened with exposure. Glumov decides to marry Mashenka immediately and so he summons Manefa the clown on to the stage and asks him to play the part of the priest.
2. The lights go down. On the screen we see Glumov's diary[19] being stolen by a man in a black mask – Golutvin. A parody of the American detective film.
3. The lights go up. Mashenka appears, dressed as a racing driver in a bridal veil. She is followed by her three rejected suitors, officers (in Ostrovsky's play there is just one: Kurchayev), who are to be the best men at her wedding to Glumov. They act out a separation scene ('melancholy'). Mashenka sings the 'cruel' romance, 'May I be punished by the grave'. The officers, parodying Vertinsky,[20]

perform 'Your hands smell of incense'. (It was Eisenstein's original intention that this scene should be regarded as an Eccentric music-hall number ['xylophone'] with Mashenka playing on the bells sewn as buttons on to the officers' coats'.

4. 5. 6. Exit Mashenka and the three officers. Enter Glumov. Three clowns – Gorodulin, Joffre, Mamilyukov – run out from the auditorium towards him. Each performs his own curious turn (juggling with balls, acrobatic jumps, etc.) and asks for his payment. Glumov refuses and leaves. (The two-phrased clowning entrées': for each exit there are two phrases of text, the clown's and Glumov's rejoinder.)

7. Mamayeva appears, dressed in extravagant luxury (a 'star'), carrying a ring-master's whip. She is followed by the three officers. Mamayeva wants to disrupt Glumov's wedding. She comforts the rejected suitors and after their rejoinder about the horse ('My friendly mare is neighing') she cracks the whip and the offi-cers scamper around the arena. Two imitate a horse while the third is the rider.

8. On stage the priest (Manefa) begins the wedding ceremony. Everyone pre-sent sings, 'There was a priest who had a dog'. Manefa performs a circus turn (the 'rubber priest'), imitating a dog.

9. Through a megaphone we hear the paper-boy shouting. Glumov, abandon-ing the wedding, escapes to find out whether his diary has appeared in print.

10. The man who stole the diary appears. He is a man in a black mask (Golutvin). The lights go out. On the screen we see Glumov's diary. The film tells of his behaviour in front of his great patrons and accordingly of his transmogri-fications into various conventional figures (into a donkey in front of Mamayev, a tank-driver in front of Joffre, and so on).

11. The wedding ceremony resumes. Glumov has fled; his place is taken by the rejected suitors, the three officers ('Kurchayev').

12. As Mashenka is simultaneously marrying three suitors, four men in uni-form carry a mullah on a board out from among the audience. He continues the wedding ceremony, performing songs parodying topical themes –'Allah-Verdi'.

13. When he has finished singing, the mullah dances the *lezginka*[21] and every-one joins in. The mullah raises the board he had been sitting on. On the back there is an inscription: 'Religion is the opium of the people'. Exit the mullah, holding this board in his hands.

14. Mashenka and her three suitors are packed into boxes (from which, unseen by the audience, they disappear). The participants in the wedding ceremony smash clay pots against the box, parodying the ancient wedding rite of 'packing off the young couple'.

15. The three participants in the wedding ceremony (Mamilyukov, Mamayev, Gorodulin) sing the wedding song 'Who here is young, who here's not wed?'

16. The wedding song is interrupted by Glumov who runs in with a newspaper in his hand: 'Hurrah! There's nothing in the paper!' Everyone makes fun of him and leaves him alone.

17. After the publication of his diary and his failure to wed, Glumov is in despair. He decides to commit suicide and asks one of the men in uniform for a 'rope'. They lower a lead to him from the ceiling. He attaches 'angel's wings' to his back and they start to raise him towards the ceiling with a lighted candle in his hands. The choir sings 'At midnight the angel flew across the heavens' to the tune of 'My beauty's heart'. This scene is a parody of the Ascension.

18. Golutvin (the 'villain') appears on stage. Glumov, seeing his enemy, starts showering him with abuse, descends on to the stage and rushes after him.

19. Glumov and Golutvin fight with swords. Glumov wins. Golutvin falls and Glumov tears a large label off Golutvin's trousers. It bears the word 'NEP'.

20. Golutvin sings a song about NEP. Glumov accompanies him. Both dance. Golutvin invites Glumov to be his 'apprentice' and go to Russia.

21. Golutvin, balancing an umbrella, walks up the sloping wire over the audience's heads to the balcony: he is 'leaving for Russia'.

22. Glumov decides to follow his example, clambers up on to the wire but falls off (the circus 'descent') with the words 'It's slippery, slippery: I'd be better off in a back alley.' He follows Golutvin 'to Russia' but takes a less dangerous route – through the auditorium.

23. Enter a clown (with red hair) on stage. He cries and says over and over again, 'They've gone and left someone behind.' Another clown descends from the balcony on the wire, holding on by his teeth.

24. 25. The two clowns start squabbling. One throws water over the other who falls over with surprise. One of them announces 'The End' and makes his bow to the audience. At this moment there is a pyrotechnical explosion beneath the seats of the auditorium.

2   The Montage of Film Attractions[1]

These thoughts do not aspire to be manifestos or declarations but they do represent an attempt to gain at least some understanding of the bases of our complex craft.

If we regard cinema as a factor for exercising emotional influence over the masses (and even the Cine-Eyes,[2] who want to remove cinema from the ranks of the arts at all costs, are convinced that it is) we must secure its place in this category and, in our search for ways of building cinema up, we must make widespread use of the experience and the latest achievements in the sphere of those arts that set themselves similar tasks. The first of these is, of course, theatre, which is linked to cinema by a common (identical) *basic* material – the *audience* – and by a common purpose – *influencing this audience in the desired direction* through a series of calculated pressures on its psyche. I consider it superfluous to expatiate solely on the intelligence of this ('agit') kind of approach to cinema and theatre since it is obvious and well-founded from the standpoint both of social necessity (the class struggle) and of the very nature of these arts that deliver, because of their formal characteristics, a series of blows to the consciousness and emotions of the audience. Finally, only an ultimate aspiration of this sort can serve to justify diversions that give the audience *real* satisfaction (both physical and moral) as a result of *fictive* collaboration with what is being shown (through motor imitation of the action by those perceiving it and through psychological 'empathy'). If it were not for this phenomenon which, incidentally, alone makes for the magnetism of theatre, circus and cinema, the thoroughgoing removal of accumulated forces would proceed at a more intense pace and sports clubs would have in their debt a significantly larger number of people whose physical nature had caught up with them.

Thus cinema, like theatre, makes sense only as 'one form of pressure'. There is a difference in their methods but they have one basic device in common: the montage of attractions, confirmed by my theatre work in Proletkult and now being applied by me to cinema. It is this path that liberates film from the plot-based script and for the first time takes account of film material, both thematically and formally, in the construction. In addition, it provides criticism with a method of objective expertise for evaluating theatre or film works, instead of the printed exposition of personal impressions and sympathies spiced with quotations from a run-of-the-mill political report that happens to be popular at a particular moment.

An attraction (NB for more details, see *Lef*, 1923, no. 3,[3] and *Oktyabr mysli*, 1924, no. 1) is in our understanding any demonstrable fact (an action, an object, a phenomenon, a conscious combination, and so on) that is known and proven to exercise a definite effect on the attention and emotions of the audience and that, combined with others, possesses the characteristic of concentrating the audience's emotions in any direction dictated by the production's purpose. From this point of view a film cannot be a simple presentation or demonstration of events: rather it must be a tendentious selection of, and comparison between, events, free from narrowly plot-related plans and moulding the audience in accordance with its purpose. (Let us look at *Cine-Pravda*[4] in particular: *Cine-Pravda* does not follow this path – its construction takes no account of attractions – but 'grabs' you through the attraction of its themes and, purely superficially, through the formal mastery of its montage of separate sequences, which by their short footage conceal the 'neutral' epic 'statement of facts'.)

The widespread use of all means of influence does not make this a cinema of polished style but a cinema of action that is useful to our class, a class cinema due to its actual formal approach because attractional calculation is conceivable only when the audience is known and selected in advance for its homogeneity.

The application of the method of the montage of attractions (the juxtaposition of facts) to cinema is even more acceptable than it is to theatre. I should call cinema 'the art of juxtapositions' because it shows not facts but conventional (photographic) representations (in contrast to 'real action' in theatre, at least when theatre is employing the techniques we approve of). For the exposition of even the simplest phenomena cinema needs juxtaposition (by means of consecutive, separate presentation) between the elements which constitute it: montage (in the technical, cinematic sense of the word) is fundamental to cinema, deeply grounded in the conventions of cinema and the corresponding characteristics of perception.

Whereas in theatre an effect is achieved primarily through the physiological perception of an actually occurring fact (e.g. a murder),*[5] in cinema it is made up of the juxtaposition and accumulation, in the audience's psyche, of associations that the film's purpose requires, associations that are aroused by the separate elements of the stated (in practical terms, in 'montage fragments') fact, associations that produce, albeit tangentially, a similar (and often stronger) effect only when taken as a whole. Let us take that same murder as an example: a throat is gripped, eyes bulge, a knife is brandished, the victim closes his eyes, blood is spattered on a wall, the victim falls to the floor, a hand wipes off the knife – each fragment is chosen to 'provoke' associations.

An analogous process occurs in the montage of attractions: it is not in fact phenomena that are compared but chains of associations that are linked to a particular phenomenon in the mind of a particular audience.† (It is quite clear that for a worker and a former cavalry officer the chain of associations set off by seeing

---

* A direct animal audience action through a motor imitative act towards a live character like oneself, as distinct from a pale shadow on a screen. These methods of theatrical effect have been tested in my production of *Can You Hear Me, Moscow?*

† In time (in sequence) clearly: here it plays not merely the role of an unfortunate technical condition but of a condition that is necessary for the thorough inculcation of the associations.

a meeting broken up and the corresponding emotional effect in contrast to the material which frames this incident, will be somewhat different.) I managed to test quite definitively the correctness of this position with one example where, because what I should call this law had not been observed, the comic effect of such a well-tried device as the alogism[6] fell flat. I have in mind the place in *The Extraordinary Adventures of Mr West in the Land of the Bolsheviks*[7] where an enormous lorry is pulling a tiny sledge carrying Mr West's briefcase. This construction can be found in different variants in any clown's act – from a tiny top hat to enormous boots. The appearance of such a combination in the ring is enough. But, when the whole combination was shown on the screen in one shot all at once (even though it occurred as the lorry was leaving the gates so that there was a short pause – as long as the rope joining the lorry to the sledge), the effect was very weak. Whereas a real lorry is immediately perceived in all its immensity and compared to a real briefcase in all its insignificance and [for comic effect] it is enough to see them side by side, cinema requires that a 'representation' of the lorry be provided first for long enough to inculcate the appropriate associations – and then we are shown the incongruous light load. As a parallel to this I recall the construction of an analogous moment in a Chaplin film where much footage is spent on the endlessly complicated opening of the locks on a huge safe* and it is only later (and apparently from a different angle) that we are shown the brooms, rags and buckets that are hidden inside it. The Americans use this technique brilliantly for characterisation – I remember the way Griffith 'introduced' the 'Musketeer', the gangleader in *Intolerance*:[8] he showed us a wall of his room completely covered with naked women and then showed the man himself. How much more powerful and more cinematic this is, we submit, than the introduction of the workhouse supervisor in *Oliver Twist* in a scene where he pushes two cripples around: i.e. he is shown through his deeds (a purely theatrical method of sketching character through action) and not through provoking the necessary associations.

From what I have said it is clear that the centre of gravity of cinema effects, in contrast to those of theatre, lies not in directly *physiological* effects, although a purely *physical* infectiousness can sometimes be attained (in a chase, with the montage of two sequences with movements running against the shot). It seems that there has been absolutely no study or evaluation of the purely physiological effect of montage irregularity and rhythm and, if it has been evaluated, this has only been for its role in narrative illustration (the tempo of the plot corresponding with the material being narrated). 'We ask you not to confuse' the montage of attractions and its method of comparison with the usual montage parallelism used in the exposition of a theme such as the narrative principle in *Cine-Pravda* where the audience has first to guess what is going on and then become 'intellectually' involved with the theme.

The montage of attractions is closer to the simple contrasting comparisons (though these are somewhat compromised by *The Palace and the Fortress*[9] where the device is naively revealed) that often produce a definitely powerful emotional effect (chained legs in the ravelin and a ballerina's feet). But we must point out that in *The Palace and the Fortress* [from which this example comes] any depen-

---

* And a large number of bank premises are shown first.

The Strike: Unrest is simmering in the factory.

dence on comparison in the construction of the shots for this sequence was completely ignored: their construction does not assist association but disrupts it and it enters our consciousness through literary rather than visual means. For example, Nechayev, seen from the waist up and with his back to the camera, hammers on a barred door and the prison warder, seen in long shot somewhere in a corner by a window, holds a canary in a cage. The chained legs are shown horizontally whereas the ballerina's points are shot about four times larger and vertically, etc.

The method of the montage of attractions is the comparison of subjects for thematic effect. I shall refer to the original version of the montage resolution in the finale of my film *The Strike:* the mass shooting where I employed the associational comparison with a slaughterhouse. I did this, on the one hand, to avoid overacting among the extras from the labour exchange 'in the business of dying' but mainly to excise from such a serious scene the falseness that the screen will not tolerate but that is unavoidable in even the most brilliant death scene and, on the other hand, to extract the maximum effect of bloody horror. The shooting is shown only in 'establishing' long and medium shots of 1,800 workers falling over a precipice, the crowd fleeing, gunfire, etc., and all the close-ups are provided by a demonstration of the real horrors of the slaughterhouse where cattle are slaughtered and skinned. One version of the montage was composed roughly as follows:

1. The head of a bull. The butcher's knife takes aim and moves upwards beyond the frame.
2. Close-up. The hand holding the knife strikes downwards below the frame.

3. Long shot: 1,500 people roll down a slope. (Profile shot.)
4. Fifty people get up off the ground, their arms outstretched.
5. The face of a soldier taking aim.
6. Medium shot. Gunfire.
7. The bull's body (the head is outside the frame) jerks and rolls over.
8. Close-up. The bull's legs convulse. A hoof beats in a pool of blood.
9. Close-up. The bolts of the rifles.
10. The bull's head is tied with rope to a bench.
11. A thousand people rush past.
12. A line of soldiers emerges from behind a clump of bushes.
13. Close-up. The bull's head as it dies beneath unseen blows (the eyes glaze over).
14. Gunfire, in longer shot, seen from behind the soldiers' backs.
15. Medium shot. The bull's legs are bound together 'according to Jewish custom' (the method of slaughtering cattle lying down).
16. Closer shot. People falling over a precipice.
17. The bull's throat is cut. Blood gushes out.
18. Medium close-up. People rise into the frame with their arms outstretched.
19. The butcher advances towards the (panning) camera holding the blood-stained rope.
20. The crowd rushes to a fence, breaks it down but is met by an ambush (two or three shots).
21. Arms fall into the frame.
22. The head of the bull is severed from the trunk.
23. Gunfire.
24. The crowd rolls down the precipice into the water.
25. Gunfire.
26. Close-up. Teeth are knocked out by the shooting.
27. The soldiers' feet move away.
28. Blood flows into the water, colouring it.
29. Close-up. Blood gushes from the bull's throat.
30. Hands pour blood from a basin into a bucket.
31. Dissolve from a platform with buckets of blood on it ... in motion towards a processing plant.
32. The dead bull's tongue is pulled through the slit throat (one of the devices used in a slaughterhouse, probably so that the teeth will not do any damage during the convulsions).
33. The soldiers' feet move away. (Longer shot.)
34. The head is skinned.
35. One thousand eight hundred dead bodies at the foot of the precipice.
36. Two dead skinned bulls' heads.
37. A human hand in a pool of blood.
38. Close-up. Filling the whole screen. The dead bull's eye.
    Final title.

The downfall of the majority of our Russian films derives from the fact that the people who make them do not know how to construct attractional schemas consciously but only rarely and in fumbling fashion hit on successful combinations. The American detective film and, to an even greater extent, the American comedy film (the method in its pure form) provide inexhaustible material for the study of these methods (admittedly on a purely formal level, ignoring content). Griffith's films, if we had seen them and not just known them from descriptions, would teach us a lot about this kind of montage, albeit with a social purpose that is hostile to us. It is not, however, necessary to transplant America, although in all fields the study of methods does at first proceed through imitation. It is necessary to train ourselves in the skill of selecting attractions from our own raw material.

Thus we are gradually coming to the most critical problem of the day: the script. The first thing to remember is that there is, or rather should be, no cinema other than agit-cinema. The method of agitation through spectacle consists in the creation of a new chain of conditioned reflexes by associating selected phenomena with the unconditioned reflexes they produce (through the appropriate methods). (If you want to arouse sympathy for the hero, you surround him with kittens which unfailingly enjoy universal sympathy: not one of our films has yet failed to show White officers juxtaposed to disgusting drinking bouts, etc.). Bearing this basic situation in mind we should handle the question of played films with great care: they wield such enormous influence that we cannot ignore them. I think that the campaign against the very notion of such films has been caused by the really low level of scripts as well as the technique of the performers. I shall return to the latter in greater detail later. As far as the former is concerned, our approach allows us to conceive of arranging something other than 'little stories' and 'little romances' with a 'little intrigue', kinds of film which on the whole (and not without reason) frighten people away. An example of this sort of arrangement may be provided by the project that I put forward for the treatment of historical-revolutionary material and that was accepted after long debates with the supporters of 'Rightist' real-life films who dream of filming the life of some underground conspirator or notorious *agent provocateur*, or an imaginary story based on real-life materials. (Incidentally, these materials are completely ignored by the 'wistful' men of cinema and left at the disposal of right-wing directors who abuse them: viz. *Andrei Kozhukhov, Stepan Khalturin*[10] and *The Palace and the Fortress!*)

The most important consideration in my approach to this theme was to give an account of and depict the *technique of the underground* and to provide an *outline of its production methods* in individual characteristic examples. How they sewed boots – how they prepared for the October Revolution. Our audience, trained to take an interest in production, is not the least interested in, and *should not be* interested in, the emotions of an actor made up as Beideman or in the tears of his bride. It is interested in the prison regime at the Peter and Paul Fortress and this is to be presented not through the personal sufferings of the hero but through the direct exposition of its methods.

It is not the life of Malinovsky the *agent provocateur* that interests us but the varieties and types (what are the characteristics of a particular type) and what makes an *agent provocateur* not the presence of someone in a deportation prison but the prison itself, the conditions there, the mores in their numerous variants. In a word, the presentation of every element of underground work as *phenomena that are represented in the greatest possible number of varieties and examples.* The conditions in which proofs were corrected, the underground printing press, etc., in the form of sequences characterising particular moments and not joined into a seamless plot centred on an underground printing press but edited with a view to the thorough exposure, for example, of the underground printing press as one of the facts of underground work. The emphasis is on the most interesting montage tasks. Without 'staging' this is quite unthinkable but in a quite different context! There is an example of the montage (e.g. in the episode of the 'flight') of pure adventure material preserving all its attractional quality in the orientation towards historical familiarisation. The theme of a strike was chosen first of all for the transition to constructions of this kind: in terms of its saturation with the mass it is most suited to the intermediate form between a film whose purpose is a purely emotional revolutionary effect conditioned by the plot and the new way of understanding its construction. For a number of reasons, dictated mainly by the material itself, it has to adhere more closely in its form to the first of these.

As far as the question of the necessity or otherwise of a script or of free montage of arbitrarily filmed material is concerned, we have to remember that a script, whether plot-based or not, is (as I wrote with reference to theatre: see *Lef*[11]), in our view, a prescription (or a list) of montage sequences and combinations by means of which the author intends to subject the audience to a definite series of shocks, a 'prescription' that summarises the general projected emotional effect on the audience and the pressure that will inevitably be exerted on the audience's psyche. More often than not, given our scriptwriters' utterly feeble approach to the construction of a script, this task falls in its entirety to the director. The transposition of the theme into a chain of attractions with a previously determined end effect is the definition we have given of a director's work. The presence or absence of a written script is by no means all that important. I think that when it is a matter of operating on the audience through material that is not closely plot-based, a general scheme of reference that leads to the desired results is enough, together with a free selection of montage material based on it (the absence of such a scheme would not lead to the organisation of the material but to hopeless Impressionism around a possibly attractional theme). But, if it is carried out by means of a complex plot construction, then obviously a detailed script is necessary. Both kinds of film have the same citizenship rights because in the final analysis we are going above all to see in *Nathan the Wise*[12] the amazing work of the cavalry, its jumping past the camera, exactly as we see it in Vertov's work at the Red Stadium.

Incidentally I shall touch here on one purely directorial moment in our work. When, in the process of constructing, shooting and moulding the montage elements, we are selecting the filmed fragments, we must fully recall the characteristics of cinema's effect that we stated initially and that establish the montage approach as the essential, meaningful and sole possible language of cinema, completely analogous to the role of the word in spoken material. In the selection and presentation of this material the decisive factor should be the immediacy and economy of the resources expended in the cause of associative effect.

The first practical indication that derives from this is the selection of an angle of vision for every element, conditioned exclusively by the accuracy and force of

41

impact of the necessary presentation of this element. If the montage elements are strung together consecutively this will lead to a constant movement of the angle of vision in relation to the material being demonstrated (in itself one of the most absorbing purely cinematic possibilities).

Strictly speaking, the montage elision of one fragment into another is inadmissible: each element can most profitably be shown from just one angle and part of the film fact that proceeds from, let us say, an inserted close-up, already requires a new angle that is different from the fragment that preceded the close-up. Thus, where a tightly expounded fact is concerned, the work of the film director, as distinct from the theatre director, requires, in addition to a mastery of production (planning and acting), a repertoire of montage-calculated angles for the camera to 'capture' these elements. I almost managed to achieve this kind of montage in the fight scene in *The Strike* where the repetition of sequences was almost completely avoided.

These considerations play a decisive role in the selection of camera angles and the arrangement of the lights. No plot 'justification' for the selection of the angle of vision or the light sources is necessary. (Apart, that is, from a case where the task involves a particularly persistent emphasis on reality. For instance, *contre-jour* lighting is by no means 'justified' in American interior shots.)

On a par with the method of staging a scene and taking it with a camera there exists what I should call the Futurist method of exposition, based on the pure montage of associations and on the separate depiction of a fact: for example, the impression of that fight may be represented through the montage of the separate elements that are not joined by any logical sequence in the staging of the scene. The accumulation of the details of conflicting objects, blows, fighting methods, facial expressions and so on produces just as great an impression as the detailed investigation by the camera of all the phases in a logically unfolding process of struggle: I contrast both kinds of montage, done separately, in the scene of the shooting. (I do not, for example, use the chain: the gun is cocked – the shot fired – the bullet strikes – the victim falls, but: the fall – the shot – the cocking – the raising of the wounded, etc.)

If we move on to the persistently posed question of the 'demonstration of real life' as such, we must point out that this particular instance of demonstration is covered by our general position on the montage of attractions: but the assertion that the essence of cinema lies only in the demonstration of real life must be called into question. It is, I think, a matter of transposing the characteristics of a '1922/3 attraction' (which was, as is always the case, a response to social aspirations – in this instance, the orientation towards construction' as the raw material for these aspirations and towards a 'presentation' that advertised this construction, e.g. an important event like the Agricultural Exhibition) to the entire nature of cinema as a whole. The canonisation of this material and of this approach as the only acceptable ones deprive cinema of its flexibility in relation to its broadly social tasks and, by deflecting the centre of gravity of public attention to other spheres (which is already noticeable), it leaves only a single aesthetic 'love for real life' (to what absurd lengths the game of love for 'machines' has been taken, despite the example of a very highly respected Soviet whodunit in which the cartridge-producing and dual-printing presses of the 'short film' begin to work for a mechanical conglomeration when the military chemical factory is set in motion!) Or we shall have to effect a 'revolution in the principles of cinema' when it will be a matter of a simple shift of attractions.

This is by no means a matter of trailing under the cover of 'agit tasks' elements that are formally unacceptable to, and uncharacteristic of, cinema in the same way as an incalculable amount of pulp literature, hack-work and unscrupulous behaviour in theatre is justified as agitational. I maintain my conviction that the future undoubtedly lies with the plot-less actor-less form of exposition but this future will dawn only with the advent of the conditions of social organisation that provide the opportunity for the general development and the comprehensive mastering of their nature and the application of all their energy in action, and the human race will not lack satisfaction through fictive energetic deeds, provided for it by all types of spectacle, distinguished only by the methods by which they are summoned forth. That time is still a long way off but, I repeat, we must not ignore the enormous effectiveness of the work of the model actor [*naturshchik*][13] on the audience. I submit that the campaign against the model actor is caused by the negative effect of the lack of system and principle in the organisation of his work.

This 'play' is either a semi-narcotic experience with no account of time or space (and really only a little off the 'place where the camera is standing'), or a stereo-metric spread in three-dimensional space of the body and the extremities of the model actor in different directions, remotely recalling some forms of human action (and perceived by the audience thus: 'Aha, apparently he's getting angry') or consecutive local contractions of facial muscles quite independent of one another and their system as a whole, which are considered as mime. Both lead to a superb division of space in the shot and the surface of the screen that follow strict rhythmic schemas, with no single 'daubing' or unfixed place. But ... a rhythmic schema is arbitrary, it is established according to the whim or 'feeling' of the director and not according to periods dictated by the mechanical conditions of the course of a particular motor process; the disposition of the extremities (which is precisely not 'movement') is produced outside any mutual mechanical interaction such as the unified motor system of a single organism.

The audience in this kind of presentation is deprived of the emotional effect of perception which is replaced by guesswork as to what is happening. Because emotional perception is achieved through the motor reproduction of the movements of the actor by the perceiver, this kind of reproduction can only be caused by movement that adheres to the methods that it normally adheres to in nature. Because of the confirmation of the correctness of this method of influence and perception I agree in this matter (this problem has been examined and elaborated in detail in my brochure on expressive movement published by Proletkult[14]) even with Lipps* who cites as proof of the correctness of his investigations into the cognition of the *alter ego* the statement that (citing Bekhterev) 'the emotional understanding of the *alter ego* through the imitation of the other leads only to a tendency to experience one's own emotion of the same kind but not to a conviction that the *alter ego* exists.'

Leaving aside the last statement, which hardly concerns us, we have a very valuable confirmation of the correctness of our approach to construction, to an 'effec-

---

* Lipps, *Das Wissen vom fremden 'Ich'* [The Consciousness of the Alien Ego].

tive construction' (in the particular instance of film), according to which it is not the facts being demonstrated that are important but the combinations of the emotional reactions of the audience. It is then possible to envisage in both theory and practice a construction, with no linking plot logic, which provokes a chain of the necessary unconditioned reflexes that are, at the editor's will, associated with (compared with) predetermined phenomena and by this means to create the chain of new conditioned reflexes that these phenomena constitute. This signifies a realisation of the orientation towards thematic effect, i.e. a fulfilment of the agitational purpose.*

The circle of effective arts is closed by the open essence of the agitational spectacle and a 'union' with the primary sources is established: I think that the celebrated dances in animal skins of the primitive savages 'whence theatre derived' are a very reasonable institution of the ancient sorcerers directed much less towards the realisation of figurative tendencies ('for what purpose?') than towards the very precise training of the hunting and fighting instincts of the primitive audience. The refinement of imitative skill is by no means a matter of satisfying those same figurative tendencies but of counting on the maximum emotional effect on the audience. This fundamental orientation towards the role of the audience was later forfeited in a purely formal refinement of methods and it is only now being revived to meet the concrete requirements of the day. This pure method of training the reflexes through performance effect deserves the careful consideration of people organising educational films and theatres that quite unconsciously cram children with an entirely unjustified repertoire.

We shall move on to analyse a particular, but very important, affective factor: the work of the model actor. Without repeating in brief the observations I have already made as to what that work is and what it should be, we shall set out our system of work, endeavouring somehow to organise this branch of our labour (reforging someone else's psyche is no less difficult and considerable a task than forging iron and the term 'playing' is by no means appropriate).

The basic premiss

1. The value lies not in the figurativeness of the actions of the model actor but in the degree of his motor and associatively infectious capabilities vis-à-vis the audience (i.e. the whole process of the actor's movement is organised with the aim of facilitating the imitative capacities of the audience).

2. Hence the first direction concerns the *selection* of versions presented to the audience: a reliance on invention, i.e. on the *combination* of the movement, required by the purpose, from the versions that are most characteristic of real circumstances (and consequently automatically imitated by the audience) and

---

* We must still bear in mind that in a spectacle of dramatic effect the audience is from the very first placed in a non-neutral attitude situation and sympathises with one party, identifying itself with that party's actions, while opposing itself to the other party, reacting from the very first through *a feeling of direct opposition* to its actions. The hero's anger provokes your own personal anger against his enemies; the villain's anger makes you jeer. The law of effect remains essentially the same.

simplest in form. The development and complication of motivations in the matter of 'delays' (as literature treats them). NB Cinema makes very frequent use, apart from delays, of montage methods and this method too. I can cite an example of a moment that is constructed cinematically in this way from my theatre production of *Can You Hear Me, Moscow?*,[15] when the *agent provocateur* is handed an empty envelope that purports to contain evidence of his provocations. (There will be no reference in this section to the film I am working on in so far as the film as a whole is not orientated in its construction towards this group of actions whereas the work of the model actor is a matter of investigating the methods of 'free work'.) Here the de-texturisation [*rasfakturennost'*] of the elements taken from the simplest versions of the movement of handing the envelope over and attempting to take it so excites the emotion of the audience with its delay that the 'break' (the transition to the murder) makes the same impression as a bomb exploding. (In a film treatment you would add a montage section following the same rhythmic module.)

3. The refinement of this version of movement: i.e. the ascertainment of the purely mechanical schema of its normal course in real life.

4. Breakdown of movement into its pseudo-primitive primary component elements for the audience – a system of shocks, rises, falls, spins, pirouettes, etc. – for the director to convey to the performer the precise arrangement of the motor version and to train these inherently neutral expressive (not in terms of plot but in terms of production) motor units.

5. Assembly (montage) and co-ordination into a temporal schema of these neutral elements of the movements in a combination that produces action.

6. Obfuscation of the schema in the realisation of the difference in execution that exists between the play of a virtuoso with his own individual reordering of rhythm [*pereritmovka*] and the play of a pupil metrically tapping out the musical notation. (NB The completion of the minor details in fixing the version also enters into this obfuscation.)

The realisation of the movement does not proceed in a superficially imitative and figurative manner vis-à-vis a real action (murder, drunkenness, chopping wood, etc.) but results in an organic representation that emerges through the appropriate mechanical schema and a real achievement of the motor process of the phenomena being depicted.

The norms of organicism (the laws of organic process and mechanical interaction) for motor processes have been established partly by French and German theoreticians of movement (investigating kinetics in order to establish motor primitives) and partly by me (kinetics in its application to complex expressive movements and the dynamics of both: see below) in my laboratory work at the Proletkult Theatre.

Briefly, they lead to the following: the basic raw material – and the actor's real work lies in overcoming its resistance – is the actor's body: its resistances to motor intentions comprise its weight and its ability to conserve motor inertia.

The methods for overcoming these resistances dictated by their very nature are based on the following premisses.

The basic premiss was stated by G.-B. Duchenne in *Physiology of Motion* as early as 1885:[16] 'l'action musculaire isolée n'est pas dans la nature',[17] i.e. a particular muscular action with no connection with the muscular system as a whole is not characteristic of nature and is found only in the pathological phenomena of cramps, hysterics and convulsions.

Furthermore, the consequences of Rudolph Bode's* premiss, the results of long years of practical research are:

1. The principle of 'totality' [*tselokupnost'*]† according to which the body as a whole participates in the execution of every movement.
2. The principle of a 'centre of gravity'. Because of the inorganic nature of the process of directing effort to individual muscles, only the centre of gravity of the entire system can serve as the sole permissible point of application. (Hence it follows that the movements of the extremities are not independent but the mere mechanical result of the movement of the body as a whole.)
3. The principle of emancipation, i.e. given general work selection, the periodic positioning – by means of the appropriate muscular relaxation [*Entspannung*] – of an extremity, of the extremities or of the body as a whole, becomes the positioning of the purely mechanical actions of the forces of gravity and inertia.

These premisses were expounded without being applied to any special kind of movement and, principally, to the norms of physical education. None the less, even the first attempts to normalise the working movements of a worker at a lathe (at that time this was mainly with a view to protecting him against occupational physical distortions of the body and the spine) led to the application of those same principles, as is clear from the motor schemas and descriptions appended to the work of Hueppe who (in 1899) first raised the question of the physical organisation of labour.

In the application of these principles to the movement being demonstrated the emphasis is on the utmost expressiveness as the bearer of the influence: I have studied this further. By expressive movement I understand movement that discloses the realisation of a particular realisable motor intention in the process of being realised, i.e. the appropriate arrangement of the body and the extremities at any particular moment for the motor execution of the appropriate element necessary for the purpose of the movement. Expressive movements fall into three[18] groups:

1. A set of rational directions in the direct execution of common motor intentions (all aspects of an appropriately constructed movement – of a boxer, a hammerman, etc. – and also reflex movements that have at some time been automated into conscious purposes – the leap of a tiger, etc.).
2. A set of instances with varying purpose with two or more motivations for their realisation when several purposes that resolve particular motivations build up in the body and, lastly:
3. The most interesting case in terms of its motor formation is the case of a

---

* R. Bode, *Ausdrucksgymnastik* [The Gymnastics of Expression] (Munich, 1921).

† *Totalität* in Sergei Tretyakov's Russian translation.

46

psychologically expressive movement that represents a motor exposure of the *con-flict* of motivations: an instinctively emotional desire that retards the conscious volitional principle.

It is realised in the motor *conflict* between the desires of the body as a whole (which respond to the tendency of instinct and represent material for the exposure of reflex movement) and the retarding role of the consciously preserved inertia* of the extremities (corresponding to the role of the conscious volitional retardation that is realised through the extremities).

This mechanical schema, first elaborated by me, for expressive movement finds confirmation in a series of observations by Klages[†] and the premises put forward by Nothnagel.[19] We value the former's statements that only the affect can serve as the cause of organic motor manifestation and not the volitional impulse whose fate it usually is to act merely as a brake on and a betrayer of intentions. The latter has stated that the actual means of communicating cerebral stimulation through the facial muscles (he is writing about mime) are achieved by quite different methods depending on whether the movement is determined by the surface of the face or as a result of affective stimulation. The latter methods involve a specific part of the brain (the so-called *Sehhügel*[20]), the former do not. As confirmation Nothnagel cites some very interesting cases of paralysis. Given the appropriate affects, the paralysed part of the face of certain patients was able to cry and laugh whereas the patient was incapable of the smallest movement of the lips or eyes consciously (freely) in the absence of affective prerequisites. Or the inverse instance when, in cases of very powerful emotional shock, a paralysed face preserved a stony immobility whereas the patient was able at will to produce any muscular contractions in his face (knit his brows, move his mouth, and so on).[‡]

It would be a great error to perceive our statement as advocating in the model actor's work the affective condition that was long ago condemned in theatre and is absolutely unthinkable in cinema, given the peculiarities of its production. It is here a matter of assessing the mechanical interactions that constantly occur within us but that flow from us in cases where a similar process has to be consciously realised in front of an audience or a camera.[§] We must also bear in mind that both series of movements that are coming into conflict are equally con-

---

* A state of tranquillity or of the preservation of the preceding movement of the object.

† Klages, *Ausdrucksbewegung umd Gestaltungskraft* [Expressive Movement and Formative Power] (Leipzig, 1923).

‡ I am quoting from Krukenberg, *Vom Gesichtsausdruck des Menschen* [Human Facial Expression] (Stuttgart, 1923).

§ The majority of movements are reflex and automatic and it was Darwin who pointed out the difficulties involved in reproducing these kinds of movements. One example is the difficulty involved in reproducing a 'premeditated' swallow. It is interesting to note the immediate departure from the laws of movement that occurs when they are consciously reproduced: whereas if the hands of an actor (which, according to the general laws, are part of his body as a whole) are in real life always engaged in motor movement, on stage 'they do not know what to do' because this law is being broken.

sciously constructed and the effect of the affective movement is achieved by the artificial mechanical setting in motion of the body as a whole and must in no way result from the emotional state of the performer. The biodynamic method of translating artificially induced movement to the conditions of the organic flow of the process of movement through a dynamic and powerful deployment of the so-called 'denying' movement (understood even by schools of movement which included it in their system merely in its spatial sense[*]) is an attitude expressed by theoreticians of theatre as long ago as the 17th century[†] and due to inertia. I shall here only remind you of the particular kind of certain neutrally affective 'working conditions' that also facilitates this translation. A detailed exposition of these questions, which are less important to cinema than to theatre, would lead us into too much technical detail.

We should do better to concentrate on selecting a particular example of this kind of expressive movement. A particularly clear example is the 'baring of teeth': in our view this is *not* a parting of the lips *but* a pushing on the part of the head which, as the 'leading' part of the body, is striving to break through the inert restraints of the surface of the face. The motor process is quite analogous to a particular psychological situation: in the final analysis the baring of the teeth is a gesture towards an opponent, constrained by consciousness for one reason or another. Thus, according to the stated premises, 'psychological expression' also leads to unique dual gymnastics in reproducing the conflict between the motor tendencies of the body as a whole and the extremities. In the process of this 'struggle' distortions arise on the surface of the face and in the centrifugal spatial trajectories of the extremities and of the interrelationships of the joints just as there will also be countless shades of expression subjected to strict calculation and conscious construction given an adequate command of this system of dual motor process. (It is very interesting that even the apparently 'intellectual' parts of the body are involved in the realisation of the delaying role of the intellect, i.e. those parts that have been emancipated with the cultivation of the individual from 'unskilled' labour in the motor servicing of the body – moving and feeding it – the hands, that we have stopped walking on, and the face, that has ceased to be a snout gulping down food – a kind of 'class struggle' in its own way!)

The material that I analysed and selected in these principles of movement is for the time being a base schema which will begin to come to life only when real forces are set in motion, and a rhythmic scale which is appropriate to the particular expressive manifestation cannot be established until that moment. (It is unnecessary to say anything about the need for a rhythmic formula in general: it is quite obvious that the same sequence of movements, with the addition of different combinations of duration, will produce quite different expressive effects.)

---

* 'Denial' in this sense in a small preparatory movement in the reverse direction to the movement being executed which serves to increase the amplitude of the movement and underline more strongly the beginning of the movement not as a starting-point but as an extreme point of denial that is no longer static but is a turning-point in the direction of the movement.

† See Vsevolod N. Vsevolodskii-Gerngross, *Istoriya teatral'nogo obrazovaniya v Rossii* [The History of Theatrical Training in Russia], vol. 2 (St Petersburg, 1913).

The principal distinction of this approach will be the establishment of temporal values, selected in a far from arbitrary way, for any elements in whatever combination, and they will represent the result of the processes of distribution of power loads for shocks, and the intensity of muscular responses; the forces of centrifugal inertia on the extremities; the neutralisation of the inertias of preceding elements of the movements, the conditions that arise in connection with the general position of the body in space, etc., in the process of realising the expressive objective.

Thus, a precise organic rhythmic schema is taking shape that corresponds to the intensity of the course of the process and itself changes in changing conditions and in the common character of the precise resolution of the objective: it is individual to each performer and corresponds to his physical characteristics (the weight and size of his extremities, his muscular state, etc.). In this context we note that in the rhythmic construction of the process of movement its degree of arbitrariness is extremely limited. In rhythmic movement we are a long way from being able to behave as we please: the actual biomechanical structure of the working organ inevitably conducts our movement towards a regular function that breaks down into the sum of simply and strictly motivated harmonic components. The role of random innervation in this process amounts to a spasmodic disturbing intervention in the organically progressing motor process and the possibility of automating this process (which represents the ultimate aim in the realisation of its conviction and is achieved by training in rehearsal) is in these circumstances excluded.*

On the other hand, to fit temporal segments artificially to a desired expressive schema is much less economical and presents enormous difficulties. I might even go as far as to say that it is impossible because of the fact that I verified this in my production of *Gas Masks*.[21] When a man suffocates in the hatch where a pipe is being mended the intervals between beats increase and their force abates. From the sound throughout the auditorium you could detect unmistakably each time the combination of the performer's beats occurred at a break in the movement and the artificial selection of the intervals between, and the intensity of, the beats and when they were part of an uninterrupted process, achieving the necessary effect by overcoming in the longer term the inertia of preceding movements through introducing successively weaker new shocks in the repeated blows. A visually similar phenomenon would strike us even more powerfully.

An example of the ideal form of the verbal-rhythmic effect of movement (constructed on the basis of matching a sound schema as we match the schema of an expressive objective) is provided by the performer in a jazz band: his command of movement consists in an amazing use of the process of neutralising the inertia of a large-scale movement into a series of pantomime and percussive movements, and in their combination with small-scale new elements of movement. If this process is replaced by a process of newly emerging innervations of certain limbs (if the jazz-player is not a good dancer), without regard for the rhythmic oscillations of the body as a whole, his exaggerated movements, ceasing to fit into an

---

* See the collection of essays by the Central Labour Institute in their application to work movement.

The Strike: The criminal underworld emerges from the cemetery of barrels to be recruited as police agents.

organic schema, would have the effect of pathological grimaces (precisely because of the inorganic character of their origin).

Even this one example should be enough to confirm the rule of the preservation of inertia, the rule that determines how convincing a motor process is by preserving the motor inertia of what becomes a single action. As an example of this use of inertia I shall cite the clowns in 'Fatty' Arbuckle's[22] film group. They employ this method in such a way that they unfailingly lend to each complex of complicated movement, liquidated in the conditions of one scene or another, a completely unfounded ending of pure movement. Given their skill this is always a brilliant little 'trick'. In mechanical terms it is this device that releases the accumulating reserve of inertia that permeates a whole complex of movement.

I shall not get involved in the details of their methodology. I shall merely point out that the basic requirement of a model actor for this kind of work is the *healthy organic rhythm* of his *normal physical functions,* without which it is impossible for him either to master this system or to perceive it via a rhythmically precise screen, despite the fact that in theatre success (i.e. emotional infectiousness) can be greater in the light of the nervous imbalance that accompanies, or rather conditions, this characteristic. (This has been tested on two of my actors: it was curiously impossible to find two or three 'unsoiled' in a row, whatever the tempo of their filmed movement, because the nervous foundation of their rhythm was so uneven.)

The question of fixation, which is so decisive for the screen, emerges here as the natural result since, whatever the outcome of the conflict depicted, that [conflict] passes through a moment of equalisation, i.e. a state of rest. If the disproportion of forces is too great there can be neither fixation nor expressive movement, for it becomes either simply an act or a simple state of rest, depending on which tendency is dominant.

Thus we can realise a montage (assembly) of movements that are purely organic in themselves. I should call them the elements of the working movement of the model actors themselves and the arrangement assembled in this way involves the audience to the maximum degree in imitation and, through the emotional effect of this, in the corresponding ideological treatment. In addition as a whole it produces (although it is possible to construct them without this) the *visual* effect of the emotion apparently experienced. We see that the methods of processing the audience are no different in the mechanics of their realisation from other forms of work movement and they produce the same *real, primarily physical* work on their material – the audience.

In this approach to the work of the model actor there is no longer any question of the 'shame' of acting (an association with the concept of acting that has taken root because of the really shameful methods of experiential schools of acting). There will be no difference in the perception via the screen of a cobbler sewing boots or a terrorist throwing a bomb (staged) because, proceeding from the identical material bases of their work, both of them first and foremost process the audience through their actions: one plays (not directly of course but through appropriate presentation by the director) on pride in work well done (more precisely on illusory co-construction) while the other plays on the feeling of class hatred (more precisely, the illusory realisation of it). In both cases this constitutes the basis of the emotional effect.

I think moreover that this kind of movement, apart from its direct effectiveness which I have verified in theatre in both its tragic and its comic aspects, will be the most photogenic in so far as one can define 'photogenic' by paraphrasing Schopenhauer's good old definition of the 'beautiful'. An idea expressed in its completeness is photogenic; that is, an object is photogenic when it corresponds most closely to the idea that it embodies.* (A car is more photogenic than a cart because its whole structure corresponds more closely to its purpose of transportation, and so on.)

That the objects and costumes of previous periods are not photogenic† can, I think, be explained by the way that they were made: for example, costumes were not produced by a search for normal clothing or by the forms of special clothing suitable for various kinds of production, i.e. for forms that corresponded most closely to the purpose they embodied, the 'idea', but were determined by purely fortuitous motivation like, let us say, the fashion for red and yellow combinations, the so-called 'cardinal sur la paille', named in honour of Cardinal de Rohan who was imprisoned in the Bastille in connection with the affair of the 'Queen's necklace'. Or lace head-dresses 'à la Fontanges', connected with the saucy episode

---

* This definition fully conforms to Delluc's observation that photogenic faces are those which first and foremost possess 'character', which, for a face, is the same as what we are saying about movement [Note in E's MS.]

The 'character' of a face is the most frequent imitation, i.e. of the motivations (Klages). [Note in Belenson version.]

† As noted, for instance, by Delluc in the journal *Veshch'*, no. 3.

between Louis XIV and Mlle de Fontanges who lost her lace pantaloons and saved the situation by hurriedly adding them to her already elaborate hair-do. The approach that makes for photogenic costume, i.e. the search for functional forms in costume, is characteristic only of recent times (noted apparently for the first time by the Japanese General Staff) so that only contemporary costumes are photogenic. Working clothes[23] furnish the richest raw material: e.g. a diving suit.

In this particular instance movements are revealed that most logically and organically correspond to the phases of the flow of a certain action. Apart from theoretical probability, a practical indication that it is precisely this kind of movement that is most photogenic is provided by the photogenic quality of animals, whose movements are structured in strict accordance with these laws and do not infringe them by the intervention of the rational principle in their automatic nature (Bode). Labour processes, which also flow in accordance with these stated laws, have similarly been shown to be photogenic.

There remains to add to the system we have elaborated only one more circumstance that formally is more critical for cinema than for theatre. For cinema the 'organisation of the surface' (of the screen) presents an even more serious problem, indissolubly linked to the organisation of the space encompassed by the frame and – and this is specific to cinema – by the fluctuation of this surface and the constant contrast between the surfaces thus organised in movement (the montage succession of shots). I think that, as far as establishing the necessary (in the sense of a correctly constructed superstructure to movement) consequent (deriving from this characteristic of cinema) spatial correctives is concerned, there is little to add to Kuleshov's 'axial system' that seemed to illuminate this problem so thoroughly. Its one fundamental error lies in the fact that those who elaborated it regard it as the basic approach to movement in general, which leads to its alienation from the mechanical and dynamic foundations of movement. In Kuleshov's view we do not have a smooth process of movement but an alternation of unconnected 'positions' (poses). The motor results of this lead to grimace instead of mime, and movement over and above the energetic purpose of material work, and the model actors, by their appearance as mechanical dolls, undermine our trust in the extraordinarily valuable methods of spatial organisation of the material on the screen. In this instance only one thing can serve as the criterion for a production: it is the director's personal taste for overturning the rhythmic schemas of quiet scenes and [creating] chaos in the motor organisation of fights and other energetically saturated places, requiring that organisation be subjugated to the schemas of force and mechanics. It is only once this has been done that they can be subjected to some kind of external moulding. Inevitably this kind of approach must, and does, lead to stylisation.

The attractional approach to the construction of all elements, from the film as a whole to the slightest movement of the performer, is not an affirmation of personal taste or of the search for a polished style for Soviet cinema, but an assertion of the method of approach to the montage of effects that are useful to our class and of the precise recognition of the utilitarian goals of cinema in the Soviet Republic.

3 The Problem of the Materialist Approach to Form[1]

The unanimous and enthusiastic reception that the press has given *The Strike,* and the actual character of that reception, allow us to perceive *The Strike* as a revolutionary victory not merely for the work itself but also as an *ideological victory in the field of form.* This is particularly significant now at a time when people are ready to trample with such fanaticism on any work in the field of form, branding it as 'Formalism' and preferring ... complete formlessness. But in *The Strike* we have the first instance of revolutionary art where the form has turned out to be more revolutionary than the content.

The revolutionary novelty of *The Strike* by no means derives from the fact that its content – the revolutionary movement – was, historically, a mass rather than an individual phenomenon (hence the absence of plot and hero, etc., that characterise *The Strike* as the 'first proletarian film'), but rather from the fact that it has promoted a *properly devised formal method of approaching* the exposure of the abundance of historical-revolutionary material in general.

The historical-revolutionary material – the *'manufactured' past* of contemporary revolutionary reality – was for the first time treated from a correct *point of view:* its characteristic movements were investigated as stages in a single process from the point of view of its 'manufacturing' essence.[2] The discovery of the manufacturing logic and the exposition of the technique of the methods of struggle as of a 'living' current process that knows no inviolable rules other than its final aim and the methods that are varied and devised at a particular moment according to the conditions and the balance of forces at that particular phase of the struggle, having depicted it in all its everyday intensity: that is the formal requirement I put to Proletkult in determining the content of the seven parts of the cycle *Towards the Dictatorship.*[3]

It is quite obvious that the specific quality of the actual *character* (the massness[4]) of this movement does not yet play any part in the construction of the logical principle that has been expounded and it is not its *massness* that defines it. The form of the plot [*syuzhet*], the treatment of the content (in this case the first use of the method of script montage: i.e. its construction not on the basis of some kind of generally accepted dramaturgical laws but in the exposition of the content by methods that define the construction of the montage as such in general terms, e.g. in the organisation of newsreel footage),* even the very correctness of the

---

* It is, however, interesting to note that, because of this feature of the actual technique of exposition of *The Strike* and the other parts of *Towards the Dictatorship,* there was, properly speaking, no script but there was a jump – subject: cue sheet – which was quite logical in terms of the montage essence of the matter.

arrangement of the visual angle towards the material were in this particular instance *consequences of the basic formal realisation of the material under consideration,* of the basic form-renewing 'trick' of direction in the construction of a film that defined it in the first instance.

On the level of the affirmation of a new form of film phenomenon as the consequence of a new kind of social command (stated baldly: the 'underground') the direction of *The Strike* followed the path that has always characterised the revolutionary affirmation of the new in the field of art, the path of the *dialectical* application, to a number of materials, of methods of treatment that were not normally used for them but that came from another field, either adjoining or opposite. Thus, the 'revolutionising' of the aesthetics of theatrical forms that have been transformed before our very eyes during the last twenty-five years has taken place under the guise of the absorption of the external characteristics of 'neighbouring' arts (the successive dictatorships of: literature, painting, music, exotic theatres in an era of conventional theatre, circus, the external tricks of cinema, etc.[5]). This involved the fertilisation of one series of exotic phenomena by another (apart, perhaps, from the role of the circus and of sport in the renewal of acting skills). The revolutionary quality of *The Strike* was exemplified by the fact that it took its renewing principle not from the ranks of 'artistic phenomena' but from those that are *directly utilitarian:* specifically, the principle of the construction of the exposition of manufacturing processes in the film, a choice that is significant because it goes beyond the limits of the aesthetic sphere (which is, in itself, quite logical for my works which are, always and in every case, orientated towards the principles not of aesthetics but of the 'mincer'), all the more so because what was in *material* terms correctly ascertained was precisely that *sphere* whose principles might alone *define the ideology of the forms of revolutionary art just as they have defined*

The Strike: An innocent child wanders among the police horses' legs.

revolutionary ideology in general: heavy industry, factory production and the forms of the manufacturing process.

When talking about the form of *The Strike* it is only very naive people who refer to the 'contradictions between the ideological requirements and the director's formal digressions'. It is time some people realised that form is *determined* much more profoundly than by any superficial 'trick', however successful.

Here we can and must talk not about a 'revolutionising' of the forms, in this particular instance of cinema, because this expression is in manufacturing terms devoid of common sense, but of an instance of revolutionary film form in general because it is in no way the result of a charlatan's 'researches', and certainly not of 'the synthesis of a good mastery of form and our content (as Pletnyov writes in *Novyi zritel*[6]). *Revolutionary form is the product of correctly ascertained technical methods for the concretisation of a new attitude and approach to objects and phenomena – of a new class ideology – of the true renewal not just of the social significance but also of the material-technical essence of cinema,* disclosed in what we call 'our content'. It is not by 'revolutionising' the forms of the stage-coach that the locomotive is created but through a proper technical calculation of the prac- tical emergence of a *new and previously non-existent kind of energy* – steam. It is not the 'research' for forms that correspond to the new content but the logical *realisation of all the phases of the technical production of a work of art consonant with* the 'new *kind* of energy' – the ruling *ideology* – that will produce the forms of revolutionary art that to the very last moment still *want like a spiritualist* to 'leave us guessing'.

So the principle of approach that I put forward and the point of view that I affirmed on cinema's use of historical-revolutionary material turned out to be correct, in terms of materialism, and was recognised as such in *Pravda* by, as one might expect, a *Communist,* who went as far as to call my (formal!) approach 'Bolshevik', and not by the *professional film critics* (who cannot see beyond the end of their noses, that is beyond my 'Eccentrism'[7]). It has been recognised even in spite of the weakness in its programme and plot: the absence of material that ade- quately describes the technique of the Bolshevik underground and of the econ- omic preconditions for the strike which is, of course, an enormous flaw in the *ideological plot* part of the content, although in this particular instance it is merely regarded as a 'non-comprehensive exposition of the manufacturing process' (that is, the process of struggle). It determined a certain superfluous refinement in forms that were in themselves simple and severe.

Massness is the director's *second conscious* trick. As we can see from the above, it is by no means a logical necessity: in fact, of the seven parts of *Towards the Dictatorship,* which are impersonal throughout, only two have a mass character. It is no accident that *The Strike* (one of them, the *fifth* in the series) was selected to be made first. The *mass* material was put forward as the material *most capable* of establishing *in relief* the ideological principle being expounded of an approach to form in the new postulation of a particular resolution, and as *a supplement to the dialectical opposition* of this principle to the *individual plot material of bourgeois cinema.* It is also consciously established in formal terms through the construction of a logical antithesis to the bourgeois West, which we are in no way *emulating* but which we are in every way *opposing.*

55

The mass approach produces in addition the maximum intensification of the emotional seizure [*zakhvat*] of the audience which, for art in general and revolutionary art in particular, is decisive.

Such a cynical analysis of the basic construction of *The Strike*, while perhaps debunking the fine phrases about the 'elemental and collective' character of its 'creation', involves at the same time a more serious and businesslike base and confirms that a formal approach that is *correctly* conducted in Marxist terms results in an ideologically valuable and socially useful product.

All this gives us grounds to apply to *The Strike* the appellation that we are accustomed to using to mark revolutionary turning-points in art: 'October'.

An October that even has its own February because what are the works of Vertov[8] if not the 'overthrow of the autocracy' of fiction cinema and ... nothing more? In this context I am speaking merely of my only fore-runner: *Cine-Pravda*.[9] But *Cine-Eye*,[10] released when the shooting and part of the editing of *The Strike* were already completed, could not have exerted any influence, and by its very essence *there was no way in which it could exert any influence* because *Eye* is the *reductio ad absurdum* of the technical methods that are valid for newsreel, of Vertov's claims that they are *adequate* for the creation of a new cinema. In fact *it is merely an act of denial* filmed by the 'running of one camera', of one particular aspect of cinema.

Without denying a certain part of the genetic link with *Cine-Pravda* (the machine-guns fired just as much in February as they did in October: the difference lay in the target!), because, like *The Strike,* it derived from manufacturing newsreels, I consider it all the more necessary to point to the *sharp distinction in principle,* that is the *difference in method. The Strike* does not 'develop the methods' of *Cine-Eye* (Khersonsky[11]) and it is not 'an experiment in grafting certain methods of construction in *Cine-Pravda* on to fiction cinema' (Vertov). Whereas, in terms of the *external form* of the construction you can point to a certain *similarity,* in precisely the most essential part, the *formal method of construction, 'The Strike' is the direct antithesis of 'Cine-Eye'.*

My starting-point is that *'The Strike' has no pretensions to being an escape from art and in that lies its strength.*

In our conception a *work of art* (at least in the two spheres in which I work: theatre and cinema) is first and foremost a *tractor ploughing over the audience's psyche in a particular class context.*

The work that the Cine-Eyes produce has neither this characteristic nor this premiss and, I think, because of a certain degree of 'mischief' on the part of these producers that is inappropriate to our epoch, their work constitutes a *denial* of art instead of a *recognition of its materialist* essence or, if not, then at least its *utilitarian application.*

This flippancy puts the Cine-Eyes in a quite absurd position because no analysis can fail to establish the fact that their works belong very much to art *and, what is more, to one of its least valuable expressions in ideological terms, to primitive Impressionism.*

With a set of montage fragments of real life (of what the Impressionists called real tones), whose effect has not been calculated, Vertov weaves the cánvas of a pointillist painting.

This is of course the most 'felicitous' form of *easel* painting, just as 'revolution-ary' in its subjects as AKhRR, which takes pride in its affinity with the Wanderers.[12] Hence the success of the *Cine-Pravdas* that are always topical, i.e. *thematically effective*, rather than of *Cine-Eye* which is thematically less satisfac-tory and which in its non-primitively agitational moments (its major part) *mis-carries because its formal effectiveness is impotent.*

Vertov takes from his surroundings the things that impress *him* rather than the things with which, by impressing the *audience*, he will plough its psyche.

The practical distinction between our approaches emerges most sharply in the limited amount of material that *The Strike* and *Cine-Eye* have in common. Vertov considers this to be virtual plagiarism (there's not much material in *The Strike* that would make you rush to *Cine-Eye*!); in particular, the abattoir that is *recorded* in *Cine-Eye* and *gorily effective* in *The Strike*. (This extremely powerful effect – 'pulling no punches' – is responsible for 50 per cent of the opposition to the film.)

Like the well-known Impressionist, *Cine-Eye*, sketchbook in hand (!), rushes after objects as they are *without rebelliously interrupting the inevitability of the sta-tics of the causal connection between them, without overcoming this connection through a powerful social-organisational motive but yielding to its 'cosmic' pressure.* Vertov uses the fixing of its external dynamics to mask the statics of a manifest pantheism (a position that in politics is characteristic of opportunism and Menshevism) in the dynamics of the methods of alogism,[13] in this context a purely aesthetic concept: winter-summer in *Cine-Pravda* no. 19,[14] or simply through the short footage of the montage fragments, and he dutifully reproduces it in sequences of quite impassive consistency.*

[All this is] instead of (as in *The Strike*) snatching fragments from our sur-roundings *according to a conscious and predetermined plan calculated to launch them at the audience in the appropriate combination, to subjugate it to the appro-priate association with* the obvious *final ideological motivation.*

You should by no means conclude from this that I am not prepared to elim-inate the remnants of the theatrical element that is organically inconsistent with cinema from my future works, perhaps through that *apology for a prede-termined plan – the 'production'–* because the important element – *the direction (the organisation of the audience through organised material)* is, in this particu-

---

* With reference to Vertov's static quality, it is in the final analysis interesting to note one instance from one of the most abstractly *mathematically* successful places in the montage: the raising of the flag over the pioneer camp (I don't remember which *Cine-Pravda* it is in). This is a striking example of resolution, not in favour of *the emotional dynamism* of the actual fact of the flag being raised, but in favour of *the statics of the examination* of this process. Apart from *this* directly sensed characterisation, there is in this context a characteristic deployment in the actual technique of montage of (for the most part, short sequences of) *static* (and, what is more, *contemplative*) *close-ups* that are, of course, because of their tri- and quatercellular quality, ill fitted to dynamism within the shot. But here, in this particular instance (and it should be noted that, generally speaking, this method is very widespread in Vertov's 'style') we have, as it were, brought into focus (the 'symbol') the relationships between Vertov and the external world that he is examining. We are face to face with precisely that montage 'elaboration' into a dynamic of static frag-ments.

We should also bear in mind that in this case, and in that of exposed montage material, the montage combination bears the *ultimate* responsibility.

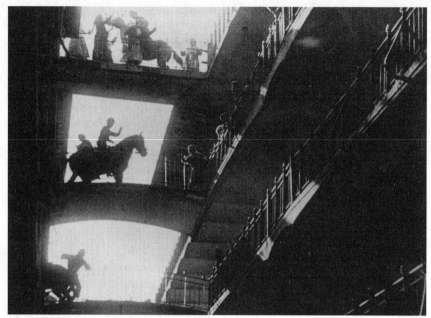

The Strike: The mounted police charge.

lar instance of cinema, possible, and not just through the *material* organisation of the effective phenomena that are filmed but *optically*, through the actual shooting. Whereas in *theatre* the director, in his *treatment*, recarves the *potential dynamics* (statics) of the dramatist, the actor and the rest into a *socially effective construction*, here in *cinema, by selective treatment*, he recarves *reality* and real phenomena through montage *in the same direction*. This is still *direction* and it has nothing in common with the *passionless representation* of the Cine-Eyes, with the fixing of phenomena that goes no further than *fixing the audience's attention*.*

---

* Justice requires me to note that Vertov is making attempts at a different, an *effective*, organisation of material, particularly in the second reel of the *Lenin CinePravda* (January 1925). It is true that here it still shows itself for the moment in the form of a groping towards ways of 'tickling' the emotions, in the creation of 'moods' with no consideration of the use that they might be put to. But when Vertov progresses beyond this first stage of mastering effect and learns to provoke the states of mind he requires in his audience and, through montage, supplies the audience with a predetermined emotional charge, then ... there will be scarcely any disagreement between us – but then Vertov will have ceased to be a Cine-Eye and will have become a *director* and perhaps even an 'artist'.

Then we could raise the question of the use by someone of certain (but by whom and which?) methods because it is only then that we shall be able to speak *seriously* of certain Vertov methods which in the meantime lead only to the intuitive method he has expounded of the practice of his constructions (which, in all probability, Vertov himself acknowledges only faintly). We must not call *practical skills a method*. In theoretical terms the doctrine of 'social vision' is nothing more than an unconnected montage of high-flown phrases and commonplaces that in montage terms yield easily to the simple montage 'sleight of hand' that he is attempting with conspicuous lack of success to substantiate and extol.

The *Cine-Eye* is not just a symbol *of vision:* it is also a symbol *of contemplation.* But we need *not contemplation but action.*

It is not a 'Cine-Eye' that we need but a 'Cine-Fist'.

Soviet cinema must cut through to the skull! It is not 'through the combined vision of millions of eyes that we shall fight the bourgeois world' (Vertov): we'd rapidly give them a million black eyes!

We must cut with our cine-fist through to skulls, cut through to final victory and now, under the threat of an influx of 'real life' and philistinism into the Revolution we must cut through as never before!

Make way for the cine-fist!

4 Constanţa (Whither *The Battleship Potemkin*)[1]

'But where does the *Potemkin* go?' That is a question that very many viewers ask. They met, they waved, they passed, but where did they go?

This is not, of course, just the average man in the street's curiosity or a worker's thirst for knowledge gaining the upper hand over his consciousness of the great public significance of the fact that the admiral's squadron did not open fire.

In the light of this revolutionary consciousness, the maximum conceivable in the circumstances, making the *Potemkin* (the moral victor over the guns of tsarism) into the occasion for an anecdote, albeit a sublime and tragic one, about a 'wandering ship' is, however, to demean the significance of this event.

We stop the event at this point where it had become an 'asset' of the Revolution. But the agony goes on.

The bewilderment of the audience does of course testify to something else: how far the squadron's refusal to open fire is seen in the present state of conscious-ness as something natural and proper rather than as something 'striking'.

Hence the inconceivability of this event today seems very 'average' to the

Filming *The Battleship Potemkin* in Odessa.

audience, who have in short 'waved', and their interest is transferred from the great significance of the event to its anecdotal aspect, 'what comes next?'

Perhaps we should prefer it if the audience did not know. Perhaps it is a matter for our conscience. But that is immaterial here.

What is material is the fact that the critics unfortunately do not act in the way my audiences do.

God Himself commanded them to examine the question, 'Where does the *Potemkin* lead?' That is, to draw conclusions from it on matters of film policy.

Instead they write me compliments or they dig out who I 'stole' it from and they do it so intensely that I begin to think of myself as a 'thief of Bagdad'.[2]

The term 'thieving' is just as appropriate here as it is to the confiscation of Church valuables. But we shall return later to the 'Church's right' to the valuables confiscated.

Now we shall try to plot the course taken by the *Potemkin* and determine its further voyage.

The time has come to establish the NEP tactic in art – and remember that, despite the NEP of the nepmen, NEP is still Ilyich's [Lenin's] most inspired tactical manoeuvre.

What characterises NEP in formal terms? It is the achievement of a particular effect by methods that are the logical opposite to the trend being followed: moving towards socialism by trading, and so on.

It is just the same in policy for the arts.

If people ask me what I myself value in *Potemkin* I tell them it is the fact that it is the first step in the 'NEP' phase of the struggle.

Because in *Potemkin* the complete review of attractions (albeit of *The Strike*) and the positive effect (the pathos) – the stern appeal to activity – are achieved by three 'negative' methods, all of them the methods of passive art: doubt, tears, sentiment, lyricism, psychologism, maternal feelings, etc. These elements are removed from the harmony of their traditional composition with the resultant 'withdrawal symptoms', with a suspension of reality and other pacifying effects (Chekhov, *The Station Master*[3]). These elements of 'right' art are dismembered and reassembled 'business fashion'. In a new setting. This is the bourgeoisie forced to work on a *subbotnik!*[4]

It is not my fault that I am not a lyric poet. But our contemporaries are even less to blame if, after the battle, they need a dose of sentimentalism. I consider that it is only through sentimentalism that they *can be given the necessary*, correct, left, active 'once over'.

Do you really think that the classic 'mists' (a masterpiece of Tisse's photography) are my 'nightingale's song'?! (It's as if, in making propaganda for co-operation, you were to set yourself the ideal of turning the future USSR into an All-Union Muir & Merrilees.[5]) Not at all, I admire them as a sharply honed razor that will cut the viewer 100 per cent in the place that needs it at a particular moment. The mists in *Potemkin* are the 'cows' in *The Strike* . . . amended for the year that has since passed!

In reflexology[6] the term 'stimulant' encompasses at the same time both the blow of a stick on the pate and the softness of pale blue light.

61

As far as *methods* of influence are concerned *Potemkin* is not a continuation of *The Strike* but a contrast to it. The full force of psychologism is here contrasted with the plotlessness, the protocolism, the abstract naturalism and, if you will, the Cine-Eye qualities [*kinoglazistost'*] of *The Strike*. In a new role, certainly, and by new methods. The object is not just an illustration acting as an object (an accordion, a toilet); the object is psychologised both by way of its positioning and in its very presentation: the rotation of the gun is an action but not by virtue of its presentation. The 'roaring lions' are the clearest instance of the new psychologism, the apogee of the psycho-effect elicited from the *object*. The skiffs and the battleship act not through *formal* juxtaposition but through a profoundly psychological contrast – the defenceless clinging to the strong. How many times have I heard how 'touching' destroyer no. 267 appeared, so 'tiny' beside the battleship. But in the encounter with the squadron the machines were almost like the heart of Harry Lloyd,[7] jumping out of his waistcoat because it was so agitated!

Let us compare the 'water hosing' sequence in *The Strike* with the 'Odessa Steps'. The difference is colossal with due regard for the technicism of public sentiment – ascertaining what was the basic emotion of the mass that was just making heroic progress with *construction* – the hosing sequence is elaborated as illustration, logically, as a technical analysis of the combination of bodies and rushing water. On the whole, that is how *The Strike* (or more accurately 'an illustration of the strike') was constructed. The 'Odessa Steps' sequence appeared at the time of an emerging flood of emotionalism. It is no accident that this flood of emotionalism overflows when women Party members leave their Party work and return to their families. A part of the worker's personality is *demobilised* for his personal life, his 'experience'. The resolution of this problem is quite different: a factual line (means and effect: there, water and bodies – here, shots and people falling) demoted to at least a secondary role, and a combination of boot and body, a combination of a 'psychological' rather than a 'production' effect, not to mention the 'episodisation' of the theme of fear that is indiscriminately resolved in *The Strike*, for instance, by a montage of the shot and the carriage.

The continuity from *The Strike* to *Potemkin* lies in the development of a pathos emerging dialectically in *The Strike* that is based on the principle of abstraction and logical technicism.

The Strike is a treatise; *Potemkin* is a hymn.

With *Potemkin* we reach a new era, that of the new psychologism.

What will it be like?

But first, a series of resolutions we must make about it:

1. There is one thing we have no right to do and that is to make generalisations. The current phase of audience reaction determines our methods of influence: what it reacts to. Without this *there can be no influential art and certainly no art with maximum influence.*

2. However much the real state of affairs may be unsympathetic to the preceding period and however much it may contradict it we are obliged to produce a slogan that derives from it. We have no right to alter our policy in the name of scholastic doctrines (and that is what even the *most topical of yesterday's slogans* is). Art

admits *all* methods except those that fail to achieve their end. It was Voltaire who said, 'Au théâtre il faut mieux frapper fort que frapper juste!' [In the theatre it is better to strike hard than true.]

3. What else do we not have a right to? In the 'slippery' methods that are standing in wait for us we must remember this with particular force. We have no right to only one thing that these dangerous attractions of tomorrow used to serve as – a means of 'lulling' the audience – and we must direct all our resources towards ensuring that art always exacerbates a current conflict rather than distracting audiences from it. The bourgeoisie is a great expert in smoothing over the critical questions of the present day which are so brilliantly resolved by the philosophy of 'happy endings'.

Hence the governing philosophy for the coming psychologism – no rigid development of psychological problems in the 'general sense' but on the level of a newspaper satire – is that you will pay some attention to the most painful current question that needs to be resolved, the question that, even though you cannot resolve it in the particular context, compels you not to 'gloss over' it but to *pose* it in concrete form.

We are, alas, on the threshold of a similar theatrical phenomenon in literature, Tretyakov's brilliant *I Want a Child*.[8] We shall see if the theatre staging it proves to be at the same peak of topicality!

It is in this that we find our guarantee against non-topicality and figurative (or, even worse, 'historical', i.e. narrative) psychologism.

4. Lastly – we must not drop the level of the qualifications of mastery and *formal* forward progress in our methods of handling the means of influence.

This concludes the concrete details on the theme 'Whither the *Potemkin*'.*

A more precise specification would be dogmatic charlatanism and playing with words. The question can be resolved only by selecting a new object from the raw material, selecting it properly from the point of view of the right theoretical presupposition and ... the right intuition in the treatment of it – an intuition that, while not yielding to dissection or close analysis, can none the less be considered a powerful but for the time being an unknown form of energy.

For those of us who take our stand on the basis of the montage of attractions, this change is neither an overturning of the foundations of cinema nor a change of course in understanding our cinema. For us it is the next consecutive change of attraction – the next tactical manoeuvre in the attack on the audience under the slogan of October.

---

* This is enough to define the raw material for the treatment.

5 Eisenstein on Eisenstein, the Director of Potemkin[9]

I am twenty-eight years old. I studied for three years until 1918; I wanted originally to be an engineer and architect. During the Civil War I was a sapper in the
Red Army. At about this time I began to devote my free time to the problems of
theatre and art: I had a lively interest in theatre history and theatre problems. In
1921 I joined the Proletkult organisation as a set-painter. It was the Proletkult
Theatre's task to find a new art form that corresponded to the ideology and the
actual state relations of the new Russia. The Theatre consisted of young workers
who wanted to create a serious art and who brought with them a really new spirit
and a new view of the world and of art. At that time these workers conformed
completely to my artistic views and requirements, although I really belong to
another class and came to the same point of view only through a purely theoretical analysis. In the years that followed I had to struggle hard. In 1922 I became sole
director of the First Moscow Workers' Theatre and I got involved in the most vio-
lent differences of opinion with the leaders of Proletkult.[10] The Proletkult people
shared Lunacharsky's view: they favoured the utilisation of the old traditions and
were not afraid of compromise when it came to the question of the relevance of
the pre-Revolutionary arts. I was one of the most uncompromising champions of
LEF, the left front, which wanted a new art that corresponded to the new social
relationships. All the younger generation and all the innovators were on our side
then, including the Futurists Meyerhold and Mayakovsky:[11] ranged in bitter opposition against us were Stanislavsky the traditionalist and Tairov the opportunist.[12]

I was all the more amused when the German press identified my 'simple people'
as actors in the Moscow Art Theatre, my deadly enemy.[13]

In 1922 and 1923 I produced three dramas for the Workers' Theatre: the principle behind their production was the mathematical calculation of their effect and
at the time I called them 'attractions'. In the first play, *Enough Simplicity for Every
Wise Man*,[14] I tried like a Cubist to dissect a classical play into its individual effective 'attractions' – the setting for the action was a circus. In the second play, *Can
You Hear Me Moscow?*,[15] I worked more with technical resources and attempted to
calculate mathematically the illusive potential of the art of drama. It was the first
success for the new theatrical effects. The third play was called *Gas Masks*[16] and it
was played in a gas works during working hours. The machines were working and
the 'actors' were working: it was the first success for absolute reality, for objective
art.

The path from this concept of the theatrical to film was now no more than
simple consequence: only the most inexorable objectivity can be the sphere of

film. My first film appeared in 1924; it was made in collaboration with the people from Proletkult and was called *The Strike*. It had no plot in the conventional sense: it depicted the progress of a strike, a 'montage of attractions'. My artistic principle was therefore, and still is: not intuitive creativity but the rational constructive composition of effective elements; the most important thing is that the effect must be calculated and analysed in advance. Whether the individual elements of the effect are devoid of plot in the conventional sense or whether they are linked together by a 'plot carcass', as in my *Potemkin,* I see no essential distinction. I myself am neither sentimental nor bloodthirsty nor especially lyrical, as has been suggested to me in Germany. But I am very well acquainted with all these elements and I know that one has only to stimulate them skilfully enough to provoke the necessary effect and arouse the greatest excitement. That is, I believe, a purely mathematical affair and it has nothing whatsoever to do with the 'manifestation of creative genius'. You need not a jot more wit for this than you need to design a utilitarian steel works.

As for my attitude to film in general, I must admit that by 'film' I understand tendentiousness and nothing else. Without a clear idea of the why and wherefore of a film one cannot, in my view, start work. Without knowing which latent moods and passions one has to speculate on (excuse this expression: it is 'not nice' but it is professional and it hits the nail on the head) one cannot create. We whip up the passions of the audience and we must therefore provide them with a safety-valve, a lightning-conductor, and this lightning-conductor is tendentiousness. I think that the avoidance of tendentiousness, the dissipation of energies, is the greatest crime of our age. What is more, tendentiousness in itself seems to me to provide a great artistic opportunity: it has by no means always to be as political, as consciously political as in *Potemkin*. But if it is completely absent, if people think of film as a plaything to pass the time, as a means of lulling and putting to sleep, then this lack of tendentiousness seems to me merely to reinforce the tendentious view that people are leading a glorious and contented existence. Just as if cinema's 'congregation', like the church's, should be brought up to be good, quiet and undemanding citizens. Isn't this the sum total of the philosophy of the American 'happy ending'?[17]

I have been criticised because *Potemkin* (and the German version has toned down the political purpose considerably) is too full of pathos. But are we not human beings, do we not have passions, do we not have aims and purposes? The [film's] success in Berlin, in post-war Europe, in the twilight of a still tottering and insecure *status quo*, had to mean an appeal to an existence worthy of mankind: is not this pathos justified? People must learn to hold their heads high and feel their humanity, they must be human, become human: the intention of this film is no more and no less.

The Battleship Potemkin was made for the 20th anniversary of the 1905 Revolution. It had to be ready in December 1925 and that gave us three months. I believe that people in Germany too will regard this as a record. I had two and a half weeks for the editing and there were 15,000 metres altogether.

Even if all roads lead to Rome and genuine works of art do in the final analysis stand on the same spiritual level, I must nevertheless insist that this work has nothing to do with Stanislavsky and the [Moscow] Art Theatre. But it has just as little to do with Proletkult: it is a long time since I worked at that theatre. I have, as it were, organically transferred to cinema whereas the Proletkult people are still wedded to theatre. But in my view an artist must choose between film and theatre: you cannot 'do' both together if you want to achieve something important.

In *The Battleship Potemkin* there are no actors. There are only real people in the film and it was the director's job to find the right people. It was physical appearances rather than proven artistic abilities that were decisive. The opportunity to work in this way is of course only available in Russia where each and everything is a matter for the state. The slogan 'All for one and one for all' was not confined to the screen. If we shoot a film about the sea, the whole navy is at our disposal; if we shoot a battle film, the Red Army joins in the shooting and, if the subject is an economic one, then the commissariats assist. Because we are not making films for me or for you or for any one person but for us all.

I anticipate enormous successes from co-operation in the film field between Germany and Russia. The combination of German technical resources and Russia's feverish creative drive is bound to produce something out of the ordinary. But it is more than questionable whether I myself might move to Germany. I should not like to leave the land that has given me both my strength and my subject matter. And I think people will understand me better if I refer to the story of Antaeos[18] rather than explaining the relationships between artistic creativity and the socio-economic base in Marxist terms. In addition it would be quite impossible for me to work, given the orientation of the German film industry towards cliché and commerce. There have of course been films in Germany that one had to respect but now people are wearing themselves out – I exclude *Faust* and *Metropolis*[19] – in absurd trivialities half-way between pornography and sentimentality. People in Germany have no guts. We Russians break our necks or we win the day and more often than not we win the day.

[I shall stay at home. I am now shooting a film about the development of agriculture in the countryside, the intense struggle for a new agriculture.[20]]

6   Béla Forgets the Scissors[21]

Balázs's article will surprise some people. Without its concluding stipulation: 'The cameraman is the alpha and omega of film.'[22]

We have such respect for foreigners that we might consider this a 'blessing'. The idiots on the Moscow evening paper who accorded recognition to the exercises by young Frenchmen that Ehrenburg brought from Paris have declared the article to be a 'revelation'.[23] These are sheer *enfantillages* –'children's playthings' – based on the photographic possibilities of the photographic apparatus. I am not exaggerating when I say that: if we have these 'children's playthings' today, tomorrow they will be used to refurbish the formal methods of a whole branch of art (for instance, the 'absolute': the plotless film of Picabia, Léger or Chomette).[24]

We are taking our conviction that light can come only from the West to the point of absurdity.

Professor Meller journeyed to London, to the egg market. To seek out standard eggs.

He found unusual ones.

A search began.

Which farms, which ranches, which plantations? Where did this unusual breed of hens come from? Through a chain of Dutch egg wholesalers, agents, contractors and intermediaries they were traced to ... the Novokhopyorsk district.[25] This 'Sirin', 'Alkonost', 'Firebird' turned out to be a peasant's hen.[26]

A peasant's hen from the Novokhopyorsk district. And a London market. ...

But the hen is not a bird and Balázs is a great authority. Such a great authority that at a stroke his book is translated, published and paid for by *two* publishers. Why not, if it's all right to make *two* films from the same material? One set at sea, one in the mountains, and so on.

To understand Béla Balázs's position you have to bear two things in mind: the first and the second. The first is the basis (not the economic one): *where* and *for whom* his report was written. *Filmtechnik* is the organ of the German cameramen's club.[27]* Give the cameraman his due or, more exactly, give him the position of respect that he deserves – that is its fighting slogan.

But that is already an integral feature of the economic basis.

The cameraman achieves. He is obliged to achieve 'self-determination'. To us this kind of programme sounds somewhat savage.

What? In the cultured West?

---

* I refer those who are interested to nos. 1 and 2, which contain a lengthy report by the most respected German cameraman Karl Freund (*Variété, Metropolis*) about the aims and purposes of the club.

Yes. In the cultured West. The steel jaws of competition in the Western metropolis are not accustomed to thinking of the 'service staff' as individuals. The director is just acceptable. But in fact the hero is of course the commercial director. And the cameraman? Round about where the camera handle ends, that's where this ... mechanic apparently begins.

In the advertisements for *Potemkin* even the heroic Prometheus[28] wanted at first to leave Eduard Tisse[29] out altogether. So strong is the tradition. That is not surprising because in the UFA-Haus – the multi-storey headquarters of Universum-Film-Aktiengesellschaft[30] – they don't even know men like Karl Freund or Rittau[31] by sight. That's how it is. They told us themselves. Whereas even we know them by sight. They are like the Novokhopyorsk eggs ... only from the Cöthenerstrasse, where UFA shares its enormous building with the 'Vaterland', the largest café in Berlin. And not for nothing. It is not coincidental that this corner is swarming with swastika-wearers (German Fascists) distributing news-sheets and leaflets. UFA will follow suit.[32]

The *Tägliche Rundschau* of 12 May 1926 writes:

> The declaration by the board of the leading German film organisation UFA of its truly national and commonsense interests is undoubtedly *a slap in the face* for the Committee of Censors: 'In view of the character of the political inclinations of the film we decline to include *The Battleship Potemkin* in the distribution plan for UFA theatres.'[33]

On the same subject *Film-Kurier* writes that, 'The wrath of a businessman who has missed the brilliant commercial success of the season is understandable.' But in other ways UFA remains true to itself. And not only UFA but Phoebus and the others, whatever they are called.

The cameramen are setting up a union to defend the character of their *activity*.

That is the first thing. It explains the emphatic nature of Balázs's positions.

The second thing concerns that same economic basis. Balázs is unaware of collectivism not just in film but also in its production, in work. There is nowhere that he can have seen it. He is due in the USSR in July. Then he'll realise. In Germany man is to man as wolf is to wolf and the link between the director and the cameraman is the banknote. Unity through non-material interest is unknown there.

Balázs's 'starism'[34] is the individualism of bourgeois countries in general. They do not think beyond this in the West. Someone has to be the 'star'. *One* person. Yesterday it was the actor. This time let's say it's the cameraman. Tomorrow it will be the lighting technician.

The idea that a film is the result of *collective* efforts goes to the devil.

What about the man who is nearly dying from the heat of the burning sun, who has to be sponged down, the man Kivilevich whom nobody has ever heard of, who is bent down under the weight of a lighting mirror and dares not move in case a shaft of light should run across little Abraham while he's being trampled on the Odessa Steps?

Or what about the heroism of the five striped assistants?! The 'iron five',[35] taking all the abuse, shouting in all the dialects spoken by the crowd of 3,000 extras who were unwilling to rush around 'yet again' in the boiling sun. Leading this human current behind them. Regardless of its mood. By their own example. And what about the Odessa crowd itself?!

What of Kulganek, Stepanchikova, Katyusha, Zhenya, who stayed up *three nights in succession* to edit the negative for the demonstration copy that was shown on 28 December in the Bolshoi. Do you realise *what* it means to edit a negative of 15,000 metres down to 1,600 ?!

Who remembers them? ... Even in our own country. Cheap overtime workers who were viewed with suspicion by the work inspectorate. Their collective enthusiasm a mere debit in the 'administrative plan'.

Balázs cannot yet conceive of the idea of the cameraman as a free member of a *union of equally creative individuals,* not the cameraman as a 'star' but the camera operator as a co-operator. There the camera crew is a transient pact between self-seeking individuals, here it is a 'creative collective'.

In his approach Balázs makes the same mistake in his theoretical principles as he makes in his section on creative organisation. Because he dissociates himself from a rigid view of the *externality* of the shot, from 'living pictures', but bases his view on the *figurative quality of the shot as the decisive factor,* he falls into rigidity himself in his definition of methods of influence.

It cannot be the decisive factor. Even though it responds to such an undeniable sign as the specific result of specific (i.e. peculiar to it alone) characteristics of the instruments of production, i.e. it corresponds to the possibilities that are the exclusive prerogative of cinema. But Balazs's individualism encourages him to dwell on this.

The shot itself as 'star'.

His stipulation about the staccato effect between 'beautiful shots' is extremely woolly even in the case of 'symbolic shots' because for Balázs the compositional harmony would be preserved in the film as a whole. He does not mention the conditions for a 'genetic' (constructive) amalgamation of the shots.

A long time ago, before *The Strike* was released, we wrote in Belenson's ill-fated book *Cinema Today*[36] opposing the individualism of the West: '*a*) down with individual figures (heroes isolated from the mass), *b*) down with the individual chain of events (the plot intrigue) – let us have neither personal stories nor those of people "personally" isolated from the mass . . . . ' It remains to add one more 'down with' – the personification of cinema in the *individualised shot.* We must look for the essence of cinema not in the shots but in the relationships between the shots just as in history we look not at individuals but at the relationships between individuals, classes, etc.

In addition to the lens Balázs has forgotten another *defining* 'instrument of production': the scissors.

The expressive effect of cinema is the result of juxtapositions.

It is *this* that is specific to cinema. The shot merely *interprets* the object in a setting to use it in juxtaposition to other *sequences.* That is characteristic. Balázs always says 'picture', 'shot', but not once does he say *'sequence'*! The shot is merely an extension of selection. That is, the selection of one object rather than another, of an object from one particular angle, in one particular cut (or *Ausschnitt*, as the Germans say) and not another. The conditions of cinema create an 'image' [*obraz*] from the juxtaposition of these 'cuts' [*obrez*] .

Because the symbolism (in the decent sense of the word!) of cinema must not be based on either the *filmed symbolism of the gesticulation* of the filmed person,

69

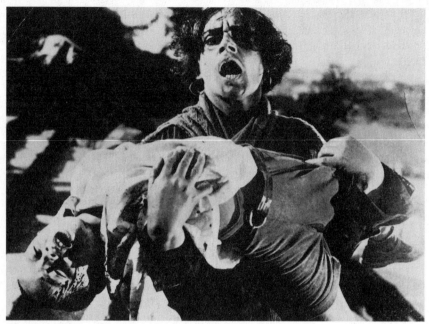

The Battleship Potemkin: Mother and dead child on the Odessa Steps.

even if there is more than one (as in theatre) or the autonomous pictorial symbolism of the emerging shot or picture (as in painting).

However strange it may seem, we must not look for the symbolism of cinema – for its own peculiar symbolism – in the pictorial or spatial arts (painting and theatre).

Our understanding of cinema is now entering its 'second literary period'. The phase of approximation to the symbolism of *language*. Speech. Speech that conveys a symbolic sense (i.e. not literal), a 'figurative quality', to a completely concrete material meaning through something that is uncharacteristic of the literal, through *contextual confrontation*, i.e. also through *montage*. In

The Battleship Potemkin: The massacre on the Odessa Steps.

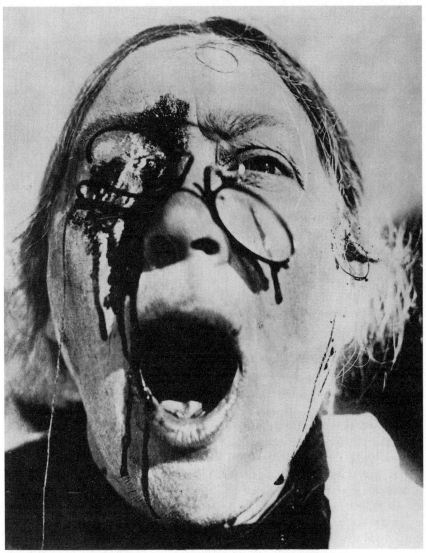

The Battleship Potemkin: The woman with the pince-nez on the Odessa Steps.

some cases – where the juxtaposition is unexpected or unusual – it acts as a 'poetic image'. 'Bullets began to whine and wail, their lament growing unbearably. Bullets struck the earth and fumbled in it, quivering with impatience' (Babel).[37]

In cases other than those of traditional juxtaposition the meaning acquires its own autonomous sense, distinct from the literal, but no longer featuring as an element of its figurative quality (no literary Darwinism!). The notion of 'swine' has its own independent legitimacy and nobody thinks of the figurative fascination of the results of 'swinish' behaviour. Why? Clearly there is little demand. But figurative expression, generally speaking, forever represents a 'mutation' that emerges only in context. When someone says, 'I feel crushed', you still do not know whether 'grief' or a 'tram' is responsible. It becomes obvious from the context.

But Balázs gets bogged down in skiffs and his own definitions which are far removed from ours: the effect of hauling down the sails (simultaneously) appears to have been *created* by the symbolism of the collective gesture *(Gebärde)* and not by the lens.[38] The way the image is cut [*obrez*] , of course, is here exactly as decisive – no more, no less – in the final analysis as the Sebastopol fishermen's union *in toto* once they are resolved and able to 'symbolise' this scene!

Nevertheless we must welcome Balázs for his good intention of constructing a cinema aesthetic on the basis of the possibilities that are unique to cinema, i.e. on pure raw material.

In this respect he has, of course, rather fallen behind the USSR. But we must not expect a man to discuss the 'montage shot' when this concept is generally unknown in Germany.

There are 'literary' shots and 'pictorial' shots, i.e. those that tell us what is happening (an acted sequence), and those that constitute a *performed* intertitle (the scriptwriter's responsibility) or a series of easel paintings (the cameraman's responsibility).

Germany is unaware of the *director's shot that does not exist independently but is a compositional shot, a shot that, through composition, creates the only effect specific to cinema thought.*

People still speak of 'American montage'.[39] I am afraid that the time has come to add this 'Americanism' to the others so ruthlessly debunked by Comrade Osinsky.[40]

America has not understood montage as a new element, a new opportunity. America is honestly narrative; it *does not 'parade' the figurative character of its montage but shows honestly what is happening.*

The rapid montage that stuns us is not a construction but *a forced portrayal, as frequent as possible, of the pursuer and the pursued.* The spacing-out of the dialogue in close-ups is necessary to show one after another the facial expressions of the 'public's favourites'. Without regard for the perspectives of montage possibilities.

In Berlin I saw the last two reels of Griffith's 1914 film *The Birth of a Nation*: there is a chase (as always) and *nothing* formally different from more recent similar scenes. But in twelve years we might have 'noticed' that, apart from its *narrative* possibilities, such – 'if you'll pardon the expression – montage' could offer the prospect of something more, something effective. In *The Ten Commandments*,[41] where there was no special need to portray the Jews separately, the 'Flight from Egypt' and the 'Golden Calf' are shown without recourse to montage but, technically speaking, by long shots alone. Hence the little nuances of the composition of the masses, that is the action of the mass, go to the devil.

In conclusion, a word about Béla Balázs's style. His terminology is unpleasant. Different from ours. 'Art', 'creativity', 'eternity', 'greatness' and so on.

Although some prominent Marxists write in the same dialect and this counts as dialectics.

It looks as if this style has become acceptable.

7 Our *October*. Beyond the Played and the Non-Played[1]

I

October is ready.

Ready and not ready.

A year of quite back-breaking toil.

A year in which coping with thirty to forty hours' shooting was regarded as the easy part of our job and most of our energy was expended on a fight with the slow, sluggish and malevolent machinery of the Leningrad studio.

Towards the end this year 'flattened' us.

We had no teeth left to bite out another ten days from the inexorable deadlines.

Ten days in which to erase the last specks of material that had not been fully integrated, to tighten the screws in the framework of the film, to eradicate the repetitions, remove some superfluous 'shock troops', some identical shots that appear

Eduard Tisse, Eisenstein and Grigori Alexandrov (front centre, left to right) and the team that made *October*.

twice, some scenes with similar rhythms – in other words, to remove everything that neither invention nor ingenuity required.

All we needed was a clear head and a little time.

We did not manage, as it were, to redeem our new-born infant.

So the film is tainted with a certain hint of negligence which in places hinders perception and everywhere provides 'dilettanti' with ammunition for their derision.

But, even if this secondary stage of work had been completed, would *October* have displayed that same taut clarity of purpose that distinguished *Potemkin?*

Potemkin.

It would be a very great mistake to judge *October* by the criteria generated by the appearance of *Potemkin.*

Just as *Potemkin* should not be judged by the rules of *Broken Blossoms.*[2] Only an extremely superficial analysis of *October* as a work would confine itself to evaluating it from the compositional point of view: even that would become a judgment on the work itself.

A cultural analysis in this particular case must address itself above all to questions of methodology.

Because the methodology of the work has taken precedence over the construction of the work.

The methodology of the work at the expense of the work as a whole has destroyed the work.

In this lies the 'tragic fault' of the direction of *October.*

In this lies its surprise for those who expected it to be, and wanted to see in it, its elder brother, *Potemkin.*

But this 'fault' is the fault of a man whose 'voice breaks' at a certain age.

October speaks with two voices.

Falsetto and bass.

'First you hear the flute and then the piano.'

The voice has a habit of 'breaking' at a transitional age.

At an age when you are growing. The transition to adulthood.

October appears at a similar turning-point for cinema.

October spans two epochs in cinema.

The poles are: AKhRR and *Zaum.*[3]

AKhRR as the forward limit of certain forms of consumerism. Of memorial tablets. Commemorative oleographs.

Zaum as that stage in the process of correctly resolving a problem when the correct forms for using the results of this resolution have by no means all yet been found.

Is *October* now unique in this respect? Or is the internal contradiction merely particularly noticeable in it?

Here we should note that development 'within the work' at *the expense of the construction* might be defined as a general characteristic of films released in the current year.

And in every instance this is a sign of internal growth.

Development to the next stage along the path of its own individual development, within the limits of its own genre.

74

October: Lenin's arrival at the Finland station.

This is accompanied by an unavoidable dialectical 'break' within the work as such, unlike the integrity of the works of the previous period.

In actual fact the complete played 'chamber' quality[4] of *The Mother* and *The End of St Petersburg*[5] is suddenly overturned in the middle of the film by a whole swarm of mass-scale and impersonally expressed methods for the social characterisation of phenomena. The disproportion in the work is unavoidable and obvious.

Measured shots, beating the intervals between the pathos-filled inter-titles in *A Sixth Part of the World*[6] like the balls of an abacus, have migrated from the Cine-Eye style to an immediate proximity to the notation marks of 'absolute' films.

The Eleventh Year[7] moves in a series of fragments from a *poem of facts* to a *symphony of facts.*

At last, the routine *Bag* has suddenly given birth to ... a mountain.

The Diplomatic Bag ... to *Zvenigora.*[8]

'An enormous distance!'[9]

75

To a polygamy of approaches, styles and genres turning upsidedown the very concept of genre.

The future researcher will of course know how to link a particular phenomenon – the move towards inward-looking, more profound study of the methods of a work at the expense of the composition as a whole – with the general trend towards cultural revolution, the trend towards more profound study of the problems of culture in general.

For the present I wanted here to point out the feature of the 'period' that even *October* succumbed to. In the next issue we shall dwell in detail on those elements of forward movement that have fallen to its lot.

II

When there are two contestants it is usually the third who is right.

In the ring now:

played and non-played.

That means that justice lies with the third.

With the extra-played.

With cinema that places itself *beyond* the played and the non-played.

With cinema that stands on its *own two* feet with its own, admittedly as yet undesignated, terminology.

The trend in cinema that places itself beyond this opposition emerges quite legitimately and opportunely.

At a time when the slogans of the previous stage have achieved 100 per cent success. At a time when they are generally recognised. At a time when these slogans are reduced – through the stages of obviousness, vulgarisation and truism – to the level of the absurd.

At a time like this there is usually a dialectical overturning of a similar stage by one that is clearly opposed to it.

A theoretical novelty – the 'non-played' film – has in due course replaced plot *by fact.*

Illusion by *raw material.*

Aesthetic fetishisation was replaced by a fetish for raw material.

But a fetish for material is not quite materialism.

In the first instance it is still after all *fetishism.*

When the question of the hegemony of 'raw material' merged into general usage, a hysterical scream, the 'cult' of raw material, it meant the end of raw material.

A new page has to unfold under the precisely inverse slogan:

CONTEMPT FOR RAW MATERIAL.*

This sounds terribly unfamiliar.

But:

slaves of the machine are becoming masters of the machine.

Slaves of raw material are becoming exploiters of raw material.

---

* Wherever 'raw material' is mentioned, it must be understood in the formal cinematic sense and not as something historical or factual.

If in the preceding period the material prevailed, the object replaced 'soul and mood', then the next stage will replace the presentation of a phenomenon (material, object) by a *conclusion* based on the phenomenon and a *judgment* on the material, given concrete form in finished concepts.

Cinema is ready to begin operating through the abstract word that leads to a concrete *concept*.

The new stage will come *under the aegis of a concept – under the aegis of a slogan*.

The period of the 'free market' in cinema is coming to an end.

The played 'I am jealous' (*Variété*),[10] the transitional 'We shall fight' *(Potemkin)* and the non-played 'I see' *(A Sixth Part of the World* and *The Eleventh Year)* remain a page of the calendar that has already been torn off.

What is more, material as material is refusing to work further.

Material is beginning to be viable only in conditions of 'exoticism'.

In *The Eleventh Year* it is already painful to watch the machines.

The shooting, montage and use of a working machine are becoming traditional for us, just as Runich and Khudoleyev[11] are.

But there was a time when the spinning of the wheels of a machine was enough 'in itself'.

Now the slogans surrounding the machine have become more complex – the *interrelationships* surrounding the machine have been made more complex.

While the wheels turn in the same simple way as they did before.

But 'in themselves', *as raw material,* they cannot give more than they have to give – as they say about the most beautiful girl.

The period of the fuss about material was the period of the recognition of the montage fragment as a word and sometimes as a letter.

In some reels *October* is trying to take the next step, trying to seek out *speech* that in its construction will wholly correspond to a similar vocabulary.

The sphere of the new film language will, as it happens, not be the sphere of the presentation of phenomena, nor even that of social interpretation, but the opportunity for *abstract social evaluation*.

On a primitive level this is the line of harps and balalaikas. The discrediting of deities. 'What we fought for' over the piles of mass-produced Crosses of St George. The Kornilov restoration.[12] The debunking of the Winter Palace: its 'moral' defeat in the assault on it, etc.

At first this method seemed to be connected to working elements of – and for the moment it works in the depiction of – the 'enemy'.

The rest adhered to the more or less pathetic tradition of previous works.

But, if the duality of the object weakens perhaps its power to shock as a whole, one corresponding dialectical rupture is compensated by another.

By the fact that it testifies to its viability. By the fact that it has perspective. That it contains both a promise and a guarantee of the film of the future.

We must not forget that the balanced integrity of *Potemkin* paid the price for its maximum effect in the utter exhaustion of its stylistic method.

There can be no further progress along *Potemkin's* path. There can only be variations in the same methods, possibly on other subjects.

We must also remember that the integrity of *Potemkin* occurred at the expense

October: A Bolshevik agitator winning over the Cossack 'Wild Division' to the revolutionary cause.

of *The Strike* which preceded it and which also displayed elements of duality and the dialectic.

I have in passing heard the view expressed that the style of *Potemkin* was missing from *October* and that *October* continues the style of *The Strike*.

This is an absolutely illiterate point of view.

It is not the *style* that *October* continues but, apart from its role as a work in its own right, it still plays the role of *The Strike* in relation to the next work, which for the moment is what it has to do.

A work in which we have perhaps already managed to approximate to genuine pure cinema, cinema beyond the played and the non-played, but equally distant from 'absolute' film.

Now that we have discovered what constitutes a word, a form, a fragment of speech in cinema language, we can begin to pose the question of what we can *express cinematically* and how.

It will be the realm of stating a concept that is free of plot and of the primitive level of 'love as I love', 'tiredness – a tired man'.

It will be the art of the direct cinematic communication of a slogan. Of communication that is just as unobstructed and immediate as the communication of an idea through a qualified word.

The epoch of the direct materialisation of a slogan takes over from the epoch of a slogan about material.

The position of the slogan as the backbone of our films, at least some of them and not just 'loyal' ones, can in no way serve as an objection to what I have stated here.

The time has come to learn to make films directly from a slogan.

To replace the formula 'deriving from raw material' by the formula 'deriving from a slogan'.

After *October* we can turn our hand to attempting the appropriate resolution of the problem. Our next work will try to resolve this problem.

It will not be *The General Line*. On that same formal level *The General Line* is the contemporary of *October*. To it will fall the role of popularising the partial *zaum* of *October* by making these methods generally more accessible.

The attempt to resolve the vast and very difficult problem that *October* proclaims can only be made by our next (planned) capital work.

Because it is only along these lines that the resolution of the problems that it sets itself can be imagined.

This 'capital' work will be made from a 'libretto' by Karl Marx and it will be called:

CAPITAL.

Since we recognise the immensity of this theme as a whole we shall shortly proceed to delimit in the first instance which of its aspects can be cinefied.

This work will be carried out in collaboration with the historian A. Efimov,[13] our consultant in the preparation of the script for *October*.

1928

8 Statement on Sound[14]

Eisenstein, Vsevolod Pudovkin and Grigori Alexandrov

Our cherished dreams of a sound cinema are being realised. The Americans, having developed the technique of sound cinema, have embarked on the first stage towards its rapid practical implementation. Germany is working intensively in the same direction. The whole world now speaks of the 'silent' that has found its voice.

We who work in the USSR recognise that, given our technical capabilities, the practical implementation of sound cinema is not feasible in the near future. At the same time we consider it opportune to make a statement on a number of prerequisite theoretical principles, particularly as, according to reports reaching us, attempts are being made to use this new improvement in cinema for the wrong purposes. In addition, an incorrect understanding of the potential of the new technical invention might not only hinder the development and improvement of cinema as an art form but might also threaten to destroy all its formal achievements to date.

Contemporary cinema, operating through visual images, has a powerful effect on the individual and rightfully occupies one of the leading positions in the ranks of the arts.

It is well known that the principal (and sole) method which has led cinema to a position of such great influence is *montage*. The confirmation of montage as the principal means of influence has become the indisputable axiom upon which world cinema culture rests.

The success of Soviet pictures on world screens is to a significant extent the result of a number of those concepts of montage which they first revealed and asserted.

And so for the further development of cinema the significant features appear to be those that strengthen and broaden the montage methods of influencing the audience. If we examine every new discovery from this standpoint it is easy to distinguish the insignificance of colour and stereoscopic cinema in comparison with the great significance of *sound*.

Sound is a double-edged invention and its most probable application will be along the line of least resistance, i.e. in the field of the *satisfaction of simple curiosity*.

In the first place there will be commercial exploitation of the most saleable goods, i.e. of *talking pictures* – those in which the sound is recorded in a natural manner, synchronising exactly with the movement on the screen and creating a certain 'illusion' of people talking, objects making a noise, etc.

The first period of sensations will not harm the development of the new art; the danger comes with the second period, accompanied by the loss of innocence and purity of the initial concept of cinema's new textural possibilities which can only intensify its unimaginative use for 'dramas of high culture' and other photographed presentations of a theatrical order.

Sound used in this way will destroy the culture of montage, because every mere *addition* of sound to montage fragments increases their inertia as such and their independent significance; this is undoubtedly detrimental to montage which operates above all not with fragments but through the *juxtaposition* of fragments.

Only the contrapuntal use of sound vis-à-vis the visual fragment of montage will open up new possibilities for the development and perfection of montage.

The first experiments in sound must aim at a sharp discord with the visual images. Only such a 'hammer and tongs' approach will produce the necessary sensation that will result consequently in the creation of a new *orchestral counterpoint* of visual and sound images.

The new technical discovery is not a passing moment in the history of cinema but an organic escape for cinema's cultural avant-garde from a whole series of blind alleys which have appeared inescapable.

We must regard as *the first blind alley* the intertitle and all the vain attempts to integrate it into montage composition as a unit of montage (fragmentation of an intertitle, magnification or contraction of the lettering, etc.).

The second blind alley comprises *explanatory* sequences (e.g. long shots) which complicate the composition of the montage and slow down the rhythm.

Every day the problems of theme and plot grow more complex; attempts to solve them by methods of purely 'visual' montage either lead to insoluble problems or involve the director in fantastic montage constructions, provoking a fear of abstruseness and reactionary decadence.

Sound, treated as a new element of montage (as an independent variable combined with the visual image), cannot fail to provide new and enormously powerful means of expressing and resolving the most complex problems, which have been depressing us with their insurmountability using the imperfect methods of a cinema operating only in visual images.

The *contrapuntal method* of structuring a sound film not only does not weaken *the international nature of cinema* but gives to its meaning unparalleled strength and cultural heights.

With this method of construction the sound film will not be imprisoned within national markets, as has happened with the theatrical play and will happen with the 'filmed' play, but will provide an even greater opportunity than before of speeding the idea contained in a film throughout the whole globe, preserving its world-wide viability.

9   Beyond the Shot[1]

It is a weird and wonderful feeling to write a booklet about something that does not in fact exist.

There is, for example, no such thing as cinema without cinematography.

Nevertheless the author of the present book has managed to write a book about the *cinema* of a country that has no *cinematography*.

About the cinema of a country that has an infinite multiplicity of cinematic characteristics but which are scattered all over the place – with the sole exception of its cinema.

This article is devoted to the cinematic features of Japanese culture that lie outside Japanese cinema and it lies outside the book in the same way as these features lie outside Japanese cinema.

Cinema is: so many firms, so much working capital, such and such a 'star', so many dramas.

Cinema is, first and foremost, montage.

Japanese cinema is well provided with firms, actors and plots.

And Japanese cinema is quite unaware of montage.

Nevertheless the principle of montage may be considered to be an element of Japanese representational culture.

The script, for their script is primarily representational. The hieroglyph.[2]

The naturalistic representation of an object through the skilled hands of Ts'ang Chieh in 2650 BC became slightly formalised and, with its 539 fellows, constituted the first 'contingent' of hieroglyphs.

The portrait of an object, scratched with a stylus on a strip of bamboo, still resembled the original in every way.

But then, at the end of the third century, the brush was invented, in the first century after the 'happy event' (AD) there was paper and in the year 220 indian ink.

A complete transformation. A revolution in draughtsmanship. The hieroglyph, which has in the course of history undergone no fewer than fourteen different styles of script, has crystallised in its present form.

The means of production (the brush and indian ink) determine the form. The fourteen reforms have had their effect.

In short, it is already impossible to recognise in the enthusiastically cavorting hieroglyph ma (a horse) the image of the little horse settling pathetically on its hind legs in the calligraphy of Ts'ang Chieh, the horse that is so well known from ancient Chinese sculpture (Fig. 9.1).

But to hell with the horse and with the 607 remaining symbols of the *hsiang-cheng*, the first *representational* category of hieroglyphs.

It is with the second category of hieroglyphs – the *huei-i,* or 'copulative' – that our real interest begins.

The point is that the copulation – perhaps we had better say the combination – of two hieroglyphs of the simplest series is regarded not as their sum total but as their product, i.e. as a value of another dimension, another degree: each taken separately corresponds to an object but their combination corresponds to a *concept.* The combination of two 'representable' objects achieves the representation of something that cannot be graphically represented.

For example: the representation of water and of an eye signifies 'to weep',
the representation of an ear next to a drawing of a door means 'to listen',
a dog and a mouth mean 'to bark'
a mouth and a baby mean 'to scream'
a mouth and a bird mean 'to sing'
a knife and a heart mean 'sorrow', and so on.
But – this is montage!!

Yes. It is precisely what we do in cinema, juxtaposing representational shots that have, as far as possible, the same meaning, that are neutral in terms of their meaning, in meaningful contexts and series.

It is an essential method and device in any cinematographic exposition. And, in a condensed and purified form, it is the starting-point for 'intellectual cinema', a cinema that seeks the maximum laconicism in the visual exposition of abstract concepts.

We hail the method of the (long since) dead Ts'ang Chieh as a pioneering step along this path.

I have mentioned laconicism. Laconicism provides us with a stepping-stone to another point. Japan possesses the most laconic forms of poetry, the *hai-kai*[3] (that appeared at the beginning of the 12th century) and the *tanka.*

They are virtually hieroglyphics transposed into phrases. So much so that half their value is judged by their calligraphic quality. The method by which they are resolved is quite analogous.

This method, which in hieroglyphics provides a means for the laconic imprinting of an abstract concept, gives rise, when transposed into semantic exposition, to a similarly laconic printed imagery.

The method, reduced to a stock combination of images, carves out a dry definition of the concept from the collision between them.

Fig 9.1

The same method, expanded into a wealth of recognised semantic combinations, becomes a profusion of *figurative* effect.

The formula, the concept, is embellished and developed on the basis of the material, it is transformed into an image, which is the form.

In exactly the same way as the primitive thought form – thinking in images – is displaced at a certain stage and replaced by conceptual thought.

But let us pass on to examples:

The *hai-kai* is a concentrated Impressionist sketch:

> Two splendid spots
> on the stove.
> The cat sits on them.
>   (GE-DAI)

> Ancient monastery.
> Cold moon.
> Wolf howling.
>   (KIKKO)

> Quiet field.
> Butterfly flying.
> Sleeping.
>   (GO-SIN)

The *tanka* is a little longer (by two lines).

> Mountain pheasant
> moving quietly, trailing
> his tail behind.
> Oh, shall I pass
> endless night alone.
>   (HITOMASO)

We see these as montage phrases, montage lists.

The simplest juxtaposition of two or three details of a material series produces a perfectly finished representation of another order, the psychological.

Whereas the finely honed edges of the intellectual formulation of the concept produced by the juxtaposition of hieroglyphs are here blurred, the concept blossoms forth immeasurably in *emotional* terms.

In Japanese script you do not know whether it is the inscription of a character or the independent product of graphics.

Born from a cross between the figurative mode and the denotative purpose, the hieroglyphic method has continued its tradition not just in literature but also, as we have indicated, in the *tanka* (not *historically* consistent but consistent *in principle* in the minds of those who have created this method).

Precisely the same method operates in the most perfect examples of Japanese figurative art.

Sharaku[4] was the creator of the finest prints of the 18th century and, in particular, of an immortal gallery of actors' portraits. He was the Japanese Daumier. That same Daumier whom Balzac (himself the Bonaparte of literature) in turn called the 'Michelangelo of caricature'.

Despite all this Sharaku is almost unknown in our country.

The characteristic features of his works have been noted by Julius Kurth.* Examining the question of the influence of sculpture on Sharaku, he draws a parallel between the portrait of the actor Nakayama Tomisaburo and an antique mask of the semi-religious No theatre, the mask of Rozo, the old bonze. (See Fig. 9.2)

Is this not the same as the hieroglyph that juxtaposes the independent 'mouth' and the dissociated 'child' for the semantic expression 'scream'?

Just as Sharaku does by stopping time so we too do in time by provoking a monstrous disproportion between the parts of a normally occurring phenomenon, when we suddenly divide it into 'close-up of hands clasped', 'medium shots of battle' and 'big close-ups of staring eyes' and produce a montage division of the phenomenon into the types of shot! We make an eye twice as large as a fully grown man! From the juxtaposition of these monstrous incongruities we reassemble the disintegrated phenomena into a single whole but from our own perspective, in the light of our own orientation towards the phenomenon.

The disproportionate representation of a phenomenon is organically inherent in us from the very beginning. A. R. Luria[5] has shown me a child's drawing of 'lighting a stove'. Everything is depicted in tolerable proportions and with great care: firewood, stove, chimney. But, in the middle of the room space, there is an enormous rectangle crossed with zigzags. What are they? They turn out to be 'matches'. Bearing in mind the crucial importance of these matches for the process depicted, the child gives them the appropriate scale.

The representation of an object in the actual (absolute) proportions proper to it is, of course, merely a tribute to orthodox formal logic, a subordination to the inviolable order of things.

This returns periodically and unfailingly in periods when absolutism is in the ascendancy, replacing the expressiveness of antiquated disproportion with a regular 'ranking table' of officially designated harmony.

Positivist realism is by no means the correct form of perception. It is simply a function of a particular form of social structure, following on from an autocratic state that has propagated a state uniformity of thought.

It is an ideological uniformity that makes its visual appearance in the ranks of uniforms of the Life Guard regiments . . . .

Thus, we have seen how the principle of the hieroglyph – 'denotation through representation' – splits into two.

Following the line of its purpose (the principle of 'denotation') to the principles of the creation of literary imagery.

Following the line of the methods of achieving this purpose (the principle of 'representation') to the striking methods of expressiveness used by Sharaku.

Just as we say that the two diverging arms of a hyperbola meet at infinity (although no one has ever been such a long way away!), so the principle of hieroglyphics, splitting endlessly into two (in accordance with the dynamic of the

---

* J. Kurth, *Sharaku*, Munich, 1929, pp. 78–80.

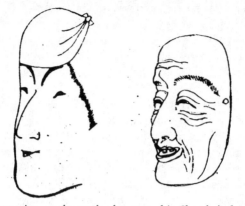

Fig. 9.2: The expression on the mask, also created in Sharaku's day, is the same as that in the portrait of Tomisaburo. The facial expression and the arrangement of masses are very similar to one another even though the mask represents an old man and the print a young woman (Tomisaburo in the role of a woman). The similarity is striking but nevertheless the two have nothing in common. Here we find a characteristic feature of Sharaku's work: whereas the anatomical proportions of the carved wooden mask are almost correct, the proportions of the face in the print are quite simply impossible. The distance between the eyes is so great as to make a mockery of common sense. The nose, in comparison with the eyes at least, is twice as long as a normal nose could possibly be, the chin is on the whole out of all proportion to the mouth: the relationships between the eyebrows, the mouth, the details in general are quite unthinkable. We can observe the same thing in all Sharaku's large heads. It is just not possible that the great master was unaware that these proportions were wrong. He quite deliberately repudiated naturalism and, *while each detail taken separately is constructed on the principles of concentrated naturalism their general compositional juxtaposition is subjugated to a purely semantic purpose. He took as the norm for the proportions the quintessence of psychological expressiveness . . . .*

signs), unexpectedly joins together again from this dual divergence in yet a fourth sphere – theatre.

Estranged from one another for so long, they are once again – the theatre is still in its cradle – present in *parallel* form, in a curious dualism.

The denotation of the action, the representation of the action, is carried out by the so-called Joruri, a silent puppet on the stage.

This antiquated practice, together with a specific style of movement, passes into the early Kabuki theatre as well. It is preserved to this day, as a partial method, in the classical repertoire.

But let us pass on. This is not the point. The hieroglyphic (montage) method has penetrated the very technique of acting in the most curious ways.

However, before we move on to this, since we have already mentioned the representational aspect, let us dwell on the problem of the shot so that we settle the matter once and for all.

The shot.

A tiny rectangle with some fragment of an event organised within it.

Glued together, these shots form montage. (*Of course,* if this is done in the appropriate rhythm!)

That, roughly, is the teaching of the old school of film-making.

Screw by screw,
Brick by brick …[6]

Kuleshov, for instance, even writes with a brick: 'If you have an idea-phrase, a particle of the story, a link in the whole dramaturgical chain, then that idea is expressed and built up from shot-signs, just like bricks'.[7]

Screw by screw,
Brick by brick …

as they used to say.

The shot is an element of montage.

Montage is the assembling of these elements.

This is a most pernicious mode of analysis, in which the understanding of any process as a whole (the link: shot – montage) derives purely from the external indications of the course it takes (one piece glued to another).

You might, for instance, come to the notorious conclusion that trams exist merely to block streets. This is an entirely logical conclusion if you confine yourself to the functions that they performed, for example, in February 1917. But the Moscow municipal authorities see things in a different light.

The worst of the matter is that an approach like this does really, like an insurmountable tram, block the possibilities of formal development. An approach like this condemns us not to dialectical development but to [the process of] mere evolutionary 'perfection', in so far as it does not penetrate to the dialectical essence of the phenomenon.

In the final analysis this kind of evolutionising leads either through its own refinement to decadence or, vice versa, to straightforward weakness caused by a blockage in the blood supply. However odd it may seem, there is an eloquent, nay melodious, witness to both these eventualities simultaneously in *The Happy Canary*.[8]

The shot is by no means a montage *element*.

The shot is a montage cell. Beyond the dialectical jump in the *single* series: shot – montage.

What then characterises montage and, consequently, its embryo, the shot? Collision. Conflict between two neighbouring fragments. Conflict. Collision.

Before me lies a crumpled yellowing sheet of paper.

On it there is a mysterious note:

'Series – P' and 'Collision – E'.

This is a material trace of the heated battle on the subject of montage between E (myself) and P (Pudovkin) six months ago.

We have already got into a habit: at regular intervals he comes to see me late at night and, behind closed doors, we wrangle over matters of principle.

So it is in this instance. A graduate of the Kuleshov school, he zealously defends the concepts of montage as a *series* of fragments. In a chain. 'Bricks'. Bricks that *expound* an idea serially.

I opposed him with my view of montage as a *collision,* my view that the collision of two factors gives rise to an idea.

In my view a *series* is merely one possible *particular* case.

Remember that physics is aware of an infinite number of combinations arising from the impact (collision) between spheres. Depending on whether they are elastic, non-elastic or a mixture of the two. Among these combinations is one where the collision is reduced to a uniform movement of both in the same direction.

That corresponds to Pudovkin's view.

Not long ago we had another discussion. Now he holds the view that I held then. In the meantime he has of course had the chance to familiarise himself with the set of lectures that I have given at the GTK since then.

So, montage is conflict.

Conflict lies at the basis of every art. (A unique 'figurative' transformation of the dialectic.)

The shot is then a montage cell. Consequently we must also examine it from the point of view of *conflict*.

Conflict within the shot is:

potential montage that, in its growing intensity, breaks through its four-sided cage and pushes its conflict out into montage impulses between the montage fragments;

just as a zigzag of mimicry flows over, making those *same* breaks, into a zigzag of spatial staging,

just as the slogan, 'Russians know no obstacles', breaks out in the many volumes of peripeteia in the novel *War and Peace.*

If we are to compare montage with anything, then we should compare a phalanx of montage fragments – 'shots' – with the series of explosions of the internal combustion engine, as these fragments multiply into a montage dynamic through 'impulses' like those that drive a car or a tractor.

Conflict within the shot. It can take many forms: it can even be part of ... the story. Then it becomes the 'Golden Series'. A fragment 120 metres long. Neither the analysis nor the questions of film form apply in this instance.

But these are 'cinematographic':

the conflict of graphic directions (lines)

the conflict of shot levels (between one another)

the conflict of volumes

the conflict of masses (of volumes filled with varying intensities of light)

the conflict of spaces, etc.

Conflicts that are waiting only for a single intensifying impulse to break up into antagonistic pairs of fragments. Close-ups and long shots. Fragments travelling graphically in different directions. Fragments resolved in volumes and fragments resolved in planes. Fragments of darkness and light ... etc.

Lastly, there are such unexpected conflicts as:

the conflict between an object and its spatial nature and the conflict between an event and its temporal nature.

However strange it may seem, these are things that have long been familiar to us. The first is achieved through optical distortion by the lens and the second through animation or *Zeitlupe* [slow motion].

The reduction of all the properties of cinema to a single formula of conflict and of cinematographic indicators to the dialectical series of one *single indicator* is no empty rhetorical pastime.

We are now searching for a single system of methods of cinematographic expression that will cover all its elements.

The reduction of these to a series of general indicators will solve the problem as a whole.

Our experience of the various elements of cinema is quite variable.

Whereas we know a very great deal about montage, we are floundering about, as far as the theory of the shot is concerned, between the Tretyakov Gallery, the Shchukin Museum and geometricisations that set your teeth on edge.[9]

If we regard the shot as a particular molecular instance of montage and shatter the dualism 'shot – montage', then we can apply our experience of montage directly to the problem of the theory of the shot.

The same applies to the theory of lighting. If we think of lighting as the collision between a beam of light and an obstacle, like a stream of water from a fire hose striking an object, or the wind buffeting a figure, this will give us a quite differently conceived use of light from the play of 'haze' or 'spots'.

Thus far only the principle of conflict acts as this kind of denominator:

the principle of optical counterpoint. (We shall deal with this more fully on another occasion.)

We should not forget now that we must resolve a counterpoint of a different order, *the conflict between the acoustic and the optical in sound cinema.*

But let us for the moment return to one of the most interesting optical conflicts:

the conflict between the frame of the shot and the object.

The position of the cinema represents the materialisation of the conflict between the organising logic of the director and the inert logic of the phenomenon in collision, producing the dialectic of the camera angle.

In this field we are still sickeningly impressionistic and unprincipled.

Nevertheless there is a clear principle even in this technique.

A mundane rectangle that cuts across the accident of nature's randomness ....

Once again we are in Japan!

Because one of the methods of teaching drawing used in Japanese schools is so cinematographic.

Our method of teaching drawing is to:

take an ordinary sheet of Russian paper with four corners. In the majority of cases you then squeeze on to it, ignoring the edges (which are greasy with sweat!), a bored caryatid, a conceited Corinthian capital or a plaster Dante (not the magician,[10] the other one – Alighieri, the man who writes comedies).

The Japanese do it the other way round.

You have a branch of a cherry tree or a landscape with a sailing boat.

From this whole the pupil cuts out compositional units: a square, a circle, a rectangle. (See Figs. 9.3 and 9.4.)

He creates a shot!

These two schools (theirs and ours) precisely characterise the two basic tendencies that are fighting one another in contemporary cinema!

Our school: the dying method of spatial organisation of the phenomenon in front of the lens:

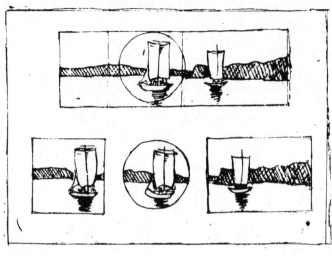

Fig. 9.3

from the 'staging' of a scene to the erection literally of a Tower of Babel in front of the lens.

The other method, used by the Japanese, is that of 'capturing' with the camera, using it to organise. Cutting out a fragment of reality by means of the lens.

Now, however, at a time when the centre of attention in intellectual cinema is at last beginning to move from the raw material of cinema as it is to 'deductions and conclusions', to 'slogans' based on the raw material, the differences are becoming less important to both schools and they can quietly blend into a synthesis.

Eight or so pages back, the question of theatre slipped from our grasp, like a pair of galoshes on a tram, slipped from our grasp.

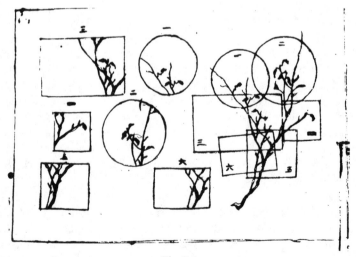

Fig. 9.4

Let us go back to the question of the methods of montage in Japanese theatre, particularly in acting.

The first and most striking example, of course, is the purely cinematographic method of 'transitionless acting'. Together with extremely refined mime transitions the Japanese actor also makes use of the direct opposite. At a certain moment in his performance he halts. The 'black men' obligingly conceal him from the audience.[11] So, he emerges in new make-up, a new wig: these characterise a new stage (step) in his emotional state.

Thus, for instance, the play *Narukami* is resolved by Sadanji's transition from drunkenness to madness.[12] Through a mechanical cut. And a change in the range (arsenal) of coloured stripes on his face, emphasising those whose duty it is to demonstrate that the intensity is greater than in the first make-up.

This method is organic to film. The forced introduction into film of the European acting tradition of fragments of 'emotional transitions' once more compels cinema to mark time. At the same time, the method of 'cut' acting provides the opportunity to devise entirely new methods. If you replace a single changing face by a whole gamut of faces of varying dispositions – typage – the expression is always more intense than that on the surface of the face of a professional actor, which is too receptive and devoid of any organic resistance.

I have utilised the distinction between the polar stages of facial expression in a pointed juxtaposition in our new film about the countryside.[13] This results in a more pointed 'play of doubt' around the separator. Will the milk thicken or not? Deception? Money? Here the psychological process of the play of motives – faith and doubt – resolves into the two extreme states of joy (certainty) and gloom (disillusionment). In addition, this is heavily underlined by light (which by no means conforms to real life). This leads to a significant heightening of tension.

Another remarkable feature of the Kabuki theatre is the principle of 'decomposed acting'. Shocho, who played the leading female roles when the Kabuki troupe visited Moscow, portrayed the dying girl in *The Mask Maker* through quite disconnected fragments of acting.

Acting with just the right arm. Acting with one leg. Acting merely with the neck and head. The whole process of the death agony was decomposed into solo performances by each 'party' separately: the legs, the arms, the head. Decomposition into shot levels. And each successive fragment became shorter as the unhappy ending – death – approached.

Freed from primitive naturalism and using this method, the actor wins the audience over completely 'with his rhythm', which makes a scene based in its general composition on the most consistent and detailed naturalism (blood, etc.) not only acceptable but extremely attractive.

Since we are no longer distinguishing in principle between montage and what happens within the shot, we can cite here a third method.

The Japanese actor in his work utilises slow tempo to a degree that is unknown in our theatre. Take the famous hara-kiri scene in *The Forty-Seven Samurai*.[14] That degree of slowing down is unknown on our stage. Whereas in our previous example we observed the decomposition of the links between movements, here we see the decomposition of the process of movement, i.e. *Zeitlupe* [slow motion]. I know of only one case of the consistent application of this method, which is technically acceptable in cinema, on a compositionally meaningful level. (It is usually deployed either for visual effect, as in the 'underwater kingdom' in *The Thief of Bagdad,* or for a dream, as in *Zvenigora.*[15] Even more frequently it is used simply for formal trifles and pointless mischief with the camera, as in *The Man with the Movie Camera.*[16]) I have in mind Epstein's *The Fall of the House of Usher.*[17] Judging by press reports, normally acted states [of mind], shot with a speeded-up camera and played back in slow motion on the screen, produced unusual emotional tension. If you bear in mind that the attraction exerted by the actor's performance on the audience is based on the audience's identification with it, you can easily attribute both examples to one and the same causal explanation. The intensity of our perception increases because the process of identification is easier when the movement is decomposed . . . .

Even instruction in handling a rifle can be drummed into the heads of the densest raw recruit if the instructor uses the method of 'decomposition' . . . .

The most interesting link is of course the one between Japanese theatre and sound film which can and must learn from the Japanese what to it is fundamental: the reduction of visual and aural sensations to a single physiological denominator. But I have devoted an entire article to this in *Zhizn' iskusstva* (1928, no. 34)[18] and I shall not return to the subject.

Thus, it has been possible to establish briefly the fact that the most varied branches of Japanese culture are permeated by a purely cinematic element and by its basic nerve-montage.

And it is only cinema that falls into the same trap as the 'left-inclining' Kabuki. Instead of learning how to isolate the principles and techniques of their unique acting from the traditional feudal forms of what they are acting, the progressive theatrical people of Japan rush to borrow the loose formlessness of the acting of our 'intuitivists'. The result is lamentable and saddening. In its cinema Japan also strives to imitate the most appalling examples of the most saleable mediocre American and European commercial trash.

Understand and apply its specific cultural quality to its own cinema – that is what Japan must do!

Japanese comrades, are you really going to leave this to us?

10 The Dramaturgy of Film Form[19] (The Dialectical Approach to Film Form)

According to Marx and Engels the system of the dialectic is only the conscious reproduction of the dialectical course (essence) of the external events of the world. (Razumovsky, *The Theory of Historical Materialism*, Moscow, 1928)

Thus:
the projection of the dialectical system of objects into the brain
– *into abstract creation –*
– *into thought –*
produces dialectical modes of thought – dialectical materialism –

PHILOSOPHY.

Similarly:
the projection of the same system of objects – in concrete creation – in form – produces

ART.

The basis of this philosophy is the *dynamic* conception of objects: being as a constant evolution from the interaction between two contradictory opposites.

Synthesis that *evolves* from the opposition between thesis and antithesis.

It is equally of basic importance for the correct conception of art and all art forms.

In the realm of art this dialectical principle of the dynamic is embodied in

CONFLICT

as the essential basic principle of the existence of every work of art and every form.

FOR ART IS ALWAYS CONFLICT:

1. because of its social mission,
2. because of its nature,
3. because of its methodology.

1. *Because of its social mission, since:* it is the task of art to reveal the contradictions of being. To forge the correct intellectual concept, to form the right view by stirring up contradictions in the observer's mind and through the dynamic clash of opposing passions.

2. *Because of its nature, since:* because of its nature it consists in the conflict between natural being and creative tendentiousness. Between organic inertia and purposeful initiative.

The hypertrophy of purposeful initiative – of the principle of rational logic –

leaves art frozen in mathematical technicism. (Landscape becomes topography, a painting of St Sebastian becomes an anatomical chart.)

Hypertrophy of organic naturalness – of organic logic – dissolves art into form-lessness.

(Malevich becomes Kaulbach,
Archipenko a waxworks show.[52])

Because:

the limit of organic form
(the passive principle of being) is

NATURE

the limit of rational form
(the active principle of production) is

INDUSTRY

and:

at the intersection of nature
and industry stands

ART.

1. The logic of organic form

versus

2. the logic of rational form produces in collision the dialectic of the art form.

The interaction between the two produces and determines the dynamic. (Not just in the sense of space-time, but also in the field of pure thought. I similarly regard the evolution of new concepts and attitudes in the conflict between normal conceptions and particular representations as a dynamic – a dynamisation of the inertia of perception – a dynamisation of the 'traditional view' into a new one.)

The basis of distance determines the intensity of the tension: (viz., for instance, in music the concept of intervals. In it there can be cases where the gap is so wide that it can lead to a break, to a disintegration of the homogeneous concept of art. The 'inaudibility' of certain intervals.)

The spatial form of this dynamic is the expression of the phases in its tension – rhythm.[21] This applies to every art form and, all the more so, to every form of its expression. Thus human expression is a conflict between conditioned and unconditioned reflex.

(I do not agree on this point with Klages[22] who

1. considers human expression not dynamically as process but statically as result and

2. attributes everything that moves to the field of the 'soul' and, by contrast, only that which restrains to 'reason', in the idealistic concept of 'reason' and 'soul' which here corresponds indirectly with the ideas of conditioned and unconditioned reflex.)

The same is equally true for every field, in so far as it can be understood as art. Thus, for instance, logical thought, viewed as art, also produces the same dynamic mechanism: 'The intellectual lives of Plato or Dante ... were largely guided and sustained by their delight in the sheer beauty of the *rhythmic relation* between law and instance, species and individual, or cause and effect.'[23]

94

This also applies in other fields, e.g. in language, where the strength, vitality and dynamism derive from the irregularity of the particular in relation to the rule governing the system as a whole.

In contrast to this we can see the sterility of expression in artificial, totally regulated languages like Esperanto. It is from this same principle that the whole charm of poetry derives: its rhythm emerges as conflict between the metric measure adopted and the distribution of sounds that ambushes that measure.[24]

The concept of even a formally static phenomenon as a dynamic function dialectically symbolises the wise words of Goethe that

'Architecture is frozen music.'[25]

We shall employ this concept further. And, just as in homogeneous thought (a monistic attitude), both the whole and the minutest detail must be permeated by a *single principle*, so, together with the conflict of *social conditionality* and the conflict of *reality*, that same principle of conflict serves as the foundation stone for the *methodology* of art. As the basic principle of the rhythm that is to be created and of the derivation of the art form.

3. *Because of its methodology*: shot and montage are the basic elements of film.

MONTAGE

Soviet film has stipulated this as the nerve of film.

To determine the essence of montage is to solve the problem of film as such.

The old film-makers, including the theoretically quite outmoded Lev Kuleshov, regarded montage as a means of producing something by describing it, adding individual shots to one another like building blocks.

Movement within these shots and the resulting length of the pieces were thus to be regarded as rhythm.

A fundamentally false notion! It would mean defining an object exclusively in terms of its external course. Regarding the mechanical process of sticking the pieces together as a principle. We cannot characterise this kind of relationship between lengths as rhythm.

It would give rise to a metre that was as opposed to rhythm as much as the mechanical-metric Mensendick system is opposed to the organic rhythmic Bode school in the case of bodily expression.

According to this definition (which Pudovkin also shares as a theorist) montage is the means of *unrolling* an idea through single shots (the 'epic' principle).[26]

But in my view montage is not an idea composed of successive shots stuck together but an idea that DERIVES *from the collision between two shots that are independent of one another* (the 'dramatic' principle). ('Epic' and 'dramatic' in relation to the methodology of form and not content or plot!!) As in Japanese hieroglyphics in which two independent ideographic characters ('shots') are juxtaposed and *explode* into a concept. THUS:

Eye + Water	=	Crying
Door + Ear	=	Eavesdropping
Child + Mouth	=	Screaming
Mouth + Dog	=	Barking

Mouth + Bird	=	Singing
Knife + Heart	=	Anxiety, etc.*

Sophistry? Not at all! Because we are trying here to derive the whole essence, the stylistic principle and the character of film from its technical (-optical) foundations.

We know that the phenomenon of movement in film resides in the fact that still pictures of a moving body blend into movement when they are shown in quick succession one after the other.

The vulgar description of what happens – as a *blending* – has also led to the vulgar notion of montage mentioned above.

Let us describe the course of the said phenomenon more precisely, just as it really is, and draw our conclusions accordingly.

Is that correct? In pictorial-phraseological terms, yes.

But not in mechanical terms.

For in fact each sequential element is arrayed, not *next* to the one it follows, but on *top* of it. *For:* the idea (sensation) of movement arises in the process of superimposing on the retained impression of the object's first position the object's newly visible second position.

That is how, on the other hand, the phenomenon of spatial depth as the optical superimposition of two planes in stereoscopy arises. The superimposition of two dimensions of the same mass gives rise to a completely new higher dimension.

In this instance, in the case of stereoscopy, the superimposition of two non-identical two-dimensionalities gives rise to stereoscopic three-dimensionality. In another field: concrete word (denotation) set against concrete word produces abstract concept.

As in Japanese (see above), in which *material* ideogram set against *material* ideogram produces *transcendental result* (concept).

The incongruity in contour between the first picture that has been imprinted on the mind and the subsequently perceived second picture – the conflict between the two – gives birth to the sensation of movement, the idea that movement has taken place.

The degree of incongruity determines the intensity of impression, determines the tension that, in combination with what follows, will become the real element of authentic rhythm.

Here we have, in the temporal sense, what we see emerging spatially on the graphic or painted surface.

What does the dynamic effect of a picture consist of?

The eye follows the direction of an element. It retains a visual impression which then collides with the impression derived from following the direction of a second element. The conflict between these directions creates the dynamic effect in the apprehension of the whole.

I. It may be purely linear: Fernand Léger, Suprematism.[27]

---

* Abel Rémusat, 'Recherches sur l'origine de la formation de l'écriture chinoise' [Research on the Origin of the Formation of Chinese Script], *Académie des inscriptions et belles-lettres, Paris: Memoires,* vol. 8(ii), Paris, 1827, pp. 1–33.

II. It may be 'anecdotal'. The secret of the fabulous mobility of the figures of Daumier and Lautrec[28] consists in the fact that various parts of the bodies of their figures are depicted in spatial situations (positions) that vary temporally. See, for instance, Lautrec's 'Miss Cissy Loftus':

A logical development of position A for the foot leads to the elaboration of a corresponding position A for the body. But from the knee up the body is already represented in position A+a. The cinematic effect of the still picture is already visible here: from hips to shoulders we already have A+a+a. The figure seems alive and kicking!

III. Primitive Italian Futurism lies somewhere between I and II: the man with six legs in six positions.[29] (Between I and II because II achieves its effects by retaining natural unity and anatomical cohesion, whereas I achieves this through purely elementary elements, while III, although undermining nature, is not yet pushed as far as abstraction.)

IV. It can be of an ideographic kind. Like the pregnant characterisation of a Sharaku[30] (eighteenth-century Japan). The secret of his extremely clever power of expression lies in the anatomical *spatial disproportion* of the parts. (You might term I above *temporal disproportion.*) Julius Kurth expresses himself thus in *Sharaku* (he is describing a portrait of an actor, comparing it to a mask):

> Whereas the anatomical proportions of the carved wooden mask are almost correct, the proportions of the face in the print are quite impossible. The distance between the eyes is so great as to make a mockery of common sense. The nose, in comparison with the eyes at least, is twice as long as a normal nose could possibly be, the chin is on the whole out of all proportion to the mouth: the relationships between the eyebrows, the mouth, the details in general are quite unthinkable. We can observe the same thing in all Sharaku's large heads. It is just not possible that the great master was unaware that these proportions were wrong. He quite deliberately repudiated naturalism and, *while each detail taken separately is constructed on the principles of concentrated naturalism, their general compositional juxtaposition is subjugated to a purely semantic purpose.*[31]

The spatial calculation of the corresponding size of one detail in relation to another and the collision between that and the dimension determined for it by the artist produces the characterisation: the resolution of the representation.

Finally, colour. A colour shade conveys a particular rhythm of vibration to our vision. (This is not perceived visually, but purely physiologically, because colours are distinguished from one another by the frequency of their light vibrations.) The nearest shade has a different frequency of vibration.

The counterpoint (conflict) between the two – the retained and the still emerging – frequency produces the dynamic of our perceptions and of the interplay of colour.

From here we have only to make one step from visual vibration to acoustic vibration and we find ourselves in the field of music. We move from the realm of the spatial-pictorial to the realm of the temporal-pictorial.

Here the same law rules. Because for music counterpoint is not just a form of composition but the basic rationale for the possibility of sound perception and differentiation. One might also say that in all the cases cited here the same *prin-*

ciple of comparison operates: it makes possible for us discovery and observation in every field. With the moving image (film) we have, as it were, the synthesis of these two counterpoints: the spatial counterpoint of the image and the temporal counterpoint of music. Characterised in film through what we might describe as:

VISUAL COUNTERPOINT

This concept, when applied to film, allows us to designate various approaches to the problem, to a kind of film grammar. Similarly with a syntax of film expressions in which the visual counterpoint can determine a completely new system of forms of expression. (Experiments in this direction will be illustrated by extracts from my films.) In all this:

The *basic presupposition* is:

  The shot is not a montage element – the shot is a montage cell (a molecule).

This formulation explodes the dualistic division in the analysis:

  of: title and shot

  and: shot and montage.

Instead it is viewed dialectically as three different *phases in the formation of a homogeneous expressive task*. With homogeneous characteristics that determine the homogeneity of their structural laws.

The relationship between the three: conflict within a thesis (an abstract idea):

1. is *formulated* in the dialectic of the *title*,
2. is *formed* spatially in the *conflict within* the shot – and
3. *explodes* with the growing intensity of the *conflict montage between the shots.*

Once again this is quite analogous to human psychological expression. This is a conflict of motives. Conceivable, likewise, in three phases:

1. Purely verbal utterance. Without intonation: spoken expression.
2. Gesticulative (mimic-intentional) expression. Projection of conflict on to the entire expressive body-system of man. ('Gesture' and 'sound gesture' –intonation.)
3. Projection of conflict into the spatial. With the growing intensity (of motives) the zigzag of mimic expression is catapulted into the surrounding space according to the same distorting formula. A zigzag of expression deriving from the spatial disposition of man in space.

Herein lies the basis for a quite new conception of the problems of film form. We cite as examples of conflict:

1. Graphic conflict (Fig. 10.1).
2. Conflict between planes (Fig. 10.2).
3. Conflict between volumes (Fig. 10.3).
4. Spatial conflict (Fig. 10.4).
5. Conflict in lighting.
6. Conflict in tempo, etc., etc.

(NB Here they are characterised by their principal feature, by their *dominant*. It is obvious that they occur mainly as complexes, grouped together. That applies to both the shot and to montage.)

For montage transition it is sufficient to imagine any example as being divided into two independent primary pieces

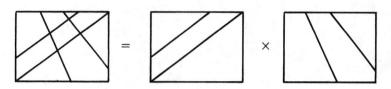

This is the graphic case. It applies also to all other cases. The extent to which the conflict concept extends in the treatment of film form is illustrated by the following further examples:

7. Conflict between matter and shot (achieved by *spatial distortion* using camera angle: Fig. 10.5).

8. Conflict between matter and its spatiality (achieved by *optical distortion* using the lens).

9. Conflict between an event and its temporality (achieved by slowing down and speeding up [*Multiplikator*]) and lastly:

10. Conflict between the entire *optical* complex and a quite different sphere.

That is how the conflict between optical and acoustic experience produces:

SOUND FILM
which is realisable as
AUDIO-VISUAL COUNTERPOINT.

The formulation and observation of the phenomenon of film in the form of conflict provides the first opportunity to devise a homogeneous system of *visual dramaturgy* for every special and particular case of the problem of film.

To create a *dramaturgy of visual film form* that is determined in the same way as the existing *dramaturgy of film material* is determined. . . .[32]

The same standpoint – viewed as an outcome for film composition – produces the following stylistic forms and possibilities and this could constitute a

FILM SYNTAX
A TENTATIVE FILM SYNTAX.

We shall list here:

A series of compositional possibilities that develop dialectically from the thesis that the concept of filmic movement (time lapse) derives from the superimposition of – the counterpoint between – two different stills.

I. *Each moving piece of montage in its own right.* Each photographed piece. The technical determination of the phenomenon of movement. *Not yet composition* (a man running, a gun firing, water splashing).

II. *Artificially produced representation of movement.* The basic optical sign is used for arbitrary composition:

Fig. 10.1. Graphic conflict

Fig. 10.2. Conflict between planes

Fig. 10.3. Conflict between volumes

Fig. 10.4. Spatial conflict

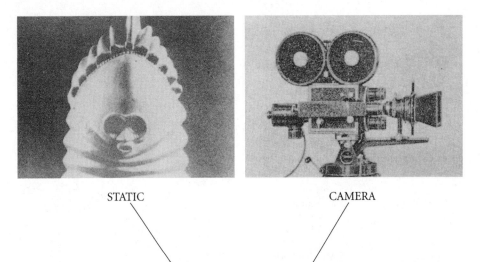

STATIC   CAMERA

CONFLICT

=

DYNAMIC

Fig. 10.5

Fig. 10.6. Logical   Fig. 10.7. Logical

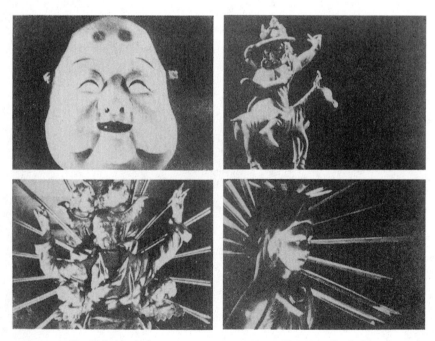

Fig. 10.8. Alogical   Fig. 10.9. Alogical

A. Logical

Example 1. *Ten Days That Shook the World (October).*
Montage: repetition of a machine-gun firing by cross-cutting the relevant details
of the firing.

Combination a):
  Brightly lit machine-gun. Dark one.
  Different shot. Double burst:
  Graphic burst and light burst.

Combination b):
  Machine-gun.
  Close-up of the machine-gunner (Fig. 10.6).
  Effect almost of double exposure with rattling montage effect.
  Length of the pieces – two frames.

Example 2. *Potemkin* (1925).
Representation of a spontaneous action, *Potemkin* (Fig. 10.7). Woman with pince-
nez. Followed immediately – without a transition – by the same woman with shattered pince-nez and bleeding eye. Sensation of a shot hitting the eye.

B. Alogical

Example 3. *Potemkin.*
This device used for symbolic pictorial expression. *Potemkin.* The marble lion
leaps up, surrounded by the thunder of *Potemkin's* guns firing in protest against
the bloodbath on the Odessa Steps (Fig. 10.10).
  Cut together from three immobile marble lions at Alupka Castle (Crimea). One
sleeping. One waking. One rising. The effect was achieved because the length of
the middle piece was correctly calculated. Superimposition on the first piece produced the first jump. Time for the second position to sink in. Superimposition of
the third position on the second – the second jump. Finally the lion is standing.

Example 4. *Ten Days.*
The firing in Example 1 is symbolically produced from elements that do not belong
to the actual firing. To illustrate General Kornilov's attempted monarchist *putsch* it
occurred to me that his militarist *tendency* could be shown in the cutting (montage),
but creating the montage material itself out of religious details. Because Kornilov
had betrayed his tsarist tendency in the form of a curious 'crusade' of
Mohammedans (!) (his 'Wild Division' from the Caucasus) and Christians (all the
others) against the . . . Bolsheviks. To this end a Baroque Christ with beams stream-
ing (exploding) from its halo was briefly intercut with a self-contained egg-shaped
Uzume mask. The temporal conflict between the self-contained egg shape and the
graphic star produced the effect of a simultaneous explosion (a bomb, a shot) (Fig.
10. 8).

Example 5. *Ten Days.*
A similar combination of a Chinese sacred statue and a madonna with a halo (Fig.
10.9). (NB As we see, this already provides the opportunity for tendentious (ideological) expression.)

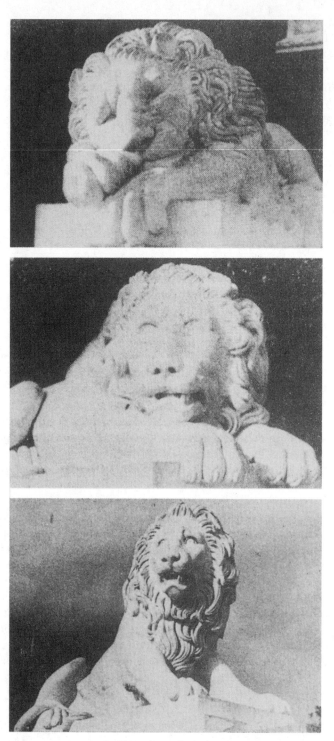

Fig. 10.10. Alogical

Another example of more primitive effect from the same place: in the simple cross-cutting between church towers leaning in opposite directions.

So far the examples have shown *primitive-psychological* cases – using *only* the optical superimposition of movement.

III. The case of emotional combinations not merely of the visible elements of the pieces but principally of the chains of psychological association. *Associational montage* (1923–4). As a means of sharpening (heightening) a situation emotionally.

In Case I we had the following: two pieces A and B following one another are materially identical. According to the position of the material in the shot they are, however, not identical:

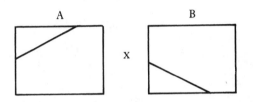

These two combined produced dynamisation in space – the impression of spatial dynamic:

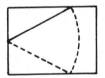

The degree of difference between positions A and B determines the tension of the movement. But let us take a new case:

Shot A and shot B are, in terms of material, *not identical*. The associations of the two shots are identical: associatively identical. By analogy this *dynamisation of the material* produces, not in the spatial but in the *psychological, i.e. the emotional, field*:

EMOTIONAL DYNAMISATION.

Example 1. *The Strike* (1923–4).
The shooting down of the workers is cut in such a way that the massacre is intercut with the slaughter of a cow. (Difference in material. But the slaughter is employed as an appropriate association.) This produces a powerful emotional intensification of the scene.

NB In this case the homogeneity of gesture plays a very great role in gen-

erally achieving the effect (the homogeneity of the dynamic gesture: movement within the shot – or of the static gesture: the graphic attitude of the
shot). Here is an excerpt from the first version of this scene in the montage
list (1923):

1. The head of a bull.
2. The butcher's knife strikes a downward blow.
3. Five hundred workers fall down a hill.
4. Fifty men get up. Hands.
5. A soldier's face. He aims.
6. Shots.
7. The bull standing. It twitches and falls.
8. Close-up. Convulsions of the hind legs. A hoof kicks into the blood.
9. Rifles.
10. Semi-close-up. People get up. Wounded.
11. Imploring hands raised towards the camera.
12. Butcher with blood-stained rope approaches the camera.
13. Hands.
14. The butcher approaches, etc.

This principle was subsequently also used by Pudovkin in *The End of St Petersburg*
(1927) when he intercut shots of stock exchange and battlefield. And, in *The
Mother* (1926), the ice breaking and the workers' demonstration.

This method may decay pathologically if the essential viewpoint – the emotional dynamisation of the material – gets lost. Then it ossifies into lifeless literary
symbolism and stylistic mannerism. We may cite the following as an example:

Example 2: *Ten Days*.
The mellifluous peace overtures of the Mensheviks at the Second Congress of the
Soviets (during the storming of the Winter Palace) are intercut with harp-playing
hands. A purely literary parallelism that does nothing to enliven the material.

Similarly in Otsep's *The Living Corpse*,[33] with the intercutting (in imitation
of *Ten Days*) of church cupolas or lyrical landscapes into the speeches of the
prosecution and the defence counsels in the court. The same mistake as that
above.

On the other hand, the predominance of purely dynamic effects may have a
positive result:

Example 3: *Ten Days*.
The pathos of the adherence of the cycle battalion to the Second Congress of the
Soviets is dynamised by the fact that, when their delegates enter, abstractly spinning cycle wheels (association with the battalion) were intercut. These resolved
the pathetic content of the event as such into a perceptible dynamic. The same
principle – the emergence of a concept, of a sensation from the juxtaposition of
two disparate events – led on to:

IV. *The emancipation of closed action from its conditioning by time and space.* The
first attempts at this were made in the *Ten Days* film.

Example 1. (*Ten Days*)
A trench packed with soldiers seems to be crushed by the weight of an enormous cannonball descending on the whole thing. Thesis brought to expression. In material terms the effect is achieved through the apparently chance intercutting between an independently existing trench and a metal object with a similarly military character. In reality they have absolutely no spatial relationship with one another.

Example 2: *Ten Days*.
Similarly in the scene of Kornilov's *putsch* attempt, which puts an end to Kerensky's Bonapartist plans. In this sequence one of Kornilov's tanks, emerging from the trench, shatters the plaster figure of Napoleon that stands on Kerensky's desk in the palace of Petrograd and has purely symbolic meaning.

This method of making whole sequences in this way is now mainly being employed by Dovzhenko: *The Arsenal* (1929). Also by Esfir Shub on her Tolstoy film (1928).[34] In addition to this method of dissolving the accepted forms of handling film material I should like to cite another example, which has, however, not been realised in practice.

In 1924–5 I was very concerned with the idea of the filmic representation of real (actual) man. At that time the prevailing trend was that living man could only be shown in film in *long* dramatic scenes. And that cutting (montage) would destroy the idea of real man.

Abram Room established the record in this respect in *The Bay of Death*[35] by using eighty metre-long uncut dramatic scenes. I felt (and feel) that such a concept is utterly unfilmic.

For what really is, in linguistic terms, a precise characterisation of man?

His raven-black hair ...

The waves in his hair ...

His flashing, bright blue eyes ...

His steely muscles ...

Even when it is not so exaggeratedly phrased, every description, every verbal representation of a man (see above!) becomes an accumulation of waterfalls, lightning conductors, landscapes, birds, etc.

Why then should cinema in its forms follow theatre and painting rather than the methodology of language, which gives rise, through the combination of concrete descriptions and concrete objects, to quite new concepts and ideas? It is much closer to film than, for instance, painting, where form derives from *abstract* elements (line, colour). In film, by contrast, it is precisely the material *concreteness* of the shot as an element that is the most difficult aspect of the process of formation. Why not then lean rather more towards the system of language, where the same mechanism exists in the use of words and word complexes?

Why is it, on the other hand, that montage cannot be avoided even in the orthodox feature film?

The differentiation in montage pieces is determined by the fact that each piece has in itself no reality at all. But each piece is itself in a position to evoke a certain association. The accumulation of associations then achieves the same effect as that provoked in the audience by purely physiological means by a theatrical play that is unfolding in reality.

E.g. Murder on stage has a purely physiological effect. Perceived in a *single* montage sequence it acts like an item of *information,* a title. It only begins to work *emotionally* when it is presented in montage fragments. In montage pieces, each of which provokes a certain association, the sum of which amounts to a composite complex of emotional feeling. In traditional terms:

1. A hand raises a knife.
2. The eyes of the victim open wide.
3. His hands clutch the table.
4. The knife jerks.
5. The eyes close.
6. Blood spurts out.
7. A mouth shrieks.
8. Drops fall on to a shoe ...

and all that kitsch! In any event each *individual piece* is already almost *abstract* in relation to the *action as a whole.* The more differentiated they are, the more abstract they become, aiming only at provoking a certain association. Now the following thought arises quite logically: could one not achieve the same effect more productively if one did not adhere so slavishly to plot but materialised the notion of *murder* in a free accumulation of associative material? Because the most important thing is to convey the representation of murder, the feeling of murder as such. Plot is only one of the means without which we still do not know how to communicate something to the audience. At any rate an attempt of this sort would produce the most interesting variety of forms. Let someone try it! Since 1923–4, when this thought occurred to me, I have unfortunately not had the time to carry out this experiment. Now I have turned to quite different problems.

But, *revenons à nos moutons,*[36] which will bring us closer to these tasks. Whereas, with 1, 2 and 3 above, the suspense was calculated to achieve purely physiological effects, from the purely optical to the emotional, we must also mention here the case in which the same conflict tension serves to achieve new concepts, new points of view, in other words, serves purely intellectual ends.

Example 1: *Ten Days.*
Kerensky's rise to (untrammelled) power and dictatorship after July 1917. Comic effect is achieved by *intercutting titles denoting ever higher rank* ('Dictator', 'Generalissimo', 'Minister of the Navy and the Army', etc.) with five or six sequences of the staircase in the Winter Palace with Kerensky ascending the *same* flight each time.

Here the conflict between the kitsch of the ascending staircase and Kerensky treading the same ground produces an intellectual resultant: the satirical degradation of these titles in relation to Kerensky's nonentity.

Here we have a counterpoint between a verbally expressed, conventional idea and a pictorial representation of an individual who is unequal to that idea.

The incongruity between these two produces a purely *intellectual* resolution at the expense of this individual. Intellectual dynamisation.

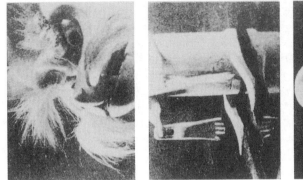

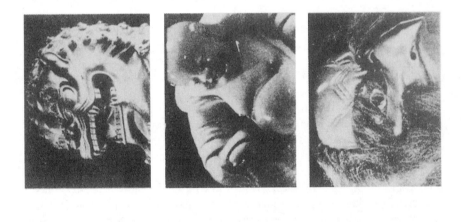
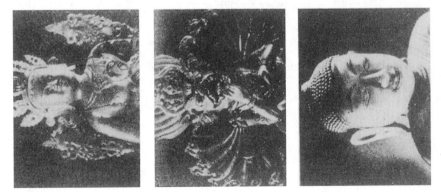

Fig. 10.11

Example 2: *Ten Days.*

Kornilov's march on Petrograd took place under the slogan 'In the Name of God and the Fatherland'. Here we have an attempt to use the representation for anti-religious ends. A number of images of the divine were shown in succession. From a magnificent Baroque Christ to an Eskimo idol. (Fig. 10.11)

Here a conflict arises between the concept 'God' and its symbolisation. Whereas idea and image are completely synonymous in the first Baroque image, they grow further apart with each subsequent image. We retain the description 'God' and show idols that in no way correspond with our own image of this concept. From this we are to draw anti-religious conclusions as to what the divine as such really is.

Similarly, there is here an attempt to draw a purely intellectual conclusion as a resultant of the conflict between a preconception and its *gradual tendentious discrediting by degrees* through pure illustration.

The gradual succession continues in a process of comparing each new image with its common designation and *unleashes a process that, in terms of its form, is identical to a process of logical deduction.* Everything here is already intellectually conceived, not just in terms of the resolution but also of the method of expressing ideas.

The conventional *descriptive* form of the film becomes a kind of reasoning (as a formal possibility).

Whereas the conventional film directs and develops the *emotions,* here we have a hint of the possibility of likewise developing and directing the entire *thought process.*

These two attempts were received in a very hostile fashion by the majority of the critics. Because they were understood in purely political terms. I willingly concede that it is precisely *this form that is best suited to express ideologically critical theses.* But it is a pity that the critics completely overlooked the filmic opportunities that could be derived from it. In both these attempts we find the first, still embryonic attempts to construct a really quite new form of filmic expression.

A purely intellectual film which, freed from traditional limitations, will achieve direct forms for thoughts, systems and concepts without any transitions or paraphrases. And which can therefore become a

SYNTHESIS OF ART AND SCIENCE.

That will become the really new watchword for our epoch in the field of art. And really justify Lenin's statement that 'of all the arts ... cinema is the most important.'[37]

One of my next films, which is intended to embody the Marxist world-view, will be devoted to an experiment in this direction.

1929

11   The Fourth Dimension in Cinema[38]

I

Exactly a year ago on 19 August 1928, before I had started work on the montage for *The General Line,* I wrote about the visit of the Japanese theatre in 'An Unexpected Juncture':

> [In the Kabuki] a single monistic sensation of theatrical 'stimulation' takes place. The Japanese regards each theatrical element not as an incommensurable unit of the various categories of affect (on the various sensual organs) but as a single unit of *theatre* . . . .
> Addressing himself to the sensual organs, he bases his calculations on the final *sum* of stimulants to the brain, ignoring *which* path that stimulation takes.[39]

This characterisation of the Kabuki theatre was to prove prophetic.

It was this method that lay at the basis of the montage for *The General Line.*

Orthodox montage is montage by dominants, i.e. the combination of shots[40] according to their predominant (principal) sign. Montage by tempo. Montage by the principal direction within the frame. Montage by length (duration) of sequences, etc. Montage by foreground.

The dominant signs of two shots side by side result in a particular conflicting relationship that produces a particular expressive effect (I have in mind here a *pure montage* effect).

This situation covers every level of intensity in montage juxtaposition or shock:

from a complete opposition between the dominants, i.e. a sharply contrasting construction,

to a scarcely noticeable 'modulation' from shot to shot. (All cases of conflict are of necessity cases of complete absence of conflict.)

As for the actual dominant, we must in no way regard it as something independent, absolute and invariably stable. There are technical ways of treating a shot so that its dominant can be more or less specifically defined, but never absolutely.

The characteristics of the dominant are variable and profoundly relative.

The revelation of its characteristics depends on the actual combination of shots for whose combination it is itself the condition.

A circle? an equation with two unknown quantities?

A dog, chasing its own tail?

No, simply a precise definition of what is.

In fact, even if we have a *series* of montage shots:

111

(1) A grey-haired old man,
(2) a grey-haired old woman,
(3) a white horse,
(4) a snow-covered roof,

it is far from clear whether this series works on 'old age' or 'whiteness'.

This series might continue for a very long time before we finally come upon the signpost shot that immediately 'christens' the whole series with a particular 'sign'.

That is why it is better to place this kind of indicator as near as possible to the beginning (in 'orthodox' construction). Sometimes it is even necessary to do this ... with an intertitle.

These reflections completely exclude a non-dialectic postulation of the question of the unambiguity of the shot in itself.

The shot never becomes a letter but always remains an ambiguous hieroglyph.

It can be read only in context, just like a hieroglyph, acquiring specific *meaning, sense* and even *pronunciation* (sometimes dramatically opposed to one another) only *in combination with* a separate reading or a small sign or reading indicator placed alongside it.

The General Line was edited in a different way from orthodox montage by individual dominants.

The 'aristocracy' of unambiguous dominants was replaced by the method of 'democratic' equal rights for all the stimulants, viewed together as a complex.

The point is that the dominant (with all due obeisance to its relativity) is far from being the only stimulant in the shot, even if it is the most powerful. For example, the 'sex appeal'[41] of the American heroine-beauty is accompanied by various stimulants: texture – like the material of her dress; light – the character of the lighting; race and nation (positive: the 'all-American type' or negative: the 'coloniser-oppressor' for a Negro or Chinese audience); social class, etc.

In a word a whole complex of secondary stimulants always accompanies the *central* stimulant (like the sexual one in our example).

This is precisely what happens in acoustics (in the particular instance of instrumental music).

There, alongside the resonance of the basic dominant tone, there is a whole series of secondary resonances, the so-called overtones and undertones. Their collision with one another and with the basic tone, etc., envelops the basic tone with a whole host of secondary resonances.

Whereas in acoustics these secondary resonances become merely 'interference', in music (which is calculatedly composed) they are one of the most remarkable means of influence for Left composers like Debussy and Scriabin.[42]

It is exactly the same in optics as well. All sorts of aberrations, distortions and other defects that are present and that can be remedied by systems of lenses, can, if calculatedly composed, produce a whole series of compositional effects (changing a 28 lens to a 310).

In combination with a calculation of the secondary resonances of the actual filmed material this produces, by analogy with music, the visual *overtonal* complex of the shot.

This is the method on which the montage of *The General Line* is constructed.

This montage is not constructed on the *individual dominant* but takes the sum of *stimuli* of all the stimulants as the dominant.

That distinctive montage *complex within the shot* that arises from the collisions and combinations of the individual stimulants inherent within it, of stimulants that vary according to their 'external nature' but are bound together in an iron unity through their reflex physiological essence.

Physiological, in so far as the 'psychic' in perception is merely the physiological process of a *higher nervous activity*.

In this way the physiological sum total of the resonance of the shot *as a whole*, as a complex unity of all its component stimulants, is taken to be the general sign of the shot.

This is the particular 'feeling' of the shot that the shot as a whole produces.

And for the montage shot this is the same as the Kabuki method for its individual scenes (see the beginning).

The basic sign of the shot can be taken to be the final sum total of its effect on the cortex of the brain as a whole, irrespective of the ways in which the accumulating stimulants have come together.

The *sum totals* thus achieved can be put together in any conflicting combination, thereby opening up quite new possibilities for montage resolutions.

As we have seen, because of the actual genetics of these methods, they must be accompanied by an extraordinary *physiological* quality.

Just like the music that constructs its works on a special deployment of overtones.

Not the *classicism* of Beethoven, but the *physiological* quality of Debussy or Scriabin.

Very many people have remarked on the extraordinary physiological quality of the effect of *The General Line*.

This is precisely because it is the first film to be edited on the principle of visual overtone.

The actual *method* of montage can be interestingly verified.

If, in the brilliant classical distances of the future, cinema uses both overtonal montage and, simultaneously, montage by dominant sign (tonic), then, as always, the new method will in the first instance always assert itself by highlighting the principle of a problem.

In the first stages of its emergence overtonal montage had to take a line in sharp *contrast* to the dominant.

It is true that in many cases, even in *The General Line*, you will find such 'synthetic' combinations of tonal and overtonal montage.

For example, the 'diving under the icons' in the 'religious procession' or the grasshopper and the mowing-machine are edited *visually* according to their *sound* association with a deliberate revelation and their spatial similarity.

But the methodologically significant constructions are, of course, those that are without a dominant. Or those in which the dominant appears in the shape of a purely physiological formulation of the task (which is the same thing). For instance, the montage of the beginning of the 'religious procession' is carried out according to the degree to which the individual shots are 'saturated with fervour' and the beginning of the *sovkhoz* sequence is graded according to its 'carnivorousness'. The conditions of the extra-cinematic disciplines that place the most unexpected signs of equality between materials are logically, formally and in an everyday context absolutely neutral vis-à-vis one another.

There is also a mass of cases of montage junctures that make a resounding mockery of orthodox scholastic montage by dominants.

The easiest way to demonstrate this is to run the film on a 'cutting table'. It is only then that the complete 'impossibility' of the montage junctures that *The General Line* abounds in is quite clearly revealed. At the same time the extreme simplicity of its metre and its scale is disclosed.

Whole long sections of reels comprise shots that are quite equal in length or of absolutely primitive repeated shortness. The entire, complex, rhythmically *sensual* nuancing of the combination of shots is carried out almost exclusively in accordance with the 'psychophysiological' resonance of the shot.

It was on the cutting table that I myself discovered the extremely sharply defined uniqueness of the montage of *The General Line*.

When I had to cut and shorten it.

The 'creative ecstasy' that accompanies the assembly of the shots and the composition of the montage, the 'creative ecstasy' when you hear and feel the shots, that moment had already passed.

Cutting and shortening do not require inspiration, only technique and skill.

There I was, winding the 'religious procession' on the table and I could not fit the combination of shots into one of the orthodox categories (where you can lord it because of your sheer experience).

On the table, *immobile*, the sign that dictated their selection was quite unintelligible.

The criteria for their assembly turned out to lie outside the usual formal cinematic criteria.

And here is revealed yet one more curious feature of the similarity between the visual overtone and the musical.

It cannot be sketched in the statics of the shot, just as musical overtones cannot be sketched into the score.

Both emerge as a real constant only in the dynamics of the musical or cinematic *process*.

Overtonal conflicts, which are foreseen but not 'recorded' in the score, emerge only through dialectical formation when the film passes through the projector or an orchestra performs a symphony.

The visual overtone proves to be a real piece, a real element … of the fourth dimension.

Of what is spatially unrepresentable in three-dimensional space and only emerges and exists in the fourth dimension (three plus time).

The fourth dimension?!

Einstein? Mysticism?

It is time to stop being frightened of this 'beast', the fourth dimension. Einstein himself assures us:

The non-mathematician is seized by a mysterious shuddering when he hears of 'four-dimensional' things, by a feeling not unlike that awakened by thoughts of the occult.

114

And yet there is no more common-place statement than that the world in which we live is a four-dimensional space-time continuum.[43]

With such an excellent instrument of cognition as cinema even its primitive form – the sensation of movement – is resolved by the fourth dimension. We shall soon acquire a concrete orientation in this fourth dimension and feel just as much at home as if we were in our bedsocks!

And then the question would arise of a fifth dimension!

Overtonal montage emerges as a new montage category in the series of montage processes that we are already familiar with.

The direct *applied* significance of this method is *immense*.

And that is just as true for the burning question of the moment in cinema – for sound film.

In the article I have already cited at the beginning, referring to the 'unexpected juncture' – the similarity between the Kabuki and sound cinema – I wrote about the contrapuntal method of combining the visual and sound image: 'To master this method you have to develop within yourself a new *sense: the ability to reduce visual and sound perceptions to a new denominator...*'[44]

Whereas *sound* and *visual* perceptions are *not reducible* to a single denominator.

They are constants in different dimensions.

But the visual overtone and the sound overtone are constants in a *single dimension!*

Because, while a shot is a visual *perception* and a tone is a sound perception, *both visual and sound overtones are totally physiological sensations.*

And, consequently, they are of *one and the same kind*, outside the sound of acoustic categories that serve merely as guides, paths to its achievement.

For the musical overtones (a beat) the term 'I hear' is no longer strictly appropriate.

Nor 'I see' for the visual.

For both we introduce a new uniform formula: 'I feel'.*[45]

The theory and methodology of the musical overtone have been elaborated and made known (Debussy, Scriabin).

The General Line establishes the concept of the visual overtone.

The contrapuntal conflict between the visual and the sound *overtones* will give rise to the composition of the Soviet sound film.

II

Is the method of overtonal montage something foreign to cinema, something artificially grafted on to it, or is it simply a quantitative regrouping of a single sign so that it makes a dialectical jump and begins to figure as a new qualitative sign?

---

* Here it is a question of the same kind of de-individualisation of the *character* of a category of feeling as you find, for instance, in a different 'psychological' phenomenon: when you feel the *pleasure* that derives from extreme *suffering*. Stekel writes of this: 'In cases of affective hypertension pain ceases to be regarded as pain, but is felt as nervous tension .... But any powerful nervous tension has a tonic effect, and the heightened tone provokes a feeling of satisfaction and pleasure.'

In other words, is overtonal montage the next dialectical stage of development of the general montage system of methods and does it stand in staged succession in relation to other kinds of montage?

The four categories of montage with which we are familiar are as follows (there is such a thing as a 'category' of montage, because we characterise montage by the specific quality of the process in various cases, and not by the external 'signs' that attend these processes):

1. *Metric Montage*

The basic criterion is the *absolute length* of the shots. The shots are joined together according to their lengths in a formula-scheme. This is realised in the repetition of these formulas.

Tension is achieved by the effect of mechanical acceleration through repeated shortening of the lengths of the shots while preserving the formula of the relationship between these lengths ('double', 'triple', 'quadruple', etc.).

The primitive form of the method: Kuleshov's montages in time, march-time and waltz-time (3:4, 2:4, 1:4, etc.).

The degeneration of the method: metric montage using a beat of complex brevity (16:17, 22:57, etc.).

This beat ceases to exert a physiological effect because it contradicts the 'law of prime numbers (relationships)'.

Simple correlations that preserve clarity of perception make for that same maximal effect.

That is why they are always to be found in wholesome classics in every field: architecture, the colour in a painting, a complex composition by Scriabin – they are always crystal clear in their 'articulation'. The geometricisation of *mises en scéne,* the clear schemes of rationalised state enterprises, etc.

Dziga Vertov's *The Eleventh Year* can serve as a similar negative example: the metric module is mathematically so complex that you can only determine its pattern 'with a ruler in your hand', i.e. by measuring rather than perceiving.

This in no way implies that the metre should be 'recognisable' at the moment of perception. Quite the contrary. Even though you are not conscious of it, it is nevertheless an indisputable precondition for the *organisation* of our feeling.

Its clarity joins the 'pulse-beat' of the film and the 'pulse-beat' of the audience 'in unison'. Without this there can be no 'contact' between the two.

Overcomplexity in the metric relationships will instead produce a chaos of perception rather than a distinct emotional tension.

A third instance of metric montage lies between the other two: it is a metric refinement in a complex alternation of shots that have a simple relationship with one another (or vice versa).

Examples: the *lezginka*[46] in *October* and the patriotic demonstration in *The End of St Petersburg.* (The second example can be considered a classic of *purely metric montage.*)

In this kind of montage what lies within each shot is completely *subordinated* to the absolute length of the shot. Hence it adheres to the primitive dominant character of the resolution (the possible 'unambiguity' of the shot).

2. *Rhythmic Montage*

Here the content within the shot is an *equivalent* element in determining the actual lengths of the shots.

Abstract scholastic determination of the lengths is replaced by a flexibility in the correlation between *actual* lengths.

Here the actual length does not coincide with the mathematical length allotted to it in accordance with the metric formula. Here the practical length of a shot is defined as the derivative of the specific quality of the shot and of the 'theoretical' length allocated to it according to the scheme.

Here it is quite possible to find a case of complete metric *identity* between the shots and the reception of the rhythmic figures exclusively through the combination of shots in accordance with signs within the shot.

Formal tension through acceleration is here achieved by shortening the shots, not just in accordance with the basic scheme's formula of repetition, but also in violation of this canon.

Best of all by introducing more intensive material into the same temporal signs.

The 'Odessa Steps' may serve as a classic example. There the 'drumbeat' of the soldiers' feet descending the steps destroys all metrical conventions. It occurs outside the intervals prescribed by the metre and each time it appears in a different shot resolution. The final build-up of tension is produced by *switching* from the rhythm of the soldiers' tread as they descend the steps to another, new form of movement – the next stage in the intensification of the same *action* – the pram rolling down the steps.

Here the pram works in relation to the feet as a direct staged accelerator.

The 'descent' of the feet becomes the 'rolling down' of the pram.

Contrast this with the previously cited example from *The End of St Petersburg*, where the tensions are resolved by cutting the *same* shots down to minimal cellular montage.

Metric montage is quite adequate for that kind of simple march-time resolution.

But it is not adequate for more complex rhythmic tasks.

Its forcible application 'come what may' to these sorts of cases leads to montage failures. That is what happened, for example, in *Storm over Asia*[47] with the religious dances. This montage, edited on the basis of a complex metric scheme that had not been adjusted to the specific weighting of the shots, could not achieve the necessary rhythmic effect.

And in many cases this provokes bewilderment among specialists and inconsistent perception among the lay audience. (This kind of case can be artificially corrected by the musical accompaniment, as happened in this particular example.)

I have called the third type of montage:

3. *Tonal Montage*

This term appears for the first time. It is the next stage after rhythmic montage.

In rhythmic montage by *movement* within the shot we mean actual transposition (either of an object within the scope of the shot or of the eye along the guiding lines of an immobile object).

But here, in this instance, movement is understood in a wider sense. Here the concept of movement embraces *all sorts of vibrations* that derive from the shot.

But to assert that, from the standpoint of perception, it is characterised by the emotional tonality of the shot, i.e. by an apparently 'impressionistic' measurement, is a simple delusion.

The characteristics of the shot can be measured just as precisely here as in the simplest instance of 'ruler' measurement in primitive metric montage.

Only the units of measurement are different here. And the actual amounts to be measured are different.

For example, the degree of light variation in a piece cannot only be gauged by a selenium light-element but can be fully perceived in all its gradations by the naked eye.

If we give a conventional, emotional designation of 'more gloomy' to a shot that is to be predominantly resolved by lighting, this can be successfully replaced by a mathematical coefficient for a simple degree of illumination (a case of 'light tonality').

In another instance, where we designate the shot as a 'sharp sound', it is extremely easy to apply this designation to the overwhelming number of acutely angled elements of the shot that prevail over the rounded elements (a case of 'graphic tonality').

A play on combinations of degree of 'soft-focus'[48] or various degrees of sharpness is the most typical example of tonal montage.

As I said above, this case is constructed on the *dominant* emotional resonance of the shot. Some examples: 'Fog in the port of Odessa' (the beginning of the 'Mourning for Vakulinchuk' sequence in *Potemkin*).

Here the montage is built exclusively on the emotional 'resonance' of individual shots, i.e. on the rhythmic vibrations that do not produce spatial transpositions.

In this regard it is interesting that, alongside the basic tonal dominant, a second, accessory *rhythmic* dominant of shots is operating in the same way.

It acts as a link between the tonal construction of this particular scene and the rhythmic tradition, whose furthest development is tonal montage as a whole.

Because rhythmic montage is a special variant of metric montage.

This secondary dominant is realised in the scarcely perceptible ripple on the water, the slight bobbing of vessels at anchor, the slowly swirling mist, the seagulls landing slowly on the water.

Strictly speaking, these too are elements of a *tonal* order. The movements are transpositions of material edited according to their tonal, rather than their spatial-rhythmic, sign. For here the spatially incommensurable transpositions are combined according to their emotional resonances.

But the principal indicator for the assembly of the shots remains entirely in the sphere of the combination of shots according to their basic optical light variations (degrees of 'obscurity' and 'illumination'). And it is in the structure of these variations that the identity with a minor harmony in music is revealed.

118

In addition, this example gives us a model of a *consonance* in internal combinations of movement as *transposition* and movement as *light variation*.

Here too the intensification of tension follows the *intensification* of the same 'musical' sign of the dominant.

The scene of the 'delayed harvest' (in the fifth reel of *The General Line*) may serve as a particularly graphic example of this build-up.

In both the construction of the film as a whole and this particular case its basic method of staging has been observed.

Namely, conflict between 'content' and its traditional 'form'.

An emotional structure applied to non-emotional material. The stimulant has been separated from its characteristic situation (e.g. the treatment of the erotic in the film) right down to paradoxical tonic constructions. The industrial 'monument' turns out to be a typewriter. There is a wedding ... but between a bull and a cow. And so on.

Thus the thematic *minor* of the harvest is resolved by the thematic *major* of the storm, the rain. (And even the harvest – a traditionally major theme of fertility under the sun's blazing rays – is used to resolve the minor theme and is in addition soaked by the rain.)

Here the increase in tension proceeds by internal reinforcement of the resonance of that same dominant chord. The growing *pre-storm 'oppressiveness'* of the shot.

As in the previous example, the tonal dominant – movement as light variation – is here accompanied by a second dominant, a rhythmic one, i.e. movement as transposition.

Here it is realised in the growing force of the wind, condensed from air 'streams' into the watery 'torrents' of rain.[49] (A complete analogy with the soldiers' feet passing to the pram.)

In this general structure the role of the rain and wind is quite identical to the link between the rhythmic rocking and the haziness of the lens in the first example. In fact, the *character* of the relationships is the direct opposite. In opposition to the consonance of the first example we have here the reverse.

The heavens gathering into a black stillness are contrasted with the strengthening dynamic force of the wind, that grows and condenses from air 'streams' to watery 'torrents' – the next stage of intensity of the dynamic attack on women's skills and the delayed rye.

Here this collision between two tendencies – the intensification of the static and the intensification of the dynamic – provides us with a clear instance of *dissonance* in tonal montage construction.

From the point of view of emotional perception the 'harvest' sequence is an example of the *tragic* (active) minor key, as distinct from the *lyrical* (passive) minor like the 'port of Odessa' sequence.

It is interesting that both examples are edited according to the first appearance of movement, which follows movement as transposition. That is, according to 'colour':

in *Potemkin,* moving from dark grey to misty white (real-life equivalent: 'dawn'),

in the harvest sequence, from light grey to lead black (real-life equivalent: 'the approaching storm'), i.e. according to the frequency of light variations, that are *increasing in frequency* in one instance and *decreasing,* according to the sign, in the other.

We have a complete repetition of the picture of simple metric construction, but perceived in a new and significantly higher category of movement.

The fourth montage category can be justly called:

4. Overtonal Montage

As we can see, overtonal montage, as I characterised it at the beginning of this essay, is the furthest organic development of tonal montage.

As I have already indicated above, it distinguishes itself by taking full account of all the stimulants in the shot.

This characteristic enhances perception from a *melodically emotional colouring to a direct physiological sensation.*

I think that this also marks an advance on the other stages.

These four categories are the *methods of montage*. They become a *montage construction* proper when they enter into conflicting relationships with one another (as in the examples cited).

In this process, replacing one another in accordance with the scheme of their interrelationships, they move towards more refined variants of montage that flow organically from one another.

Thus, the transition from the metric to the rhythmic method arose from the emergence of conflict between the length of the shot and movement within the shot.

The transition to tonal montage resulted from the conflict between the rhythmic and tonal principles of the shot.

Lastly, overtonal montage resulted from the conflict between the tonal principle of the shot (the dominant) and the overtonal.

These considerations provide us in addition with an interesting criterion with which to evaluate montage construction from the standpoint of its 'pictorial quality' [*zhivopisnost*']. Pictorial quality as opposed to cinematic. Aesthetic pictorialism as opposed to physiological animation.

To pass judgment on the pictorialism of a *shot* in cinema is naive. It is for people with a reasonable knowledge of painting but absolutely no qualifications in cinema. This kind of judgment could include, for example, Kazimir Malevich's statements on cinema. Not even a film novice would now analyse a film shot as if it were an easel painting.[50]

I think that the criterion for evaluating the 'pictorialism' of a montage construction, in the broadest sense of the term, must be this: is the conflict resolved within one of the montage categories, i.e. without a conflict arising between different montage categories?

Cinema begins where the collision between different cinematic measures of movement and vibration begins.

For example, the 'pictorial' conflict between a figure and the horizon (whether static or dynamic is irrelevant), or the alternation of differently lit shots purely according to the conflicts between the light variations, or between the forms of the object and its illumination, etc.

We should also note the characteristics of the effect of individual montage variants on the 'psychophysiological' complex of the perceiver.

The first category is characterised by the primitive motor of effect. It is capable of leading the audience into specific outwardly motor states.

This is how the hay-making sequence in *The General Line*, for example, is edited. The individual shots move – 'unambiguously' – in a single movement from one side of the frame to the other, and I really laughed when I watched the more impressionable section of the audience as they rocked slowly from side to side with the increasing acceleration or when the shots got shorter. The effect was the same as that of a drum and brass playing a simple march.

We call the second category rhythmic, although it could also be called primitive emotional. Here the movement is more subtly calculated, because the emotion is also the result of movement, but of movement that never reaches the primitive external transposition.

The third category – tonal – could be called melodic emotional. Here the movement, which in the second case had already ceased to be transposition, clearly passes over into emotional *vibration* of a still higher order.

The fourth category – a new influx of pure physiologism – repeats with the greatest intensity the first category, once more finding a new stage in the intensity of the direct motor effect.

In music this is explained by the fact that, from the moment when overtones appear in parallel with the underlying resonance, there also appear so-called beats, i.e. kinds of vibrations that once again cease to be perceived as tones but are perceived rather as purely physical 'parallaxes' on the part of the perceiver. This applies to strongly pronounced timbre instruments where the overtonal principle is greatly preponderant.

They sometimes achieve the sensation of physical 'parallax' almost literally: very large Turkish drums, bells, organ.

In some places in *The General Line* I managed to achieve conflicting combinations of the tonal and overtonal lines. Sometimes they also collide with the metric and rhythmic lines. For example, individual junctions in the religious procession: 'diving' beneath the icons, the melting candles and the panting sheep at the moment of ecstasy, etc.

It is interesting that, while making our selection, we quite unconsciously produced evidence of the essential equality between *rhythm* and *tone*, establishing the same kind of staged unity between them as I had previously established between the concepts of *shot* and *montage*.

Hence, tone is a stage of rhythm.

For those who are afraid of such gradational reductions to a common denominator and of the extension of the characteristics of one stage into another for the purposes of research and methodology, I shall recall a quotation concerning the basic elements of the dialectic:

> These, apparently, are the elements of the dialectic. These elements may be presented in a more detailed way thus: . . .
> (11) an endless process of deepening the human cognition of objects, phenomena, processes, etc., from appearances to essence and from the less profound to the more profound essence.

(12) from coexistence to causality and from one form of connection and interdependence to another, deeper and more general.

(13) repetition, at the highest stage, of certain traits, characteristics etc. of the lowest stage and

(14) return, as it were, to the old....[51]

After this quotation I think that there will be no objection to the next order of

Eisenstein meets Mickey Mouse, 'my best friend in the USA', in Hollywood, September 1930.

montage, established as an even higher category of montage, i.e. intellectual montage.

Intellectual montage is montage not of primitively physiological overtonal resonances but of the resonances of overtones of an intellectual order,

i.e. the conflicting combination of accompanying intellectual effects with one another.

The gradation is here determined by the fact that there is no difference in principle between the motive force of a man rocking to and fro under the influence of primitive metric montage (viz., the hay-making example) and the intellectual process within it, for the intellectual process is the same oscillation – but in the centres of higher nervous activity.

Whereas in the first case under the influence of 'tap-dance montage' [*chechetochnyi montazh*] the hands and feet quiver, in the second case this quivering, provoked by an intellectual stimulant combined differently, produces an identical reaction in the tissues of the higher nervous system of the thought apparatus.

Whereas, judged as 'phenomena' (appearances), they seem in fact to be different, judged as 'essence' (process), they are, of course, identical.

The application of the experience of work on lower lines to categories of a higher order gives us the opportunity to carry the attack into the very heart of objects and phenomena.

Hence, the fifth category was the case of the intellectual overtone.

The sequence of the gods in *October* may serve as an example of this. In it all the conditions for their juxtaposition are conditioned by the class-intellectual (class, because, whereas the emotional 'principle' is universally human, the intellectual principle is profoundly coloured by class) resonances of the shot of 'god'.

These shots were assembled on a descending intellectual scale and lead the notion of god back to a block of wood.

But this, of course, is not yet the intellectual cinema that I have been announcing for some years now.

Intellectual cinema will be the cinema that resolves the conflicting combination of physiological overtones and intellectual overtones,[52] creating an unheard-of form of cinema which inculcates the Revolution into the general history of culture, creating a synthesis of science, art and militant class consciousness.

As we see it, the question of the overtone has enormous significance for the future.

We must examine the problems of its methodology all the more attentively and conduct a thorough investigation of it.

1934

12 'Eh!' On the Purity of Film Language[1]

My surname begins with an E. None the less, it is quite immaterial who first says 'Eh!' to the question.[2] The question of the purity of film language.

But one way and another we must all comment on Gorky's statement on language and literature with our reflections on film language.

Film language as a defining concept rather than a critic's turn of phrase is to a certain extent connected with my works and commentaries on them.

For this reason I shall take on the role of sniping at myself.

I do not intend to talk about the talking film. Or rather about the talking part of talking film. It speaks for itself. It even shouts. And its quality, even before we assess it from a cinematic point of view, has so many infelicities of a purely literary sort that its pretensions to cinematic quality can wait a while.

It is not about this language that I want to speak. (It would be absurd for me to do so given my fairly well-known literary style!) I want to talk about the uncultured cinematic language of films as they appear on our screens today.

In the field of film language our cinema has done a great deal for film culture. Much more than fashion has done.

It is true that in the West many of the means of expression that are specifically ours have taken no deeper root than fashion. Little snippets of film, spliced together with the aid of that stuff that smells of pears,[3] appear on the film menu under the name 'russischer Schnitt' or 'Russian cutting' in the same way as the term 'salade russe' is retained on restaurant menus for various vegetables prepared and seasoned in a particular way.

Fashion.

Fashions pass – culture remains. Sometimes the culture behind the fashion remains unnoticed. Sometimes the cultural achievement is thrown out with the outmoded fashion.

As in the West.

Negro sculpture, Polynesian masks or the Soviet way of editing films – for the West these are, first and foremost, exotica. And just exotica.

No mention can of course be made of the extraction of general cultural values, of the assimilation of principles, of the use of these achievements to move culture forward in principle.

What would it all be for?! Tomorrow the fashion magnates – the Patous, Worths, Mme Lanvins in various fields – will launch a new style. From somewhere in the Congo they will bring ivory tusks that have been carved by colonial slaves in some new way. Somewhere on the plains of Mongolia some yellowed bronze plates made by the slaves of some long past epoch are being dug up.

All is well. It is all to the good. It all helps profits.

The growth of culture? Who cares?

It would seem that this attitude towards culture and cultural achievements has long since come to an end with the October Revolution.

You cannot even force your way into the museums on your day off: the worker and his wife and children are queuing for the Tretyakov Gallery.

You cannot even squeeze into the reading room: there are so many people.

Readings and lectures are all overcrowded. Everywhere you find interest, attention, thrift. A proprietary interest in pre-Revolutionary achievements.

But in cinema there is a purely bourgeois absence of good management. And not only in the estimates. There is thoughtlessness. And not only in the schedules.

There is a complete disregard for, and neglect of, everything that has been done in the field of film culture in the Soviet period, by Soviet hands, on Soviet material and in accordance with Soviet principles.

Splendid: 'We have mastered the classics'.[4] (Whether or not it is splendid is another question – and a very debatable one at that!) Let us enter that on the credit side.

But this in no way invalidates the question. Why must we make these films with the complete disregard for all cinema's expressive means and possibilities that they demonstrate when flashed up on the screen?!

We have mastered theatre actors (better than the classics). Splendid!

But the question again arises: 'Should we hold on to auntie's tail?'[5]

Even if this auntie is as fine an actress as Tarasova![6]

Or would cinema culture harm her acting rather than promoting it?

Meanwhile the shots are 'rubbish'. The combination of the shots is a 'mess'. And the montage obviously 'jumps about'.

As a result, looking at the screen, you experience a sweet sensation, as if your eye had been gripped by sugar-tongs and ever so gently turned first to the right, then to the left and finally turned full circle and then put back into a confused orbit. They say: 'That's how your eyes are', 'That doesn't matter to the audience', 'The audience doesn't notice', 'The audience won't shout'. Quite right. The reader doesn't shout either. But what is needed is not a shout but a terrifying shout. Gorky's authoritative shout to make literature notice the elements of its own undoing. The reader will not die of the 'mess'. 'Rubbish' will not kill him. And neglect of literary language will not push him into the grave.

None the less it was deemed necessary to take the reader's literary hearing into protection. How does the reader's vision deteriorate when he becomes a film viewer?

How much worse is his ear in conjunction with his eye when he is present at some audio-visual catastrophe that has pretensions to audio-visual counterpoint?

Characteristically, films have begun to be called 'sound' films. Should this mean that what you see does not deserve attention?

But that is how it is.

In this context people say viciously: 'Well, the old devil, he's whining about montage.'

Yes, montage.

For many people montage and the Left deviation in Formalism are synonyms.

But in the meantime. . . .

Montage is not that at all.

For those who know, montage is the most powerful compositional means of realising plot.

For those who know nothing about composition, montage is the syntax for the correct construction of each particular fragment of a film.

Lastly, montage is simply the elementary rules of cinema orthography for those who mistakenly put together the fragments of a film the way one would mix potions according to a fixed recipe, pickle cucumbers, marinate plums or soak apples in cranberry juice.

[And the button, the sash, the suspenders, if they also become an end in themselves, can lead to absurdity.][7]

Not just montage. . . .

But I should like to see the freedom of expressive activities of man's hands relieved of these supporting aggregates in the lower part of his toilet.

In films you do encounter individual good shots but in these circumstances the independent pictorial qualities of the shot and its value stand in mutual contradiction. As they are not linked by montage thought and composition, they become mere playthings and an end in themselves. The better the shots, the closer the film comes to being a disjointed collection of beautiful phrases, a shop window of unrelated objects or an album of postage stamps with views.

We do not by any means stand for the 'hegemony' of montage. The time has passed when, for pedagogical and educational purposes, it was necessary to perform a tactical and polemical manoeuvre to ensure the broad mastery of montage as one of cinema's means of expression. But we are duty-bound to confront the problem of literacy in film language.[8] We must demand that the quality of montage, film syntax and film speech not only matches the quality of earlier works but exceeds and surpasses them. That is what the battle for the high quality of film culture requires of us.

It is easier for literature. When you criticise it, you can stand it alongside the classics. Its heritage and achievements have largely been examined down to the tiniest microscopic detail. The analysis of the compositional and image structure of Gogol's prose carried out by the late Andrei Bely stands as a living reproach to any literary flippancy.[9]

None the less, Gogol has also been used in cinema. The last, as it were, flash of purity of montage form in sound cinema was, before it descended into complete formlessness, like a transposition of a Gogol text into visual material.

You could, I think, successfully accompany the magnificent visual poetry of the Dnieper in the first reel of Dovzhenko's *Ivan* by declaiming Gogol's 'Wonderful Dnieper'.[10]

The rhythms of moving shots. Sailing along the shore. Motionless expanses of water cutting in. The magic of Gogol's imagery and his turns of speech are captured in their alternation and changing. All this 'neither stirs nor thunders'. All this 'you see and do not know whether its immense expanse is moving or not and it seems as though it is made of glass', etc. Here literature and cinema provide a model of the purest fusion and affinity. And these fragments also recall Rabelais.

His poetic anticipation of the 'imaging' of the theory of relativity in his description of the island '*des chemins cheminants*':

> Seleucus had been of the opinion that the earth really revolved around the poles, rather than the heavens, although the contrary seems to us to be the truth – just as, when we are on the River Loire, the trees along the bank seem to be moving, whereas it is not the trees at all, but ourselves upon the boat, who are in motion.

We have dwelt on this example because it seems like a swansong for the purity of film language on our contemporary screen. Even for *Ivan*. Its later reels nowhere rise to the perfection of this fragment.

People will say: but 'The Wonderful Dnieper' is a poem.

That is not the point at all. On this basis we should have to assume that the structure of the prose of, for instance, Zola would unfailingly display signs of 'naturalistic chaos'.

Yet in one study I happened to see his pages broken up into the strophes of an epic poem. These pages of *Germinal* were recited with almost as much severity as Homeric hexameters.

They covered the episodes leading up to the sinister scene when, during the disturbances before the arrival of the gendarmes, the mob destroys the shop of the usurer and rapist Maigrat. When the infuriated women, under the leadership of La Brute and Mouquette, 'emasculate' the corpse of the despised shopkeeper who, in escaping, had stepped from the roof and broken his skull on the kerbstone. When the bloodied 'trophy' is hoisted on a pole and carried in procession.

> 'What is it they have at the end of that stick?' asked Cécile, who had grown bold enough to look out.
> Lucie and Jeanne decided that it must be a rabbit-skin.
> 'No, no,' murmured Madame Hennebeau, 'they must have been pillaging a pork butcher's, it seems a remnant of a pig.'
> At this moment she shuddered and was silent. Madame Grégoire had nudged her with her knee. They both remained stupefied.[11]

This scene, like the previous scene in which the crowd of women tries to flog Cécile publicly, is itself, of course, related to the stylised quoted transplant of episodes that obviously struck Zola in the annals of the French Revolution.

The women's attempt to abduct Cécile echoes the well-known episode of the execution of Théroigne de Méricourt.[12]

The second scene forces us to recall involuntarily a perhaps less well-known and popular episode from Mercier's materials. When the people's hatred for the Princesse de Lamballe, Marie-Antoinette's closest intimate, burst and the popular anger made short work of her at the gates of La Force prison, one of the participants 'cut out her virginal parts and made himself a moustache'.[13] The later commentary on this affair by the journal *Intermédiaire* in 1894 is interesting:

> We are told all about the unfortunate princess's fate. But collectors have no respect for anything! About twenty years ago in one of the chateaux in the neighbourhood of Liège in Belgium I saw the reverentially preserved, completely withered organs of the Princesse de Lamballe, spread out on a satin cushion.

127

The title of the novel, *Germinal*, deliberately chosen from the names given to the months in that earlier period, suggests a previously stylised adaptation of the episodes.[14] Whereas this reference for purposes of temperament and pathos to an earlier pathos-filled epoch played a considerable part in defining the rhythmic clarity of the form of its literary language, its spread to the treatment of minor episodes is not very felicitous.

Our film *October* suffered in a similar way in the sequence dealing with the events of July 1917. At all costs we wanted the historical incident of the worker Bolshevik who was beaten and murdered by the brutalised bourgeoisie to be imbued with the 'tone' of the Paris Commune. The result was the scene with the ladies hitting the worker with their parasols: the scene is quite different in spirit from the general mood of the period before October.

This passing observation may not be unhelpful. We have to make frequent use of our literary heritage and the culture of the image and language of earlier periods. In stylistic terms it often determines our works quite considerably. And it does us no harm to note our failures as well as our positive models.

Returning once more to the question of the purity of film form, I frequently come across the objection that the craft of film language and film expressiveness is still very young and has no models for a classic tradition. They say that I attack, without contrasting the positive models, getting away with literary analogies. Many even express a doubt as to whether there is anything similar in this 'half art', as many people still think of cinema.

Forgive me. That is how things are.

At the same time our film language, although it has no recognised classics, has acquired great severity of form and expression. At a certain stage our cinema displayed the same strict responsibility for each shot admitted into a montage sequence as poetry did for each line of verse or music for the regular movement of a fugue.

We may cite quite a number of instances from the practice of our silent cinema. As I do not have the time now specially to select other models, I shall permit myself to cite here a sample analysis from one of my own works. It is taken from the materials for my book *Direction* (Part II: *Mise en cadre*),[15] which I am finishing, and it concerns *Potemkin*. In order to demonstrate the compositional interdependence of the plastic aspect of the changing shots I have deliberately chosen an example at random rather than from a climactic scene: fourteen consecutive fragments from the scene that precedes the shooting on the Odessa Steps. The scene where the 'good people of Odessa' (as the *Potemkin* sailors addressed their appeal to the population of Odessa) send skiffs with provisions alongside the mutinous battleship.

The sending of greetings is constructed on a distinct intersection between two subjects:

1. The skiffs speed towards the battleship.
2. The people of Odessa wave.

In the end the two subjects merge.

The composition is basically on two planes: depth and foreground. The subjects dominate alternately, advancing to the foreground and pushing one another into the background.

The composition is constructed: (1) on the plastic interaction between both planes (within the shot), (2) on the change in line and form on each plane from shot to shot (by montage). In the second case the compositional play is formed from the interaction of the plastic impression of the previous shot in collision or interaction with the succeeding one. (Here the analysis is by purely spatial and linear sign. The rhythmic temporal relationship will be examined elsewhere.)

The movement of the composition (see the attached table, p. 133) takes the following course.

I. The skiffs in motion. A smooth movement parallel to a horizontal cross-section of the shot. The whole field of vision is occupied by the first subject. There is a play of small vertical sails.

II. The intensifying movement of the skiffs of the first subject. (The entrance of the second subject facilitates this.) The second subject comes to the fore with a strict rhythm of motionless vertical columns. The vertical lines sketch the plastic disposition of future figures (IV, V, etc.). The interplay of horizontal waves and vertical lines. The skiff subject is pushed into the background. The plastic subject of the arch appears in the bottom half of the shot.

III. The plastic subject of the arch expands into the whole shot. The play revolves around the change in the frame's articulation from vertical lines to the structure of the arch. The vertical subject is maintained in the movement of small-scale people moving away from the camera. The skiff subject is finally pushed into the background.

IV. The plastic subject of the arch finally occupies the foreground. The arch structure moves into the opposite resolution: the contours of a group forming a circle are sketched in (the parasol completes the composition). The same transition to an opposite also occurs within the vertical construction: the backs of the small-scale people moving into the background are replaced by large-scale static figures filmed from the front. The subject of the movement of the skiffs is maintained by reflection in the expression of the eyes and in their movement along the horizontals.

V. In the foreground a common compositional variation: an even number of people is replaced by an uneven number. Two becomes three. This 'golden rule' in changing the *mise en scène* is supported by a tradition that dates back to the Italian *commedia dell'arte*[16] (the direction of the glances also intersects). The arch motif is once more straightened out, this time into an opposite curve. Repeating and supporting it, there is a new parallel arch motif in the *background*: a balustrade. The skiff subject in motion. The eye passes over the whole breadth of the shot along the horizontal.

VI. Sections I–V provide the transposition from the skiff subject to that of the onlookers, developed in five montage sections. The interval V–VI produces a sudden transition back from the onlookers to the skiffs. The composition, which strictly follows the content, suddenly turns all the signs back in the opposite direction. The line of the balustrade is brought suddenly to the foreground, and repeated in the line of the boat's gunwale. It is echoed by the line where the boat comes into contact with the surface of the water. The basic compositional articulation is the same but the treatment is the opposite. V is static. VI is sketched out through the dynamic of the boat in motion. The division into 'three' along the vertical is maintained in both shots. The central element is texturally similar (the woman's blouse and the canvas of the sail). The elements at the sides are sharply contrasted: the dark shapes of the men beside the woman and the white spaces beside the sail. The articulations along the vertical are also contrasted: three figures cut off by the bottom of the frame become a vertical sail cut off by the top of the frame. In the *background* a new subject appears: the battleship seen from the side, cut off at the top (a preparation for Section VII).

VII. Another sudden change of subject. The background subject, the battleship, moves forward into the foreground (the thematic jump from V to VI serves as a kind of *Vorschlag*[17] to the jump from VI to VII). The angle is turned through 180°: the shot from the battleship towards the sea is the reverse of VI. This time the side of the battleship is in the *foreground* and is cut off by the *bottom* of the frame. In the background is the sail subject, working in verticals. The vertical of the sailors. The static gun-barrel continues the line of movement of the boat in the preceding section. The side of the ship appears to be an arch becoming a straight line.

VIII. This repeats IV with greater intensity. The horizontal play of the eyes spreads into a vertical of waving hands. The vertical subject moves from the background into the foreground, repeating the thematic transfer of attention to the onlookers.

IX. Two faces closer up. Generally speaking, an unfortunate combination with the preceding section. A shot with three faces should have been inserted between them. A repetition of Section V, for instance, but also with greater intensity.

This would have produced a 2:3:2 structure. Moreover the repetition of the familiar group IV–V ending with a new IX would have heightened the perception of the last shot. The situation is saved by a slight enlargement of the close-up.

X. Two faces become one. The arm is raised very energetically up and out of the frame. A correct alternation of faces (if we adopt the correction between VIII and IX): 2:3:2:1. The second pair of shots with the correct enlargement of scale vis-à-vis the first pair (a proper repetition with qualitative variation). The line of odd numbers varies both in quantity and quality (the dimension of the faces is different as is their number, while observing the general characteristics of odd numbers).

XI. Another sudden change of subject. A jump that repeats V–VI but with greater intensity. The vertical *thrust* of the previous shot is repeated in the vertical *sail*. But the vertical of this sail scuds past horizontally. A repetition of the subject of VI with greater intensity. And a repetition of the composition of II with the difference that the subject of the horizontal of the skiffs' motion and the vertical of the motionless columns is here fused into a single horizontal transposition of the *vertical* sail. The composition repeats the thematic line of the unity and identity between the skiffs and the people on the shore (before we move on to the final theme of merger: the shore and the battleship via the skiffs).

XII. The sail in XI dissolves into a multitude of vertical sails, scudding along horizontally (a repetition of Section I with heightened intensity). The small sails move in the opposite direction to the large sail.

XIII. Having dissolved into small sails, the large sail is once more reassembled, this time not into a sail but into the flag flying over the *Potemkin*. There is a new quality in this shot because it is both static and mobile, the mast being vertical and motionless while the flag flutters in the breeze. In formal terms Section XII repeats XI. But the change from sail to banner translates the principle of plastic unification into an ideological and thematic unification. This is no longer just a vertical that in plastic terms joins the separate elements of composition: *this is a revolutionary banner uniting the battleship, the skiffs and the shore.*

XIV. From here there is a natural return from the flag to the battleship. XIV repeats VII. Also with heightened intensity.

This section introduces a new compositional group of *interrelationships between the skiffs and the battleship* as distinct from the first group of *skiffs and the shore.* The first group reflected the subject: 'the skiffs are bringing greetings and gifts from the shore to the battleship'. The second group will express the *fraternisation between the skiffs and the battleship.*

The mast with the revolutionary flag serves as a compositional watershed and at the same time as the ideological uniting face for both compositional groups.

Section VII, repeated by the first shot in the second group in Section XIV, appears as a sort of *Vorschlag* for the second group and as an element linking the two groups together, like a 'patrol' sent out by the latter group to the former. In the second group the same role will be performed by the shots of the waving figures, cut into the scenes of fraternisation between the skiffs and the battleship.

You must not think that both the shooting and montage for these sequences were done according to tables calculated a priori. Of course not. But the assembly and the interrelationship of these fragments on the cutting table were clearly dictated by the compositional requirements of film form. These requirements dictated the selection of these fragments from all those available. They established the regularity of the alternation between shots. Actually these fragments, if viewed merely from the standpoint of plot and story, could be arranged in any combination. But the compositional movement through them would scarcely prove in that case to be as regular in construction.

We should not complain of the complexity of this analysis. In comparison with analysis of literary and musical form my analysis is still quite obvious and easy.

Setting aside for the moment problems of rhythmic examination, I have in my analysis also examined the alternations of sound and word combinations.

An analysis of the actual objects of shooting and their treatment through camera angle and lighting, deriving from the requirements of style and of the character of the content, would correspond to an analysis of the expressive quality of the actual phrases, words and their phonetic indication in a literary work.

We are convinced that the requirements that film composition sets itself are just as great as the requirements of the corresponding sections of literature and music.

The audience is, of course, least of all able to verify with a pair of compasses the regularity of the construction of successive shots in montage. But its perception of regular montage composition involves the same elements as those that distinguish stylistically a page of cultured prose from a page of Count Amori, Verbitskaya or Breshko-Breshkovsky.[18]

Now Soviet cinema is historically correct in joining battle for plot. There are still many obstacles along the path, many risks of a false understanding of the principles of plot. The most terrible of these is the underestimation of the opportunities that a temporary emancipation from the old traditions of plot has given us:

the opportunity to re-examine in principle and once more the bases and problems of film plot

and advance in a progressive cinematic movement not 'back' to plot but 'forward to plot'.

There is no clear artistic orientation at the moment along these paths although individual positive phenomena are already being sketched in.

But, one way or another, we must meet the moment when we master the clearly recognised principles of Soviet plot cinema fully armed with an irreproachable purity and culture in our film language and speech.

We value our great masters of literature from Pushkin and Gogol to Mayakovsky and Gorky not just as masters of plot. We value in them the culture of masters of speech and word.

The time has come to pose the acute question of the culture of film language.

It is important that all film-makers should express their views on the matter.

Above all in the language of montage and the shots of their own films.

The sequence from *Potemkin* to which Eisenstein refers above (pp. 124–32).

1937

13   The Mistakes of *Bezhin Meadow*[1]

How could it have happened that more than ten years after the victory of *The Battleship Potemkin*, on the twentieth anniversary of *October*, I came to grief with *Bezhin Meadow*? What caused the catastrophe that overtook a picture I had spent about two years working on? Where lay the original error in my world-view that flawed the work, so that, despite the sincerity of my feelings and my dedication, it turned out to be patently groundless politically; and anti-artistic in consequence?

Asking myself that question again, and with much soul-searching, I have begun to see my error and to understand it.

My error is rooted in a deeply intellectual, individualist illusion. An illusion which starts off on a small scale but can lead to major and tragic mistakes and consequences. An illusion that Lenin did not approve of and that Stalin has constantly unmasked. An illusion that you can make something that is genuinely revolutionary purely 'off your own back', rather than in the thick of a collective, marching resolutely in step with it.

That is where the mistake lurks. And that is the first thing that I should admit when asking myself in all seriousness about the origins not just of the mistakes in the present work but also of a series of mistakes in past works.

This intellectual illusion explains for the most part the flawed Quixotic detours and erroneous diversions and the failure to set questions and answer them properly. This leads to a summation of the individual diversions which constitutes the political distortion of the event portrayed and a politically incorrect treatment of the subject.

The spirit of elemental revolution lies where Bolshevik consciousness and the disciplining of that consciousness are long overdue – that is where mistakes are born; despite all good intentions and endeavours, that is where what is subjectively flawed and simply objectively harmful can break out, surface with increasing frequency.

What happened to me, in my understanding of the teaching of realism, sprang from the same source.

My stylistic endeavours and my inclinations draw me strongly toward the general, the generalised, toward generalisation. But is that the generalisation, the 'general' that Marxist doctrine has taught us? No. Because in my work, generalisation absorbs the particular. Instead of being detected through what is concretely particular, the generalisation dissipates into fragmented abstraction. That was not the case with *The Battleship Potemkin*. The strength of that film lay in the fact that through this particular, single event I managed to convey a generalised idea of 1905 as a 'dress rehearsal' for October. This particular episode could absorb what was typical of that phase of the revolutionary struggle. And what was selected for this episode was typical, and the interpretation of it was generalised, characteristic. This was in no small measure due to the fact that *Potemkin* was first conceived as one episode in a major epic about 1905, only later becoming an independent work, but one that absorbed the whole build-up of emotions and resonances that had been intended for the larger film.

This did not happen with *Bezhin Meadow*. Even the episode that lies at the heart of it, the dramatic episode, is not in the least bit characteristic. The kulak father murdering his son, a Young Pioneer, is not an impossible episode: such things had happened. But it is not a typical episode. Quite the opposite: it is exceptional, unique and uncharacteristic. Furthermore, its position at the centre of the screenplay confers upon it the status of something independent, self-sufficient and generalised. This confusion completely distorts a valid and realistic picture and the state of the class struggle in the country. This is concealed behind a pathologically distended portrayal of the father's 'execution' of his son which is more reminiscent of Abraham's 'sacrifice' of Isaac than it is of the themes which are bound to stir the viewer: the final battles to ensure the lasting triumph of collective farming. From this perspective the first version of the screenplay was entirely flawed, as it treated this episode as the key and central one.

The second version of the screenplay and its treatment tried instead to stop the drama between father and son from becoming 'a thing in its own right' and to show it as an episode in the general progression of the class struggle in the countryside. This was not done thoroughly or decisively enough: the break with the original concept was not entirely final, neither in the screenplay nor in the director's realisation of it.

And if a social situation has been accentuated wrongly, that is bound to lead to a false psychological interpretation. The psychological question of infanticide becomes the focus of attention. And this generalised question pushes the main problem – the depiction of the struggle between the kulak and the forces of collectivisation – downstage. The situation is resolved in a psychological abstraction, not by a realistic examination of reality.

The first version removes every last trace of humanity from the father: it is an unconvincing and stilted show of brutishness. The second version goes too far in the opposite direction: class hatred of the kulak, whose unbridled anger even leads him to murder his own son in his fight against socialism, lies beyond the 'human drama' of the murder and vanishes from view.

Abstracted from reality, the psychological conception results in political bankruptcy: hatred of the enemy evaporates and the psychological ramifications extend the theme to that of a father murdering his son 'in general'.

The mistakes – the isolation of a concrete event from reality – of generalisation within the actual theme are just as jarring in the methods of its realisation.

The first thing is the isolation of an idea from a concrete example of it.

And this leads to an underestimation of man and inattention to the creator of the image of man in a picture – the actor.

Hence also attention is focused not on the people whose roles are politically significant, but on those who have the most interesting personalities.

The brutish appearance of the father gives him a disproportionately important role. The head of the political section is pale, dull and pompous.

Filming the filmed in *Bezhin Meadow*.

At the same time the village Pioneer, the hero of the film, is exaggerated beyond any realistic measure of his social significance. This produces the impression that the class struggle in the countryside is being waged only by Pioneers – or in our picture by only one Pioneer (this is true of the first version in particular).

The same thing applies to the artistic structure of the film. Once attention is no longer focused entirely on one person, on his character and actions, then the role of props and secondary means grows enormously. Hence the exaggeration of the expressiveness of the surroundings: a lair instead of a hut; a distorting camera angle and unnatural lighting. Set, shot and lighting do the acting instead of the

136

actor. Even in regard to the appearance of the cast. These were not living faces but masks: the ultimate generalisation of 'typicality',[2] as distinct from a real face. In their behaviour, the emphasis was on stasis, where the static frozen face was like 'the mask of a gesture' just as a mask was the ultimate generalisation of a dead face.

All these elements in the realisation, which were so justifiably severely criticised, especially in the first version of the film, derived entirely from the premises enumerated at the beginning.

I can write about this with complete frankness because over the course of two years' work I myself, helped by the unremitting criticism of those in charge of the film industry, tried to overcome these features. But I could not do so entirely. Everyone who has seen all the footage of film, from beginning to end, has commented that there was an undoubted shift towards realism and that the complex of 'night' scenes demonstrates that the author was already abandoning the weak positions he had adopted while working on the first version.

The exaggeration of generalisation, detached from a particular event and from concrete reality, inevitably sent a whole system of images flying in the only possible direction: towards figures and associations fashioned after mythology (Pan, Samson – the destroyer of the Temple – the 'lad' in the first version). If, in the 'rout of the church', this was done with conscious irony – Biblical associations clashed with actions that were not characteristic of them (once I had abandoned the attempt at a realistic portrayal there was nothing for it but to work on a game of speculation) – in the serious part this sent the images and characters to their destruction without the author being conscious of it. The full-blooded comprehensiveness of a tragic collision petered out into monochromatic 'black and white' melodrama; the reality of a class struggle turned into a cosmically generalised battle between 'good and evil'. To imagine that the author consciously aimed at myth is simply not reasonable. We see once again how a method for a workable portrayal of reality, which was not fully realised or assimilated in practice, took the author's mistake well beyond the limits of aesthetics and artistry and caused the work to strike a false note politically.

But who made the first mistake? And can it be said that a political flaw is a 'disaster' and the consequence of a flawed creative method? Of course not. The flaw in the creative method takes its source from the flawed world-view.

The flaws in the world-view lead to the flaws in the method. The flaws in the method lead to objective political error and bankruptcy.

If this is logically apparent for every even minutely aware creative worker in our country, myself included, then in order not merely to understand that finally, but to feel it all in the whole depth of my emotions, I needed the withering and harsh criticism with which the catastrophe of *Bezhin Meadow* was discussed in the press and among the activists of GUK and Mosfilm.[3]

Extended viewing at Mosfilm of all the reels of the picture laid bare for me too the flawed perspective from which I had viewed the subject. The criticism of my comrades helped me towards a clear perception of how wrong my slant on the matter had been.

What had led to this? The failure to uncover the principal motive forces and the actual situation of the class struggle in the villages. The situations of the film did not flow from these presuppositions. Quite the reverse: the film's situations were self-referential. All in all, this was not only incapable of conveying the positive revolutionary effect present in the author's emotions and purposes. Quite the reverse. The errors on this level were capable of arousing an objectively opposite effect on the viewer. This was compounded by errors in the method: the unrealistic treatment of the overwhelming majority of the material (with the exception in particular of the last third of the material for the new version, which shows a shift in method). Even if you had not seen all of the material, you might reach a similar conclusion about it from the screenplay and a description of the reels alone.

Blindness, negligence and absence of vigilance can be attributed to all those who guided and carried out the work. Work should have been stopped. No amount of takes or retakes could have saved it. I can now see clearly that not only a series of details but also the conception of the work as a whole were flawed. It grew out of a screenplay but the director's interpretation could not stand up to those elements and went on to repeat the original errors despite the possibilities offered by the second version.

The unfolding course of discussions about *Bezhin Meadow* further enlightened me on the principal questions: how could it have happened that an obviously incorrect conception could develop in production?

I shall be clear and direct in my answer. In recent years I have become self-absorbed. I have retreated into my shell. The country fulfilled its Five-Year Plans. Industrialisation took giant steps forward. I remained in my shell. My alienation from life was, it is true, not complete. It was in those years that I was intensively involved with the younger generation, devoting all my energies to my work at the Institute of Cinema.[4] But this was also a retreat within the walls of an academic institute; there was no broad creative exit towards the masses, towards reality.

The twentieth anniversary of Soviet cinema has given me a real shock. In 1935 I threw myself into my work. But the habit of self-absorption and alienation had already taken hold. I worked shut away with my film crew. I created the picture not out of the flesh and blood of socialist reality, but out of a tissue of associations and theoretical conceptions relating to that reality. The results are obvious.

And that is the upshot of this harsh criticism, criticism that is truly Bolshevik; that is, friendly and intended to help, well-intentioned not malicious. Speeches by our Mosfilm collective of workers saved me from the worst – saved me from being wounded by everything that occurred as a result of my errors in *Bezhin Meadow*. The collective helped open my eyes above all to my own mistakes, to the mistakes in my method and the mistakes in my socio-political conduct. All this overshadows even the natural grief over the loss of two years' work, to which I had devoted so much energy, love and effort. Why am I firm and calm? I understand my own mistakes. I understand the meaning of the criticism, self-criticism, examination and self-examination which grips the whole country following the decisions of the Central Committee of the Party.[5]

I feel very acutely the necessity finally to overcome the errors of my world view; the necessity for a radical reconstruction [*perestroika*] and mastery of Bolshevism.

And in this light I face the question: how may I do all this in the fullest, most profound and responsible way?

This is not possible in isolation from concrete and practical tasks and perspectives. What should I do?

Work seriously on my own world view and delve deeply into new themes from a Marxist angle. Study reality and the new man in concrete fashion. Direct my attentions towards a concretely chosen, strong screenplay and subject.

There is only one possible subject for my next work: spiritually heroic, following the Party's ideology, treating of war and defence, and popular in style – independently of whether the material will be about 1917 or 1937 – it will serve the triumphant passage of socialism.

In preparation for the making of this film, I see the path through which I shall obliterate the last traces of elemental anarchy from my world-view and my creative method.

The Party, the cinema's leadership and the creative collective of film-makers will help me to make the new and accurate pictures that we need.

14 Alexander Nevsky and the Rout of the Germans[1]

Bones. Skulls. Scorched earth. The charred remains of human habitation. People led away to slavery in a distant land. Ruined towns. Human dignity trampled underfoot. Such is the terrible picture of the first decades of the 13th century in Russia that stands before us. The Tatar hordes of Genghis Khan had rounded the southern shores of the Caspian and penetrated the Caucasus. Destroying the flourishing culture of Georgia, this horror, death and insanity – the source of their strength – launched themselves on Russia. The rout of the Russian soldiers who had come to meet them, in the battle of Kalka in 1223, was only a prelude to the bloody epic of Khan Batu's invasion which stirred up all Europe.

Russian princedoms and towns were ready, one after the other, to repulse the terrible enemy. But they had not reached the stage of maturity where they realised that a powerful state, capable of opposing any invasion, cannot be created amidst civil strife and infighting. Disunited and solitary, town after town showed itself a model of great fortitude. But, one after the other, they fell in unequal struggle. The Tatars advanced with terrible force and threatened to rout Europe. In a Europe driven mad by horror, isolated calls to give a collective rebuff were made. But these appeals hung in mid-air. Germany was not moved by a summons to universal armament. Germany was immersed in factionalism and political competition between the Emperor and Rome. Only the Slav peoples undertook the defence and salvation of Europe from the Tatars. The Russians sacrificed themselves and their towns to this cause.

And – an irony of fate! – it fell to the Czechs to save Germany from death and destruction. The Czech king Wenceslas was her saviour from Batu's hordes; with his regiments he blocked off the route into Germany. The Czech warrior Jaroslav of Sternberg, during the siege of Olmütz, brought down destruction upon Batu's troops.[2]

The Ukraine, and other constituent parts of the future great land of Russia, lay for long years beneath the heel of the Tatar yoke, suffering all the victor's greed as he stood upon the ruins of the Russian principalities that he had routed and crushed. Such was the fearful face of long-suffering Rus of the 13th century. Without a complete picture of all of this you will not understand the full magnitude of the heroism with which the Russian people, enslaved by an Oriental barbarian, was able with Alexander Nevsky as general to rout the Western barbarian – the Teutonic Knights who were trying to tear off a slice of enslaved Russia. But where had these knights come from?

At the start of the 12th century the 'House of the Teutons' arose first in

Jerusalem and then in the setting of the Crusaders' siege of Ptolemais.[3] This House, like the 'Brown House' in Munich all those years later,[4] was destined to be the cradle of one of the most terrible scourges of humanity; like leprosy, it held Western and Eastern Europe in its rapacious grasp.

The 'House of the Teutons' represented at first nothing more than a field hospital; however, the German marshals of the Crusades took the most active part in it. On 6 February 1191, with the blessing of Rome, a new order of knights came into being. On 12 July of the same year, Ptolemais fell to the Crusaders. The new order took possession of a sizeable share of the spoils and the ownership of the territory, by settling in number on the land that had been conquered. It could now easily go about the business of organising itself, and the Teutonic Order became a focus for German influence not only in Palestine, but in the whole of Europe. Its composition was uncompromisingly nationalistic and aristocratic: only Germans who were also members of the oldest of the noble families were entitled to join. The political importance of similar little islands of German orientation in various countries was as clear to the politicians of the 13th century as it is to the masters of contemporary Germany. Initially, the knights confined themselves to starting to trade on their military strength and strategic skills. They began to play a policing role, as guard dogs for the various rulers of Europe.

But there soon began a prolonged and systematic invasion of the East. One by one, Prussians, Livonians, Estonians, Zhmuds fell prey to them.[5] Vying with the Tatars in cruelty and ruthlessness towards their subjugated peoples, the Teutons had by this time joined forces with other, monastic orders who were no less rapacious and considerably more terrifying than the Tatars.

The Tatars were satisfied with incursions, pillage and destroying the subjugated lands; they did not settle on them, but went back into the heartlands of Asia or to the khanates in the south-east, extorting a heavy, and sometimes crippling, tribute.

It was quite a different matter with the Teutonic and Livonian 'Knights'. We are dealing here with a consistent colonisation in the form of a complete enslavement of its subjects and the destruction of the features of their aboriginal religious and social structures which characterised the colonists' plunder for centuries to come.

With military techniques and an organised military strength that was superior to their subjects', the 'devout brothers' would stoop to any tactic: the first was the widely established system for recruiting traitors. The chronicles have brought to us not only the names of our country's heroic defenders, but also those of its vile betrayers. There is the prince, Vladimir of Pskov, and his son Yaroslav Vladimirovich who was such a traitor. Here at last is also the colourful figure of the governor of Pskov, Tverdila Ivankovich, who betrayed Pskov to the Germans out of selfish personal interests.[6]

The centre, where the first defence of the Russian lands against the Western barbarians – and later the organised counter-attack against them – originated, was then Novgorod ('Lord Novgorod the Great', as it was christened in those days).[7] The glorious name of Novgorod has forever been linked with the heroic defence of the land of Russia and the rebirth of its national independence which especially farsighted and vigorous princes had fought for. Pride of place among them belongs to the Novgorod prince Alexander Nevsky, whose strength lay not only in

Prophetic warnings of German atrocities in *Alexander Nevsky*.

his personal genius but in his deep inner bond with the people's volunteers, 'Russian muzhiks' (as Marx wrote of them), whom he led in victorious campaigns.[8] His closeness and his blood tie with the people set his unerring course through the complex international politics of the day. It enabled Alexander to choose the one historically correct political line. Currying favour with the Tatars and trying by all means possible to 'cope with' them, Alexander thereby set his hands free to deal with the West: there lay the greater menace to the people's originality and the first growths of national self-awareness which was emerging as a natural reaction to the incursions from the West and the East. Alexander launched his main strike against the West.

Alexander and the armed forces of Novgorod attained the high point of their military success and glory in the defence of the nation on this path, in the battle on Lake Peipus, famous as the Battle on the Ice, which took place on 5 April 1242. It was the finale of a brilliantly conceived military campaign against the invaders and involved regaining Coporia from the Germans, winning back Pskov, skirmishes with the Germans at Izborsk and a raid along the shores of Lake Pskov (which was joined to Lake Peipus) with the aim of smashing the Germans' plans – they wanted to keep Alexander's main troops at Izborsk, so that they could entrap his principal forces in an encirclement. Alexander guessed the Germans' plan; in an unexpected manoeuvre he used his vanguard to cut off their route on the west bank of the lake, somewhere near the Embakh estuary. These advance troops, led by the valorous Domash Tverdislavich and Kerbet, suffered defeat at the hands of superior German forces. But Alexander retreated on to the ice of Lake Peipus; without going on to the eastern, Russian shore he faced the Germans' strike at Raven Rock near the narrow strait connecting Lake Peipus with Lake Pskov. The Germans advanced in a terrifying formation, a cavalry wedge.[9]

We will try to imagine what that hitherto invincible military formation was like. Picture the prow of a modern battleship or a very powerful tank, enlarged to the size of a hundred armoured knights on horseback. Imagine this gigantic iron triangle galloping at full tilt, building up furious energy. Imagine this force cutting through a circle and into the mass of the enemy, who are dumbstruck by the terrible, impersonal mass of iron bearing down upon it. The knights' faces cannot be seen: instead there is a wall of iron with small slits forming a cross, for them to see and breathe. The 'wedge' breaks up the enemy's front and immediately breaks up into separate 'spears'. The 'spear' – a knight in armour, the prototype of the 'tanketka' – bursts into the mass of living flesh of the enemy scattering them left and right. Penetrating even deeper, the 'spear' is not only a knight; it may be a whole group, sometimes as many as thirteen men, a military crew: armour-bearers, pages, and horsemen comprising, with a knight at its centre, one whole.

To face an onslaught from a 'wedge' head-on, in an open field, with the state of troops being what it then was, was as unthinkable as trying unarmed to stop a tank would be now.

And Alexander got even with the Germans using the same manoeuvre of genius that Hannibal used and with which he covered himself with undying glory at Cannae.[10] Knowing that the centre ('forehead') could not resist an onslaught by a 'wedge', he did not even attempt to: he deployed all his strength on the flanks (the regiments of the 'left' and 'right' hand). The intentionally weakened centre yielded to the wedge's attack, but at the same time encouraged its pursuit. Alexander was successful. To the envy of future warriors who aspire to realise the dream of all commanders of all ages, he accomplished a complete encirclement of the enemy from both flanks. We have information that a detachment lying in ambush even cut into the enemy from the rear. The treacherous enemy, crushed on all sides, was subjected to a complete rout. Never before had there been such a battle. The Germans had never known such defeat. The din and the groans of the unforgettable conflict come to us through the pages of the chronicles: 'the crack of shattering lances, the clash of swords – it was as though the frozen lake was moving. . . . The ice was hidden, everywhere awash with blood . . . and the Russian soldiers cut them to pieces, pursuing them as though through the air, and there was nowhere for them to hide. . . . They slew them on the ice, over the seven versts to the Subolich shore . . .'

We must explain why the battle took place on the ice. There are many theories about this. First, the smooth surface of the frozen waters made it possible to meet the enemy in battle face to face; there would be none of the unexpected ups and downs of the shoreline (and Russians were used to fighting on the smooth surface of frozen lakes). Then there was the possibility of deploying the sections of his troops skilfully. Third, the slippery surface made the going harder for the horses. Finally, there was the consideration that the ice would have to give beneath the weight of the more heavily armed Germans. This actually happened, chiefly, during the pursuit; the April ice, thin near the shore, could not support the weight of the knights who were gathering in large numbers at the western bank, whose steep sides made a quick flight impossible. The remainder of those fleeing perished in the waters that opened up beneath their feet. But just looking at the map, we can see that the key thing here is not the icy surface of the lake, but its geographical location. The boundary of the Russian lands follows the eastern shore of the lake and the surface of the frozen lake is in the first place not our territory. The ice, in contrast to the eastern shore, is a foreign expanse, a foreign land. And the decisive rout of the invaders in the battle on Lake Peipus was determined to no small extent by this circumstance.

The actual rout on Lake Peipus was an unexpected and staggering miracle. The chronicles sought to explain it by supernatural phenomena and some sort of heavenly force that was said to have taken part in the battle. But the answer does not lie of course with these dubious precursors of aviation. The only miracle in the battle on Lake Peipus was the genius of the Russian people, who for the first time began to sense their national, native power, their unity: a people able to draw from this awakening self-awareness an indomitable strength; able to advance, from their midst, a strategist and commander of genius, Alexander; and with him at their head, to defend the motherland, having smashed the devious enemy on foreign territory and not allowed him to spoil by his invasion their native soil. 'The swine were finally repulsed beyond the Russian frontiers', wrote Marx. Such will be the fate of all those who dare encroach upon our great land even now.[11]

For, if the might of our national soul was able to punish the enemy in this way, when the country lay exhausted in the grip of the Tatar yoke, then nothing will be strong enough to destroy this country which has broken the last chains of its oppression; a country which has become a socialist motherland; a country which is being led to unprecedented victories by the greatest strategist in world history – Stalin.

15 The Problems of the Soviet Historical Film[1]

I do not know if it is proper for me to be the first to speak, especially with the lofty designation of principal speaker, because I am not going to give a solemn speech, nor one that generalises broadly; instead it will be fairly down-to-earth and cover a wide range of matters which are often ignored. It will be about the particular individual problems that have arisen in connection with historical films and that we are now able to discuss. Theoretical abstractions have no place in this discussion, which is based upon the different elements that have arisen in our historical films.

The question of historical films is one that must be examined: first, because of what they tell us about history; second, because the cycle of historical films over the last five years has done much to develop Soviet cinema in general; and third, because of a large number of specific problems connected with historical films which [these films] have touched on, raised, or revealed. I shall have to refer to some pictures, to talk about them, but that does not mean that each of these pictures has solved these problems in one way or another. However, some of these films have posed these problems, and to some extent raised these questions.

The films we have seen are not of equal value, if considered from these three standpoints. I think that one big mistake in the evaluation of our films is the way that films are always assessed in an undifferentiated way. If a film is good in general, then the tendency is to think that all its elements are faultless and fine. This was once a perfectly accurate device for confusing the critics, and the dictum about the unity of form and content was used as a distraction to prevent valid examination of a wide range of creative problems that a film might throw up. The rule was that if a film was generally good, then it was considered bad form to talk about individual elements in the film which fell short of the mark.

But if a film is considered from different points of view, that is, what it contributed, what it introduced, what it did, in different areas, then it must also be evaluated with respect to these different areas. For example, we know what happened with the reviews of *Stepan Razin*.[2] When we read two different reviews of the same film, the evaluations concerned different aspects of the film and, I think, if we are to examine our films, it is worth adhering to this procedure.

There is a similar discussion (sadly a rather subdued one) about a quite indisputably fine work – *Lenin in 1918*.[3] A number of criticisms have been made by comrades which are seldom voiced on platforms, which are spoken of fairly frequently, and which for some reason are not raised at public debates, but remain outside criticism, rather than being incorporated into an academically rigorous system: namely, that the picture *Lenin in 1918* is in some elements, such as the historical-revolutionary, irreproachable and faultless, whereas in regard to some aspects of the construction of the film as such it has definite shortcomings.

I frequently had to sit in on discussions and to defend *Lenin in 1918*; the picture was attacked with extraordinary harshness by the panel at Dom Kino, who took no account of the fact that the film was, by the standards it set itself, of extraordinarily high quality.[4]

I think that we must return to this question in the future: when we examine a picture we must not let ourselves be distracted by how good, or faultless, it may be from the standpoint of what it teaches us about history, but from the point of view of the interpretation of the historical landscape, for example, and whether that is flawed.

That is the first stipulation I should like to make.

I do not think that it is worth spending too much time on the question of the importance of the study of history for the present and for building the future: everyone knows that much. I shall only say that there is a very good Party document: the Resolution of the Council of People's Commissars and the Central Committee of the All-Russian Communist Party (Bolsheviks) of 16 May 1934.

It explains, states precisely that the final aim of this study is the Marxist understanding of history, and it indicates the routes towards this aim: the correct selection and generalisation of historical events. The essential conditions: the accessibility, clearness and concreteness of the historical material. It also indicates the essential premises in studying: '... observing a historical and chronological consistency in setting out the historical events, and students of important historical phenomena must have the historical figures, and chronological dates fixed in their minds.' All this in lively, engaging style.

This document even indicates errors which were allowed earlier: an abstract quality, sketchiness, vagueness in defining a socio-economic structure, and so on.

If we take education as the principal and fundamental purpose of a work of art, then these provisions are of crucial importance for works of art too. We know that a work of art pursues the same aims, but does so using figurative and artistic means.

Hence, the importance of these guidelines, including the note about chronology. We can remember individual elements of history, but chronology helps by establishing the date and showing us where concurrent episodes intersect, and allows us a much fuller appreciation of the epoch.

For example, if we remember that Shakespeare was born in the year Michelangelo died, that he was thirty when Ivan the Terrible died; that Giordano Bruno perished at the stake between the premières of *Twelfth Night* and *Hamlet*; the historical Boris Godunov died a year after the première of *Lear* and *Macbeth*; that the Three Musketeers turn out to be contemporaries of Ivan Susanin, etc. – a whole number of things, when seen in their chronological perspective, give an unexpected twist to one's sense of what the world was like at that time.[5]

You might remember that Goethe died three years after Griboyedov.[6]

The difference between a history textbook and a historical film is that a history textbook summarises and generalises a given period after describing it.

The key thing about a historical film is for the generalising summary to emerge from the vivid play of passions and the unfolding events that pass before the viewer.

Poor films belong to the first type: they are built upon a moralistic script or a special dialogue which generalise the events. In this respect they become history textbooks, at the same time that a vivid history textbook will convey the essence, in images, of the events which it sets out.

I have attended lectures in higher mathematics whose delivery made you wish you had studied the history of literature. But Goldschmidt's biology textbook *Ascarides* almost turns biology into a novel, without losing any scientific rigour.[7]

The basic, essential premiss for a historical film is historical truth. All societies are interested in their history. And each class aims at interpreting its past so that it can justify the rationale for its existence.

In these cases, the bourgeoisie is compelled to lie about the past and distort it, as it looks for justifications for its existence which it cannot justify at all.

One of the most outrageous examples of a class lying about history is *Viva Villa!*, a very well constructed film that is dramaturgic in other respects too. It had to prove that the people cannot govern the state, and this is demonstrated with great vividness in the closing episodes.[8]

Two historical figures have been brought into the single character of Villa himself, although they are essentially mutually exclusive. There is the charming Villa, who can do almost anything, and who has a vague programme which satisfies the interests of the Mexican farm labourers. It should be said that the actual Villa was an adventurer, a general who staged a *putsch*. But his agrarian programme, which is more or less feasible to us, has been taken from the programme of a completely different kind of peasant leader, Emiliano Zapata.[9]

The union of these two figures in one character is not merely false: it also discredits Zapata's programme, which in many of its provisions approached the Communist programme.

Not to mention the figure of Madero, who was incredibly distorted, and who was one of the most implausibly repellent historical figures of Mexico.[10]

This example shows how the bourgeoisie is forced to distort and twist historical material to make it justify the methods by which it works.

This gives rise to the notorious motto: 'History is politics projected into the past', which sums up bourgeois attitudes to history.[11]

Our attitude, as a class, to history is objective veracity and objective truth [that] historical truth can only be revealed on the basis of Marxist historical science. There is no divergence between the objective truth and our understanding as a class.

But historical truth should not be confused with historical naturalism. In some cases a naturalistic, simple twisting of the facts and a realistic interpretation of the past may become almost mutually exclusive.

Here I can refer to the example of *Potemkin*. We know the mutiny on the 'Potemkin' was crushed as a single instance. It could be considered a defeat, but nevertheless in the film we consciously ended with [a different] scene on the 'Potemkin', the moment of victory, bearing in mind that what was important to me was to discover the generalised idea, the valid realistic meaning: a great victory in the general movement in the history of the Revolution, and not the fate of a

147

battleship which would have had, a few weeks later, to have been returned to the tsarist government.

It must be said that the majority of our historical films have grappled particularly successfully with the first aim – to educate and make aware. There are no distortions of history.

The next question that I wanted to touch on is the role of historical films within our cinema.

When we started to take a particularly strong interest in history, when that turn towards the study of history happened, cinema reacted; and very soon after the government's decision it managed to respond with the first historical films.

But, apart from this, the historical film has another great role to play.

The main task facing us is making contemporary films. And it is in the creation of contemporary films that the experience of a historical film is of colossal importance, because we would rather see a contemporary film not as a self-contained episode from the present day, nor as individual characters, but as individual characters elevated to major historical generalisation. [It is necessary] to know how to show a historical fact not as a solitary fact, but as a major generalised event.

Approaching this in *A Great Citizen*, we had to study this experience in the past, in its sweep of events and grasp of individual images and individual personae.[12]

So it must be said that the role of the historical film is vital precisely for making contemporary films and, generalising the experience of historical films, it should always be borne in mind that this material can be used for making a contemporary film too. It is natural in this respect to look at the way that different masters treat the materials of the historical past.

If we look at current bourgeois traditions in this matter, then we can see that on the one hand there are buskins; and on the other, a dressing-gown and nightcap. On the one hand, the past is elevated to extraordinary heights, and idealised to an extraordinary degree; and on the other hand, the attempt is made to bring it as low as possible.[13]

This is nothing new. Marx wrote about this in *The Eighteenth Brumaire of Louis Bonaparte*, and Pushkin wrote about it apropos of the publication of notes by Samson the executioner.[14]

Pushkin wrote:

After the seductive *Confessions* of eighteenth-century philosophy, came the no less seductive revelations about politicians. We were no longer content with seeing famous people in their nightcap and gown; we wanted to follow them into their bedrooms, and beyond.[15]

If we look at [German] cinema, during the years of social democracy, we see that it was just then that the films *Bismarck* and *Fridericus Rex* enjoyed their greatest success.[16]

There has been a sharp increase in the practice of cutting down great figures from the past to commonplace proportions. This has given rise to the publication of intimate diaries, and also a film about Parnell, where the leader of Ireland is shown primarily from the perspective of the amorous escapades that led to his death.[17] He has lost his aura as a historical figure.

Both approaches represent, as I say, an artificial levelling of previous epochs with our own.

Carlyle writes about this – and none too badly, incidentally – in his book on Oliver Cromwell.[18]

He writes about England, for example, thus:

> The Genius of England no longer soars Sunward, world-defiant, like an Eagle through the storms, 'mewing her mighty youth', as John Milton saw her do: the Genius of England, much liker a greedy Ostrich intent on provender and a whole skin, mainly, stands with its *other* extremity Sunward; with its Ostrich-head stuck into the readiest bush, of old Church tippets, King-cloaks or what other 'sheltering fallacy' there be, and *so* awaits the issue.[19]

Carlyle tended to heroicise the past, but he could not see leaders and heroes in the light in which he should have seen them.[20]

I will not keep you any longer with this: you can read it for yourselves.

We have a different attitude to events and historical figures, since we can converse with past epochs on equal terms. We do not need to reduce the heroes of the past, nor do we need to stand on tiptoe in order to seem their peers.

I think that the best example for understanding heroes in our sense would be Chapayev in our cinema.[21] [Chapayev] is remarkable precisely because he was shown as an heroic figure whom everyone felt he could identify with.

And had somebody else fallen into that same situation, he would have been that Chapayev. The absence of buskins was one of the achievements of this magnificent film, and contributed something new to our cinema.

The key task facing our film is to elevate our theme of the present to the heights of historical generalisation. So far this has only been done in approximation. But I must say that in many cases we have not wholly brought this off.

What then is our aim when we work on film?

Pushkin once neatly formulated this aim. He asked: 'What is unfolding in a tragedy? What is its purpose? Man and the people. The fate of a man, the fate of a people.'

This latter is especially true today.

If we look at our films from that angle, we see a remarkable division.

Let us take [the films] *October* and *Lenin in October*.[22] Some of the elements concerning the masses and [the situation of] Petrograd in 1917 appeared in *October*, but there are no historical personalities or a historical leader [in that film]; on the other hand, *Lenin in October* omits those very elements present in *October*. After watching the film *The Strike*, the actor Saltykov characteristically said: 'that should all have been a background for me.'

That wounded me at the time, but it has to be said that he was to a certain extent right. *The Strike* and *October* are undeniably canvases that lack a major historical figure. These days we have the major historical figure, but no historical canvas. This is particularly true of films about the Civil War.

When I had to study materials about Frunze, I was unexpectedly struck by the scale of the Civil War.[23] I realised that I had become used to seeing the Civil War in our films in the images and on the scale that our films have given it. You always have the feeling that *Chapayev* and *Shchors* are excellent; but the colossal

149

resonance of the epoch is missing. Our films do not convey this scope. They are better at conveying the man than the historical sense of the scale of the events. When it happened that I saw real events, it seemed that 10,000 men fell in one assault near Perekop. We know that steamships left with Wrangel. I thought there would have been about a handful. But it was 150 vessels, carrying 150,000 men. If you add up the number of people travelling southwards across Russia to the northern Crimea during the Civil War, there were six million men headed for southern Russia during the Civil War.

With no disrespect to our pictures, I ask you: do our films give you the sense of such a colossal sweep of events? That does not mean that you should film crowd scenes six million strong; but our films about the Civil War give no feeling of the scale on which these events took place.

They depict individual people perfectly, but this approach prevents us from showing the colossal scale.

What models does historical film have to learn from? I think that a brilliant work to study would be *Boris Godunov* – a national drama about Tsar Boris, which supplies two examples of depicting a character: the monologue 'I have attained the greatest power', and the famous 'The people is silent'.[24] These are the ultimate limits of the work of the solo artist and the chorus; and, furthermore, 'The people is silent' is open to several different interpretations. The fact that this passage has been discussed in the history of literature shows to what extent this stage direction gave the masses an image. I do not want to talk about how the dismembered image of the crowd, who come on at the end, has been apportioned amongst all the possible types of characters who pass through the tragedy. It is a concentration at the finale [of the tragedy]. If we measure our films against *Boris Godunov*, then it must be said that one part of them inclines towards the 'greatest power'; and the other [towards] 'The people is silent'.

If we take *Peter the First* and *Alexander Nevsky*, it is obvious that the former is very close to *Boris Godunov*, and the latter is the opposite.[25] This happens because the films set themselves somewhat different aims. It was important to define the image of Peter and give an idea of the national movement in the 18th century, and this is connected with the traditions from which they came. *Peter the First* came from literary and dramaturgical traditions connected with the activities of the author, whereas *Alexander Nevsky* followed cinema epic. *Minin and Pozharsky* had to combine these two elements within itself, as it drew on both literary and filmic traditions.[26]

Unfortunately, the synthesis proved inadequate but, [I repeat], our films have done much to facilitate the principal task: to construct films about the present.

These are the general issues that I wanted to touch on here. I also want to dwell on particular questions that have arisen within the context of our historical films.

The first thing to mention is the connection between cinema and literature. A lot was said about this at one time. Now less is said, and so one should pay particular attention to this because, if our cinema tends to fall into two genres – film drama and film epic, then both of these are linked extremely closely with literature, albeit in different ways. The fact is that the film epic is fundamentally linked with the method of literary forms. You may recall that we have spent much time thinking about metaphor in cinema and a whole series of things connected with the internal mechanism and the internal life of literature. When we adopt the position of film drama, then it must be said that there the closeness of the work to literary form [is also essential]; without close contact with the experience of literary forms, the plot of a drama cannot advance further. If we take the majority of successful films, we see that the most successful images (and I stress this) occur when there are literary prototypes available. Let us begin with *The Mother*,[27] *Chapayev* and *Peter the First*. Even individual images from *Alexander Nevsky*, who were based on prototypes, always turned out full of life. The same thing happened in American cinema. Take the hit *Juarez*.[28] That was based on the play *Maximilian and Juarez*. Or *The Trial of Zola*, which was shown in [the thirties].[29] I know this very well because Paramount's first proposal was that I direct *The Trial of Zola*. It was the same with *The Coward*, etc.[30] Why is this so important? Because this gives the director one possibility he would not otherwise have. If the author is the interpreter of life, then the director does not only interpret these phenomena on the basis of his own experience, but he interprets the work as well. It is fascinating that a director's real creative fulfilment [occurs] when he is wrestling with the author's conception; when he tries to comprehend, discern it. Anyone who has worked with high-quality plays or novels will know the colossal creative enjoyment and fulfilment you feel when you analyse the various twists and turns, guess at the [author's] intention, discover the meaning there. If we were to consider not the image of man, but the image of an epoch, we might mention *Potemkin*, which managed to capture a whole year, 1905. How did it do this? Because *Potemkin*, as anecdotes about its past have made widespread, was constructed from one half of the second part. But the various episodes of *Potemkin* succeeded in amassing the generalising features of 1905. If we take the Odessa Steps, that did not merely depict an episode that took place on the Odessa Steps, but an infinite number of similar episodes that typified 1905. That is, the result was a synthetic depiction of 1905 in general.[31]

Successes in our screenplays, like *Shchors*, or *Maxim*,[32] or *A Great Citizen* or *Lenin*, occur when the scope and time of the work are on the same grand scale as for a high-quality literary work.

What is the Achilles' heel of screenplays? It is that they must be extremely laconic. A screenplay has to depict both the character of an epoch and the character of the personae in two or three decisive strokes, because of the amount of time and the film footage. There is a simple approach: you take stroke 1, stroke 2 and stroke 3 and you splice them together, and nothing, other than a living image, will result (my own experience has taught me this, so – no objections, please). But there is another means whereby one image of a living man and the image of the epoch are created and then everything is reduced to two or three decisive scenes. I know, for example, how we spliced *Alexander Nevsky* and joined it together, but I cannot say why neither you nor I was satisfied with it. It is of course true that the part where there was to have been a Shakespearean turn in character was cut out – the ending, to do with Alexander Nevsky's journey to the enemy. But this is a local affair, and not worth going into in detail here.[33]

So, what it all means is that the method that should have been followed here was to interpret it as an historical actor would have done. We know that in a film, an image should be created when working with an actor. Then this [invented] image can act out various situations. Does this make sense? It is not a question simply of rehearsing the five or six episodes shown in the film, but of building a person capable of performing these five or six scenes in character. And for the screenplay, it would be proper to devise a person who could then provide two or three crucial features. In relation to Chapayev's character, literary and dramatic works proved of great advantage when it came to creating a cinema image that was to outdo Chapayev's image in literature or drama.

Hence it must be said that episodic roles are often done very well in screenplays; episodic, because there is no complex character, only a couple of crucial features. So they usually work well.

All this to say that we would remain for the most part audio-visual symphonists, were it not for the experience of literature. We have very obligingly already learned how to do this; but it does not of course satisfy us to any extent. Because, referring again to American literature, it must be said the strength of American cinema is that there are mountains of relevant literary genres behind almost every genre and every model of film play. The theme, approach, and solution of some or other situational passages have already been resolved down to the finest detail. There is an unbelievable abundance of genres, and an unbelievable abundance of models within these genres. It must be said that genres in these areas – these prototypes – are not in any way appropriate in our case; but we should make our literature work for us, and think about literary prototypes that are appropriate for us.

I want now to move on to an entirely specialised question, namely: how you should rework the various elements of a historical film; how they should be made. And this is something very narrow – how to work with a historical landscape, with a character, music and the various scenes, and so on. In fact, it is obvious here that the fundamental rule to be obeyed is seemingly one and the same for all the elements, and we can begin with the simplest and the most convenient.

I shall permit myself to begin with the historical landscape – I shall talk about my feelings on this, and cite several examples. Scenes from *Minin and Pozharsky* that stuck in my memory were when Minin stood above the Volga, and when Roman was galloping along on his horse, and also that scene from *Alexander Nevsky* showing the frozen boats. Why are these scenes memorable, and what do they remind you of? It is the feeling that they have not been perceived historically. When I saw my landscape of frozen boats and little fir trees, I could see that it might have been a market selling fir trees, or, at best, an ice-rink at Sokolniki,[34] but it certainly did not make me think of the 13th century.

You might be wondering what this is about, and whether you can talk about the historical feeling of fir trees, and unhistorical feelings?

There is an anecdotal story about Ilya Repin and the scholar Bruni,[35] who had criticised one of his paintings with the words: 'You've caught plenty of the genre there; those bushes are very alive, ordinary-looking, like the ones growing at Petrovsky.' (But Repin had brought his *Diogenes*.) 'The rocks, too ... This is no good at all for a historical scene ... historical pictures need historical landscapes.' The advice Bruni gave the young Repin does not withstand criticism. He said: 'Go to the Hermitage, pick any landscape by Nicolas Poussin, and copy the part you need for your painting.'[36] We sometimes do that ourselves, but the crux of the

152

matter lies elsewhere. What is the essence of the thing? The first question you should ask is whether the landscape has its character; only then can you say that it must have an historical image. About the image of landscape, I shall quote some passages from the young Engels. In his *Wanderings in Lombardy* (1841) Engels writes as follows:

> Where nature displays all its magnificence, where the idea that is slumbering within it seems, if not to awaken, then to be dreaming a golden dream, the man who can feel and say nothing except 'Nature, how beautiful you are!' has no right to think himself superior to the ordinary, shallow, confused mass.[37]

In another work from 1840, *Landscapes*, Engels wrote (and I apologise for quoting at such length, but it will help me say less on my own account):

> Hellas had the good fortune of seeing the nature of her landscape brought to consciousness in the religion of her inhabitants. Hellas is a land of Pantheism; all her landscapes are – or, at least, were – embraced in a harmonious framework. And yet every tree, every fountain, every mountain thrusts itself too much in the foreground, and her sky is far too blue, her sun far too radiant, her sea far too magnificent, for them to be content with the laconic spiritualisation of Shelley's spirit of nature,[38] of an all-embracing Pan. Each beautifully shaped individual feature lays claim to a particular god, each river will have its nymphs, each grove its dryads – and so arose the religion of the Hellenes. Other regions were not so fortunate; they did not serve any people as the basis of its faith and had to await a poetic mind to conjure into existence the religious genius that slumbered in them. If you stand on the Drachenfels or on the Rochusberg at Bingen,[39] and gaze over the vine-fragrant valley of the Rhine, the distant blue mountains merging with the horizon, the green fields and vineyards flooded with golden sunlight, the blue sky reflected in the river – heaven with its brightness descends on to the earth and is mirrored in it, the spirit descends into matter, the word becomes flesh and dwells among us – that is the embodiment of Christianity. The direct opposite of this is the North-German heath; here there is nothing but dry stalks and modest heather, which, conscious of its weakness, dare not raise itself above the ground; here and there is a once defiant tree now shattered by lightning; and the brighter the sky, the more sharply does its self-sufficient magnificence demarcate it from the poor, cursed earth lying below it in sackcloth and ashes, and the more does its eye, the sun, look down with burning anger on the barren sand – there you have a representation of the Jewish world outlook.[40]
> ... To continue with the religious character of various regions, the *Dutch* landscapes are essentially Calvinist. The absolute prose of a distant view in Holland, the impossibility of its spiritualisation, the grey sky that is indeed the only one suited to it, all this produces the same impression on us as the infallible decisions of the Dordrecht Synod.[41] The windmills, the sole moving things in the landscape, remind one of the predestined elect, who allow themselves to be moved only by the breath of divine dispensation; everything else lies in 'spiritual death'. And this barren orthodoxy, the Rhine, like the flowing, living spirit of Christianity, loses its fructifying power and becomes completely choked up with sand. Such, seen from the Rhine, is the appearance of its Dutch banks ... [42]

That is how Engels wrote about the feeling of images of nature.

It is easy to see that he has made it a two-fold question: on the one hand, in this case a system, Calvinism, say, gives him a perfectly distinct, plastic sensation; on the other hand, the landscape fits into a synthesising physiognomy, a synthesising image, and it finds a correspondence to the image which the landscape is talking about; the image, which the idea is talking about and which he himself is thinking about, and that is one art which we must master to a great extent.

What is the particular task of the image which must lie on the historical landscape? I think that one circumstance characterises the historical landscape. That is the feeling of remoteness. I think that the problem of remoteness may be embodied in the landscape because in an historical landscape the first thing that must be preserved are those elements which are connected with the landscape when it is viewed from a distance; that is, one of the first conditions is a small number of details that may be seen in this landscape. That is the quick answer. Or if more detail is required, then landscape has to work in an historical picture through its generalised and generalising features.

If we take pictures by Roerich or Serov, Serov does, in essence, venture into historical pictures.[43] If you take a prehistoric painting by him, *The Rape of Europa*, and remember the landscape in it, the principal impression left by the landscape is of some generalising circular movements depicting the movement of the primordial sea that this charming bull is swimming in.

If we progress from this prehistoric landscape to a more historical one (*Odysseus and Nausicaa*) – the horizon is set extraordinarily low, the sea and the smooth bank with its two figures are shown in two or four strokes and spots – then we can see that this condition of remoteness and generality has been observed once again. You could of course say: Greece – well, that's what it's like, you can't do anything about it. But Serov observes that same law in a less emphatic way when he comes to show an historical landscape with a royal hunt, where our ordinary, mundane Russian landscape is given in the same elements, brought into extraordinarily sharply defined generalising features.

If that is the aim for middle-distance works, then for close-up they must preserve the same law; that is, the film must not be filled with an excessive number of defining details if it is to preserve the elements of generality.

A very curious question arises here, about the tasks of so-called stylisation in historical films. These tasks have the aim of showing the natural environment through contemporary eyes, as the people of the epoch we are portraying would have seen them.

That of course is the limit of what is permissible, and one thing here is to be avoided at all costs, namely second-hand stylisation. That is when the artist's feeling is not his spontaneous interpretation of nature at that time, as he believes it was seen, but when he uses somebody else's interpretation. We are all guilty of that: some do it in the style of Roerich, others in the style of Surikov, and this is hard to avoid.[44] Indeed, it is impossible not to think of 'Morozova, the Boyar's Wife' when you've got an old-fashioned type of sleigh.

But there is another question too. I ran up against it when I was travelling to Uzbekistan.[45] Everyone is familiar with Persian miniatures and the large number of features characteristic of them. A figure, sitting on a rug, stretches forwards so that the entire length of his body lies, flat, within its borders. I always thought that if you could begin filming like that, then it would be in the style of Persian artists.

But when I reached Uzbekistan, it turned out that there was no distortion of reality at all. That is merely the way the various things and objects are arranged there. And if you look directly at what you can see, there really does turn out to be a colossal quantity of things there, which you can see set out like that. . . .

If you go to an old, good tea shop, and drink tea on the fourth platform up, then you will be able to see all the figures arranged like that sharply defined miniature.

If you ride out to the paddy fields, which are also arranged in terraces, you will get the same impression.

We are all used to the stylised forms of trees on miniatures – circular, oval and so on. But if you go past mulberry trees of a certain period, you will see that they have been pruned in just that way.

You can see on a miniature a ram, half white and half black; or a horse, with its patches of colouring arranged with almost geometrical precision. I must say that I have met both a ram and a horse like that.

So miniaturists, without losing their eye for other types of painting, were able to look at the special features of points of view which were created around them.

The same thing happened with me and a painting by Van Gogh.[46] His cottages, rivers and sky appear with absolutely pure tonality. If you find yourself in Van Gogh's native country and travel around Holland, you could be convinced that they are little short of photographic fragments, so pure the tonality and so transparent is the air there.

This aspect should not be baulked at when it is shaped by nature and not by the idiosyncrasies of one particular artist.

It is worth examining another example. If you have anything to do with landscapes of the Quattrocento,[47] you will be struck by the great size of the figures relative to the architecture, which is shown in the distance and uniformly small, never taller than knee height.

The explanation for this is that at that period they were not able to draw the elements of buildings: one door, one window, one portico. At that time, they could not separate the various elements in their all-embracing perception and the buildings had to be shown in full. And since they would not fit as they were, they had to be reduced in size, hence the effect of distance.

In this respect I have something to say about our films.

There are times when you are showing a real landscape, but its image does not correspond with what you feel. There are two pictures about the Far East: *The Volochayev Days* and *Aerograd*.[48] In *Aerograd* it is the shots filmed in the Crimea that most convey the feeling of the Far East. *The Volochayev Days* always conveys the feeling of Pargolov. You can of course tell me that the foliage and tree size reproduce the flora of the Far East precisely; but in this case as a lowbrow viewer I did not sense the character of the Far East.

The landscape in *Minin and Pozharsky* is done superbly in this respect, capturing the historical sense – the flight from Moscow, with the racing sleighs. It was done superbly. And why? Because here the sense of distance and separation is conveyed.

In *Alexander Nevsky* we tried to follow this for the city landscape, and the landscape of Pereslavl. The ultimate was achieved on Lake Peipus, with the ice and grey sky. Try to examine it when you see this scene.

Actually, if I had to film such a battle on ice – and the Red Cavalry fought roughly the same sort of battle at Bataisky, near Rostov – the need would immediately arise not to denude the landscape of details as I did at Lake Peipus, but to fill it with a wealth of details coming nearer, details in close-up.

If we are talking about foliage and tree size, a generalised tree form will be a lot of use in a historical film whereas it is the foliage that says more in a genre film.

If we take the film *Engineer Kochin's Mistake*, a fine film in relation to the genre, [we can see that] for the first time, foliage has been filmed very well in this work.[49] But to saturate our historical films with foliage of this sort would tire the eyes.

Let me omit two sections, on the historical character and the historical subject. Let us move on to battle scenes.

The greatest experience that we have gained from historical films concerns battle scenes, and since we will have to make a great many historical films with a great many battle scenes, then something can be learned now, and this should be mentioned at this point.

Battles were treated and fought differently at different stages of history. I do not say this because the picture should reproduce the way of fighting in a given period; but so that there is a clearer idea of the principal notions.

Originally, a battle was the totality of single combats. In Mexico I saw a Spanish dance that showed how the Moors won control of Spain. Thirteen people stood in a row facing another thirteen and they moved together: each engaged his opponent in armed combat, always successfully.

Then battles developed into combat between organised masses; and the third type was battle as single combat, the harmonious action of military formations using a different kind of weaponry.

There are three types of construction in this respect.

The first is when the battle is shown as a montage of the various single encounters. The last act of *Macbeth* illustrates this very well, and [there are examples] in other plays by Shakespeare. I have a detailed copy of the fifth act which shows how the various scenes follow one another, and how the various fights follow one another. There is no need to read this out now; it will be provided in the short-hand transcript.

Let us move on to the second type, the second scenario – the battle scenario, where large masses come into conflict.

Incidentally, there are some very interesting devices here, which Pushkin used to good effect in the battles in *Ruslan and Lyudmila*.

This is how it is done: the separate, different episodes are depicted as though they were one act of single combat; that is, he shows the twists and turns of one duel; he provides several battle scenes, but they are so put together that it seems there is just one duel happening – this is the battle with the Pechenegs.

They met – and the battle commenced.
Sensing death, the steeds reared up,
There was the ring of swords on plate,
A cloud of arrows hissed upwards,
And the plain was awash with blood ...

That is a perfectly succinct opening.

The comparative element: the excited horses and the sound of the swords.

Then there is the upwards motion.

Then the downwards motion.

It goes on:

The riders were racing full tilt,
Cavalry sections were mingled;
Unit was hacking with unit
In a regular, close-knit block.

Infantry and cavalry. Next comes battle with cavalry and infantry:

Then foot-soldier grapples with knight;
The terrified steed hovers there ...

Close examination of these lines shows a possible outcome of the battle: [whether] the knight or [the foot soldier] will be killed.

There Russian fell, there Pecheneg ...

The possible outcome: either the Russian or the Pecheneg died.

Then it abandons the close-up.

The reason I stress this so much is that we all tend to forget these connecting passages of middle shot, being so carried away by the intensity of a scene.

The last moment is the finale: the foot-soldier is slaughtered. But this moment is underlined with particular skill: the horse crashes down on the shield with all its force.

The composition of an entire battle might in some cases be constructed on just such an element. And when we talk about the clarity of a picture, this is precisely the kind of thing that should be remembered.

Milton's *Paradise Lost* provides examples of the combination of different kinds [of battle]. There, battles are done brilliantly from the point of view of a battle picture. I regret reading Milton after I had done *Alexander Nevsky*, as I could have taken some elements for the scene where the ice gave way.

Last, the 'triumphs' of the types of weaponry.

I had the opportunity to apply this in *Potemkin*. When cannon are before the cameras, the engines are not shown; when the engines are on, the sea is not shown; when the sea is on, the battleship is not shown. This was also observed with fairly strict consistency in the 'Battle on the Ice', both when the cavalry wedge broke through, and in the individual phases of the battle where the functions of the battle were distributed evenly. When the cavalry is winning, the infantry is kept out of view.

One more characteristic device is that of the chance participant or the civilian in a battle.

In *War and Peace*, Tolstoy provided the classic example of this: Pierre Bezukhov.

I did a scene which has not been shown: we wanted [to show] the liberation of the Winter Palace through the character of an officer. There was a lieutenant,

Sinegub, who recorded how everyone left the Palace and [how] he was the only worried one. I wanted to show all the elements of the life and destruction of the Palace through him.

And also through one participant who found himself with a regiment in the Winter Palace. He was a civilian who had absolutely no connection with the battle. He was walking through the Palace, looking at things, and at last reached Nicholas's study where he found an album of titillating pictures.

Some general compositional features of a battle scene.

The first essential is a distinct sense of the images of the battle – how it is going to look. There should be a perfectly precise mental picture of the feeling that the battle as a whole must transmit, not merely as a description of the events, but as an emotionally imagistic complex. Without this, the most important thing will remain out of reach and there will be no coherence in the course of the battle. Coherence in the course of the battle is the coherence of the successive phases.

For example, the conflict in the 'Battle on the Ice', that was much too drawn-out (although this was not my fault; I was not allowed to cut 200 metres), was constructed from the horn of the Germans which brought the whole mass together, to the horn which went off into the water. And the theme – the leitmotif of the horn – informs this whole story. And the sense of this outline was dictated by the succession of phases in the battle. It was left insufficiently distinct, since I had not been allowed to cut almost 200 metres.

The second condition is clarity: who does what to whom and when; because the majority of scenes so confuse the action that you lose track of it and do not know whom to follow. At that point you should amend the situation, from the point of view of screenplay and plot, and this is a powerful strong point. Or you should pay attention to the plastic elements. In this regard, I could refer to the beautiful use of 'colour' in *Shchors*, and to the distinction made in *Alexander Nevsky* where there is always black and white colouring.

Apart from plastic and plot elements, there are also the characteristics of rhythm. Here I could mention the metaphorical battle on the Odessa Steps, where there is the characteristic of rhythm, both of the soldiers and those who escape to safety off the steps. And in *Chapayev* there is rhythm on the one hand, and broken rhythm on the other; that is, you can recognise the opponents not only by their surnames, but by the rhythmic leitmotif which each side has been given.

There is another important circumstance: the clarity of dislocation and of the strategic battle picture. This is what decides the fate of the struggle because, if it is not clear, then there can be an implausible mixture of ideas on stage. Here, the means of revelation are various, but the universally used means is the council of war, with people talking either looking at a map, or simply clarifying what is going to happen. But we endeavoured with *Alexander Nevsky* to show this council in a different way, and we stuck to narrative. I was interested in what made Alexander think about a wedge being pressed from two sides. We spent a long time looking, looking for a material subject that could supply the basis. We even took an axe and went walking on the ice, but nothing satisfied us until I remembered the tale of the Vixen and the Hare.[50]

It was not possible to rely on this episode as the episode that could give the picture its strategic plan. If we could have spent another month working on it, then we would have found a solution that met all the requirements.

A map can play a very important role, and if there is a map, if it is possible from time to time to show how a phase of the battle is turning out, using a bird's-eye view, that is better still. In this regard, battle pictures of all ages have much to offer – including those of Callot,[51] who showed the siege of the Breda fortress where the foreground (medium shot and close-up) – showed the combatants; the middle distance had the small embattled groups, and the background had a map showing where the different sections were positioned. Cinema demands skilful montage cuts, and one should know how to make them easy for the audience.

One very important matter is that the crowd scenes should also work figuratively in the shot; that is, the movement of one mass against the other, their encounters and so on, should be done not only in close-up, but they should be clearly shown in long shots too. I learned this at my own expense. I had to retake an entire crowd scene, since one body was not clearly shown to be advancing or moving into the other body, and this did not give the impression of a real fight.

A few more words about emotionality. The first thing to be taken into account is that all manner of emotional devices should prepare the way for the battle. I cannot agree with part two of *Peter the First*,[52] where the whole thing just starts with the battle of Poltava. Seventy-five per cent of the emotional charge that will be developed in the battle is lost to no purpose, because you cannot expect the audience to remember everything that they saw in part one eighteen months ago.

Well, there is no mystery about the need to vary not only the phases of the battle but also its rhythmical characteristics. Unchallenged in this respect is Pushkin's battle of Poltava which can be examined as an ideal screenplay which can be used to examine a battle.[53]

In conclusion, I should like to reiterate that our fundamental, chief and general aim is the depiction of the present, of contemporary man, elevated to a broad, historical generalisation. The historical film is of great use in this, and I am certain that we will succeed in showing our great epoch thus.

16 Stalin, Molotov and Zhdanov on *Ivan the Terrible* Part Two[1]

We were summoned to the Kremlin for a meeting at 11 p.m. At 10.50 we entered the reception room. At precisely eleven o'clock, Poskrebyshev came out to take us into the study.[2]

Stalin, Molotov and Zhdanov were at the back of the study.[3] We went in, shook hands, and sat at the table.

STALIN. You wrote a letter. The answer has been somewhat delayed. I thought of replying in writing, but then decided that it would be better to talk it over, as I am very busy and have no time; I decided after considerable delay to meet you here. I received your letter in November.

ZHDANOV. Yes, you were still in Sochi when you got it. [...]

STALIN. Have you studied history?

EISENSTEIN. More or less.

STALIN. More or less? I too have a little knowledge of history. Your portrayal of the *oprichnina* is wrong. The *oprichnina* was a royal army. As distinct from a feudal army, which could at any moment roll up its banners and leave the field, this was a standing army, a progressive army. You make the *oprichnina* look like the Ku-Klux-Klan.

EISENSTEIN. They wear white headgear; ours wore black.

MOLOTOV. That does not constitute a difference in principle.

STALIN. Your Tsar has turned out indecisive, like Hamlet. Everyone tells him what he ought to do, he does not take decisions himself.

Tsar Ivan was a great and wise ruler and, if you compare him with Louis XI (you have read about Louis XI, who prepared the way for the absolutism of Louis XIV?), he dwarfs Louis XI. Ivan the Terrible's wisdom lay in his national perspective and his refusal to allow foreigners into his country, thus preserving the country from the penetration of foreign influence. In showing Ivan the Terrible the way you did, aberrations and errors have crept in.

Peter I was also a great ruler, but he was too liberal in his dealings with foreigners, he opened the gates too wide and let foreign influences into the country, and this allowed Russia to be Germanised. Catherine even more so. And later – could you really call the court of Alexander I a Russian court? Was the court of Nicholas I really Russian? No, they were German courts.

Ivan the Terrible's great achievement was to be the first to introduce a monopoly on foreign trade. Ivan the Terrible was the first, Lenin was the second.

ZHDANOV. Eisenstein's Ivan the Terrible comes out as a neurasthenic.

MOLOTOV. There is a general reliance on psychologism; on extraordinary emphases on inner psychological contradictions and personal experiences.

STALIN. Historical figures should be portrayed in the correct style. In Part One, for instance, it is unlikely that the Tsar would kiss his wife for so long. That was not acceptable in those days.

ZHDANOV. The picture was made with a Byzantine tendency. That was also not practised.

Ivan the Terrible: The shadow of Ivan and the chess set he presents to Elizabeth I of England.

MOLOTOV. Part Two is too confined to vaults and cellars. There is none of the hubbub of Moscow, we do not see the people. You can show the conspiracies and the repressions, but not just that.

STALIN. Ivan the Terrible was very cruel. You can depict him as a cruel man, but you have to show why he *had* to be cruel. One of Ivan the Terrible's mistakes was to stop short of cutting up the five key feudal clans. Had he destroyed these five clans, there would have been no Time of Troubles.[4] And, when Ivan the Terrible had someone executed, he would spend a long time in repentance and prayer. God was a hindrance to him in this respect. He should have been more decisive.

MOLOTOV. The historical events should have been shown in the correct interpretation. Take Demyan Bedny's play, *The Knights*, for example. In that play, Demyan Bedny made fun of the conversion of Rus to Christianity, whereas the acceptance of Christianity was a progressive event at that particular historical period.[5]

STALIN. We are not of course particularly good Christians. But it is wrong to deny the progressive role of Christianity at that stage. It had great significance, as it marked the point where the Russian state turned away from the East and towards the West.

On relations with the East, Comrade Stalin said that,

recently liberated from the Tatar yoke, Ivan the Terrible was very keen to unite Russia as a bulwark against any Tatar invasions. Astrakhan had been subdued, but could at any point attack Moscow. As could the Crimean Tatars. Demyan Bedny has misrepresented the historical perspectives. When we moved the monument to Minin and Pozharsky nearer to St Basil's, Demyan Bedny wrote me (Comrade Stalin pointed at himself) a letter of protest to the effect that the monument should be scrapped altogether and Minin and Pozharsky consigned to oblivion.[6] I addressed my reply to 'Ivan, ancestry forgotten'. We cannot scrap our history.

Then Comrade Stalin made a series of remarks about the treatment of the

161

character of Ivan the Terrible, stressing Malyuta Skuratov's importance as a military leader and his heroic death in the war with Livonia.

Comrade Cherkasov, answering the claim that criticism was useful and that Pudkovkin had, following criticism, made a good film, *Admiral Nakhimov*, replied:

> I am sure that we shall do just as well, because I am working on the character of Ivan, not only in cinema but also in theatre; I like the character very much and I am sure that our re-working of the script may turn out to be correct and truthful.

To which Comrade Stalin said: 'Well, let's give it a try.'

> CHERKASOV. I am sure that the re-working will be a success.
> STALIN (*laughing*). God willing, every day would be like Christmas.
> [. . .]

Eisenstein asked if there were specific instructions about the film.

Comrade Stalin replied: 'I am not giving instructions so much as voicing the thoughts of the audience.'
[. . .]

Comrade Zhdanov said that Eisenstein's fascination with shadows distracted the viewer from the action, as did his fascination with Ivan's beard: Ivan lifted his head too often so that his beard could be seen.

Eisenstein promised that Ivan's beard would be shorter in future.

Comrade Stalin, recalling the individual actors in *Ivan the Terrible* Part One, said:

> Kurbsky was splendid. Staritsky (played by Kadochnikov) was very good.[7] The way he caught flies was very good. He was a future tsar but caught flies with his hands. You need details like that. They reveal a man's true character.

> STALIN. Well then, that is sorted out. Comrades Cherkasov and Eisenstein will be given the chance to complete their project and the film. [He added:] Pass that on to Bolshakov.[8]

Comrade Cherkasov asked about some details of the film, and Ivan's physical appearance.

> STALIN. His appearance is fine and does not need changing. Ivan the Terrible's physical appearance is good.
> CHERKASOV. Can we leave the scene of Staritsky's murder in the film?
> STALIN. Yes. Murders did happen.
> CHERKASOV. There is one scene in the script where Malyuta Skuratov strangles Metropolitan Philip. Should we leave that in?
> STALIN. It must be left in. It was historically accurate.

Molotov said that the repressions could and should be shown, but it should be made clear what caused them and why. This required a portrayal of how the state worked rather than scenes confined to cellars and enclosed spaces. The wisdom of statesmanship needed to be depicted.

Nikolai Cherkasov as Ivan the Terrible.

Cherkasov voiced his ideas on the re-working of the script.

Stalin asked how the film would end. How the other two films – i.e. Parts Two and Three – could be better made, or how we envisaged doing this in general. [...]

STALIN. How will your film end?

Cherkasov said that the film would end with the rout of Livonia, the heroic death of Malyuta Skuratov and the expedition to the sea, where Ivan the Terrible would stand surrounded by his soldiers and say: 'We stand on the seas and always will.'

STALIN. Which is what happened. And more besides.

Cherkasov asked whether an outline of the future script needed to be shown to the Politburo for reading and approval.

STALIN. There is no need to submit it for approval. Sort it out for yourselves. It is always difficult evaluating a script; it is easier to talk about a finished work. (*Turning to Molotov*) You of course very much want to read the script?
MOLOTOV. No, I specialise in a somewhat different area. Let Bolshakov read it.

Murder in the cathedral: sketch and still of the mystery play in *Ivan the Terrible*.

Eisenstein said that it would be better not to rush the production of this film.

Everyone heartily concurred with this remark. Comrade Stalin said 'On no account rush it; as a rule we cancel films being made in a hurry and they never go out on release. Repin spent eleven years painting *The Zaporozhian Cossacks*.'

Everyone came to the conclusion that it did indeed take time to make a good picture. With respect to *Ivan the Terrible*, Comrade Stalin said that, if it took eighteen months, two or even three years to produce it, then go ahead, make sure of it, let it be 'like a work of sculpture'.

STALIN. The overall task now is to improve the quality. Higher quality, even if it means fewer pictures.

He said that Tselikovskaya had been good in other roles. She acted well, but she was a ballerina.[9]

Murder in the cathedral: sketch and still of the mystery play in *Ivan the Terrible*.

We said that no other actress could make the journey from Moscow to Alma-Ata.

Comrade Stalin said that a director must be unyielding and demand whatever he needed but that our directors compromised too readily.

Comrade Eisenstein said that it had taken two years to find an Anastasia.

Comrade Stalin indicated that the actor Zharov had not brought sufficient gravity to his role in *Ivan the Terrible* and the result was wrong.[10] He was not serious enough for a military commander.

ZHDANOV. He was not Malyuta Skuratov, more of a flibbertigibbet.

Comrade Stalin said that Ivan the Terrible was more of a national tsar, more circumspect. He did not admit foreign influences into Russia; it was 'that Peter who opened the gates on to Europe and let too many foreigners in'.

The conversation ended with Comrade Stalin wishing us luck and saying, 'May God help you.'

We shook hands all round and went out. The discussion was over by ten past one.[11]

There follows an appendix:

Comrade Zhdanov also said that the film overdid the use of religious ceremonies.

Comrade Molotov said that this gave a mystical edge which should not have been so prominent.

Comrade Zhdanov also said that the scene in the cathedral with the 'bloody deed' was filmed too broadly, which was a distraction.

Comrade Stalin said that the *oprichniki* looked like cannibals when they were dancing, reminiscent of Phoenicians or Babylonians.

When Comrade Cherkasov said that he had been working on the character of Ivan the Terrible for film and stage, Comrade Zhdanov said: 'I have held power for six years myself, no problems.'

Comrade Cherkasov reached out for the box of cigarettes, asking Comrade Stalin, 'Is it all right if I smoke?'

Comrade Stalin said, 'There's no ban on smoking, as such. Perhaps we should take a vote on it?' He allowed him to smoke.

INSERT [on the script]:

When the conversation came round to submitting the script for approval, Comrade Molotov said, 'There is no need to submit it for approval, especially as I expect Comrade Eisenstein will have thought out all the details about Ivan the Terrible by then.'

Stalin enquired after Eisenstein's heart and thought that he looked very well.

1947

17 From Lectures on Music and Colour in *Ivan The Terrible*[12]

... You tell the composer, who is to write the music for your film, what he must base his composition on. A really great composer may not discuss it with you at all, but will reply: 'I understand everything myself.' Avoid composers of that sort. But there are marvellous composers who say: 'Tell me exactly how much you want, and of what.' These are exasperating! ... Have you read the script for *Ivan the Terrible*? There is a song about a beaver. Prokofiev wrote the score to a written text. I will tell you how this happened.

There were some lines of text and I felt it was important that these lines should be accompanied by music that perfectly matched the actress's emotional state and performance. The song could have been neutrally written, for the actress to perform it with a particular subtext; that is, thinking in a precise way what she was singing about. I was more interested in a different approach. I wanted the thought of the singer to be expressed first in the orchestra, then in her voice.

> Washing in the icy stream
> Of the Moscow River,
> Black of fur, swam a beaver
> Washing all the mud away.
> Then off it went, all clean, uphill;
> It climbed the towering hill.
> It dried itself, shook itself,
> And looked around, turned its head –
> Was someone coming, seeking?

These words were taken from a folk song. There are several variations of it. I found it for the scene where Yevfrosinia Staritskaya sings Vladimir a lullaby. I imagined that, if the old woman were singing this song, then the black beaver and the towering hill would be associated with her deepest thoughts. She was upset that Ivan was on the throne and she had to persuade her son to take his place. These neutral words would stir up within her associations with Ivan.

I told Sergei Sergeyevich [Prokofiev] my intention, and asked if he could do that for me.

As the song begins, you can hear the folk melody. 'The Beaver' – the same one. But when it comes to 'black of fur', that is where the first frisson should be felt.

Sergei Sergeyevich asked, 'Where do you need this frisson?'

'On the word "black".'

Later I said, 'Between the lines, when Yevfrosinia first feels afraid of the Tsar, so that it seems to be in her head.'

Sergei Sergeyevich asked, 'And for how long will it be in her head?' And I replied, 'This long.'

'Washing all the mud away' – on these words, Yevfrosinia is overcome by hatred, and she forgets to sing this part. There are colloquial words in the music here, and these are not sung.

'Then off it went, all clean, uphill; it climbed the towering hill.' This reprises the theme of the coronation. This is a moment of elevation.

Sergei Sergeyevich asked, 'How much of an accent do you need on "towering"?' 'This much,' I answered.

Further: 'It dried itself, shook itself, and looked around, turned its head,' I asked for this part to be treated as a Russian dance. And in that part of the song the old lady is terribly evil.

That was how the whole mood was developed musically in its psychological subtext. And, when Yevfrosinia sings, and the music echoes her with unbelievable force, and when additionally the orchestra plays Ivan's theme, the effect of this piece is instantly horrifying.

And that is how a rhythmical drawing should be given to a composer.

'It dried itself, shook itself, and looked around, turned its head' – this moment does not have to turn into a staccato dance. But it is here that the old lady's intonation is very good. So what, you could say: he is still on the throne, settling scores .... But if this music was not for this moment, then you could treat these words fluidly.

'Was someone coming, seeking?' This line has to sound out. 'The hunters whistle, seeking a black beaver' – now the theme is of hunting. I requested Sergei Sergeyevich to make this part 'Wagnerian'.

'They want to kill and skin the beaver, for a fox fur trimmed with beaver.' These words convey the theme of Ivan's murder. Traditionally, the last line reads: '... for a gift for someone.' It is a ceremonial song. We therefore had 'as a cloak for Tsar Volodimir'.

The words 'for a fox fur trimmed with beaver' begin with that same intonation as the start of the song. It is most horrifying when Staritskaya whispers these words in Vladimir's ear, hunched right over him, as though it were a mere lullaby. He slowly wakes and begins to understand what the point of it is. And when she starts to wail: 'as a cloak for Tsar Volodimir', it becomes clear to him that he must murder Ivan. Then he begins to wail uncontrollably: this is picked up by the choir.

And so, at the end of the song, comes the return to the lullaby motif, which is then broken by a shout, the abrupt end of the song and terrifying chords. And Yevfrosinia starts shouting, 'I could endure the agonies of birth a hundred times over for you!' This is how it happened, in a relatively *recherché* case. But in principle, each scene does and should have the same rhythmical structure. Where you set action to music or song, you lead it towards a purely musical resolution. Where this is not done directly through the music, there must be an inner, musical sketch.

When I worked with him, Sergei Sergeyevich always asked that his task be laid down as precisely as possible, and the more complex that task was, the more rigid its parameters and the more enthusiastically did he work. Such tasks gave him a genuine basis on which to begin work.

When objects on stage have been placed there earlier, you can no longer act 'however you like', but instead you construct your action to take account of these objects. It is hardest of all to work on an empty stage: then you have no element on which you can rely. You set yourself an artificial focus for movement – a place that serves as an anchor.

It is just the same when I work with an actor. He takes this rigid framework as his foundation, on which he develops his own personal understanding. When you say: 'There must be a dance motif here', then this apparently says everything. But here there could be anything at all; that is to say the range here is all-encompassing, but it has certain limitations. It is very bad if an actor who has reached an agreement with the director about the outline of the role only performs it satisfactorily. The actor must know how to invest it with all his emotional resources, so that the rhythm and spatial outline can be not merely observed, but filled with a plenitude of emotions.

... Just as Prokofiev liked composing for a very precise theme, and this fascinated him and was one of his particular strengths, this must also hold for actors. It is exactly the same for stage designers as well. Suppose that you have to give the set designer a plan of what you need, with an approximate setting. There we need a platform, here a flight of steps, and so on. A good set designer uses this as his foundation. You must never constrict his artistic imagination – how the steps will look, how they will join the colonnade, the style of the windows, and what will be behind them. This he must be left to do. In this regard, you can follow Meyerhold's example when he worked with the designer Golovin, on the set of *Masquerade*.[13] Using the precise *mise-en-scène* of the director, the sets produced were unrivalled. But, when Meyerhold worked with a lesser designer on *La Dame aux camélias*, it transpired that the plan, as set out by the director, was still plainly visible – the designer had done no more than colour it in.[14] In cases such as these the director has either to go beyond the limits of the creative meaning that is his territory, or be content with a set of this kind. When you deal with an eminent designer, you can pose any problem. He will be as 'bound' by it as the director is 'bound' by plot and situation. In these the director senses an anchor. Which is why I have always written scripts for myself, although I cannot stand writing 'to myself'. ...

... Prokofiev had a striking talent for creating images in music. And I do not mean by this that he did so as an illustrator. How would a pedestrian composer write the music for an autumn landscape? He would take the rustle of leaves, then a light breeze would pick up, and blow about. But Prokofiev had first and foremost a very sophisticated perception of the visual image. The different shades of colour would also play a role in his transcription into musical imagery. Any composer can translate the rustle of leaves into his music. But to translate the rhythm of a shot's yellow tone into the accompanying musical tone takes talent. Prokofiev was amazingly adept at this.

I remember how he wrote the song 'Ocean Sea, Sea so Blue', which did not make it into the film. When it was being recorded with the orchestra, he used to say, 'Now that is the sea's depth you can hear, that is a splash, those are the waves, and that is the bottom.' But this does not happen all at once, and the whole orchestra does not do this at the same time. There are extraordinarily complicated, different passages, and the result is a collective image of the ocean. Some sounds evoke the sense of depth, or the feeling of a tempest.... That is how we act when we film various objects from different points. You do not film a fortress, say, just from 'head-on'. You give it a turret, drawbridges, a moat, and from the combination of the different shot angles, the result is an impression of a fortress. That is how Prokofiev worked in music. If the entire orchestra played only 'the depth', or only 'the blueness', the music would be comparable to filming from one angle: it would convey information, not emotion.

Whichever area of work we choose, they literally all meet up in our working method.

... Suppose that Prokofiev's music is difficult for an ordinary dance. Its range of application is different from that of Tchaikovsky which seems to have been devised to make you move to it. Prokofiev's music is strikingly well suited to montage movement. As far as the rhythm of moving arms or legs is concerned, it is very difficult. When Prokofiev himself dances, he always treads on his partner's toes. He is so used to expanding a rhythm that he finds a normal, ordinary human rhythm difficult and his feet cannot manage it.

I understand something of rhythm, to judge from my films. But, when I joined Meyerhold's directing workshops, I failed the part on rhythm.[15] All my marks in this subject were unsatisfactory. My work is on a different element of rhythm. Rhythmic gymnastics, which I failed, should properly have been called metrics.[16] This is not a living rhythm, which approaches regularity, but the tap of a metronome.

The same thing happened with dance. When I learned how to dance, I could not grasp certain figure-dances at all, and I was wildly delighted when the fox-trot appeared, where you can move however you like according to the sense of the music rather than the various steps.

There are the same distinctions in montage too. There is montage built on a uniform sense of rhythmical movement; and montage built on metrical relationships.[17] I do not know anything about the metrical length of the montage fragments in my constructions. These fragments come not by the metre, but by the feeling. I never check by calculation. But, if you take Pudovkin, he has always used a metre rule, and he still does. On many an occasion, if there was any unused piece of film left, he could always determine precisely its place in the edited film. But he can also unite the metrical and rhythmical passages. Dziga Vertov also uses a typical, metric montage.

I do not mean that this method is flawed, but it is not organic. For no absolute measure for length exists: so much depends on the content within the frame. Whether a section is filmed in close-up or medium shot, or whether it is the third time that it appears in the montage – all these influence the length. There is no single gauge for length. Does this mean that you need to multiply the internal 'mass' of a section by the length of time it is to be seen? But this is a purely 'physical' method. And why do that, when you can sense it? You need to cultivate an internal sense of rhythm. In that way, you obtain precise rules of measurement.

... I was saying that Prokofiev liked a rigid montage framework in which to project his fantasy. But, when working with a composer, the converse may be true, when you need to edit, using a finished piece of recorded music. Here it is essential to adjust the pieces of filmed material, which must be carefully examined to see that they match exactly the beats in the music. This is an awful job. You have to observe all the laws of plastic connection between the fragments, taking into account both the informational and the purely plastic aspects. All of this must be projected on to pre-recorded music. Sometimes you can just insert the pieces, but at crucial moments you can do next to nothing. If you do not work on the metrical relationships between depiction and music, that is, if there is no primitive, direct relationship between the musical and the visual accents, between the 'lines' of music and the montage segments of expression, that makes it doubly difficult. In this respect, work on the colour sections of *Ivan the Terrible* was very complex. The music for the dance of the *oprichniki* was commissioned earlier; it was filmed with that music and then edited.

I was talking about the external and primitive metrical correspondence between music and depiction; and about the more complex rhythmical correspondence. But the most splendid approach is the melodic approach – that is the most splendid correspondence.

In this sense, Disney is a unique master of the cartoon film.[18] Nobody else has managed to make the movement of a drawing's outline conform to the melody. In this Disney is inimitable. But, when he made the transition to colour, it seemed he could not make it 'work' musically, even in *Bambi* [USA, 1942]. True, I have not studied his *Fantasia* [USA, 1940] in this sense. But in other works he failed to make a 'colour melody' to ensure that there was not only an emotional correspondence between the colour and the music, but a precisely formulated musical correspondence. But that is the second stage, when colour is connected not so much to the melody as to the orchestral hues.

When you handle this whole range, when you make a colour film, it is as complex as hell. You have to handle extraordinarily large numbers of correspondences. But why should it be any easier for you than for the general who has to deploy infantry, artillery, tanks and transport? The most brilliant and intelligent strategy is built on a combination of different weaponry, on the relationship between the various types of forces in action. Which is why any respectable director must also know how to be a 'general'.

The trouble with colour cinema is that colour cannot meet expressive demands. If there are no demands for expressiveness in colour, then there are no parameters to support you. And there must be expressive movement of colour – it is very difficult, but necessary.

In the last lecture I spoke about music and how movement and action translate into a musical construction.

In this study, we saw that music demands to be set free from the purely routine and to transpose the theme on to a somewhat different plane, a somewhat different dimension.

Then in the example of the song about the beaver, we investigated how various sections of music are written, and so apparently you now have a full idea of how you tackle work with music.

Could you pick out the actual secret of the process? How the shift into music occurred, when we were doing this exercise?

That is the most important thing: not so much knowing about it, as feeling, because it will be the same thing in all the most serious of cases.

When making a montage construction, you must also assemble and disassemble the segments, combining them until you reach the point where the combination 'begins to sing out' because, while you are merely using montage to explore the consistency of plot and the consistency of the various segments, you are doing nothing that could be termed 'artistic'. This is purely an informational report. But, when the combination of sections starts to attain the regularity of a musical construct, you have the germ of what you need.

What is important to me is that you also understand that this same process applies to work on colour film. The most serious thing is to understand what makes 'music in colour' distinct from the ordinary colouring of a work.

Suppose that you have black, blue and red – for the colouring of costumes, furniture, and so on. What is important when you start handling colour film, is that the themes of black, blue and red should become independent expressive themes. The real black polish of boots could be elevated to the meaning of blackness, which you are using in this case as a tragic colouring.

You have to know how to arrange things so that the blue colour of wallpaper or furniture upholstery does not remain merely the colour of wallpaper or furniture upholstery, but that, whenever necessary, it should have its own emotional value, connected with a precise idea.

Colours are perceived very individually. Red evokes certain associations in some people, different ones in others.

Suppose that, for me, red was associated with certain revolutionary ideals and notions. Since their youth, people have been accustomed to red at festivities and demonstrations. But take another 'sector' where red drives a bull – or equally Churchill – mad. There are psychological predispositions at work there too.

There are more or less common facts about colours. Black is connected with darkness, night, cold and, like it or not, it evokes negative feelings. Since childhood, blue has for us been associated with the sky, fresh air, and with a whole number of accepted things and it has a certain psychological effect. Yellow and gold are associated with sunlight and warmth. This does not mean that there is a catalogue of colours which invariably act in a certain way. Far from it.

It is also the case that different countries have different notions of colour. For example, white here is not associated with grief, whereas for the Chinese it is the colour of mourning.

What matters is that you have a conception of a coloured object, or a number of coloured objects, as a sense of the colour as a whole; this sense of colour can then be interpreted emotionally in its own way.

There is no difference at all between working with colour and with music. Once you have understood how you should treat the musical resolution, you have laid the groundwork for handling colour too. Because music in sound film begins at the point where the usual pairing of sound and image gives way to an arbitrary unity of sound and depiction; that is, when actual synchronisation ceases to exist. As long as the depiction of a boot is linked to the sound of a violin, then it can have no relationship to the creative process but, when the violin is separated from the boot, and rests on the face of the person speaking, that is when your action starts: there is something that you want to express. Ordinary synchronisation is done away with and you combine sound and image in the way that your creative intention suggests.

Almost the same thing happens with montage too. Essentially, as long as you simply film the whole scene just as it happens and in sequence, there is no artistic involvement with what you see. But when you begin to film using montage, you marry your understanding of the reality that you are filming to the sequence, to the change in scales, to the accentuation. A person filmed in long shot is generally just a person. But what do you do if you want to characterise him using montage? You define his features and show these details in a certain sequence. Suppose you show him groomed, powdered and so on, with an unbelievably 'luxurious' Lvov or Białystok hat and a German dust-coat over his arm. You thereby create a specific impression. Or show that his trousers are tattered and his shirt is badly worn. His character will be shown by a second series of details. This is where your dramatic presentation of the man starts. You reveal his character by the sequential portrayal of these things. If these details are thrown up by chance, and not sequentially, the impression of revelation is lost. That is, you take apart and put together the usual pairing of elements in the way you think necessary.

This is done more easily in music, because sound goes by one route, and image by another. They might coincide, or they might not.

It will be harder with colour, because the colour is inherent in the object, and you cannot separate the two as you can sound. Therefore the filming requires a much greater sense of forethought.

For the moment, remember the rule: you take apart an existing link, and creatively try out various combinations. Always remember the violin for the shoes or boots. This is the original formula by which you may be guided.

I now want to finish what we embarked upon last time, regarding the feeling of music and dance, and then say a few words about rhythm.

By rhythm we mean a temporal correspondence between the different parts. Is that clear? Any questions?

From the floor Just as in music there is a common plan, and a secondary one, which exists alongside the music, that must somehow correspond to the colour resolution. Now colour is resolved completely head-on. Even the attempt to achieve a colour resolution is primarily a question of colour. So it looks as though this is also one of the forms of musical connection.

Eisenstein Right. Just as theme and accompaniment work in music. In contemporary music they often change places, the theme becoming the accompaniment. But the fundamental feature of course is that it works on two levels.

There is also polyphonic montage in colour. There is a line of colours, one black, one blue, and so on; there will be this second stage. I want you to understand for the present that what is relevant is not that there is a blue shirt in one episode, but that a blue shirt is, apart from that, also a definite blue sound among the colours;[19] that it is not only a manufactured item, but a perfectly defined complex of sounds. Since you have chosen a blue shirt, it is bound to influence the colour solution of the other elements. But the most that colour cinema is capable of at present is every now and then in one frame to make the other shirts not too dazzling. But to make three quarters blue, and one quarter gold – this has not yet been done – is difficult. Another reason for not doing it is that there is no thematic interpretation for blue and gold.

If you are not trying to resolve a dramatic problem using blue, be it a problem of expression or of content, then why increase or decrease the amount of blue? If it does not have any meaning, say, for the accumulation of blue sounds, which drown the gold sounds, if there is no connection here between the two, then there is no point in doing it.

Again, 'a little spot of music, for its own sake' is of no use to us. Music is fine in a film, when it has a dramatic function. It does not mean that it must repeat directly what the actor is doing. Imagine that the actor is angry. Does that mean that the orchestral music must be angry too? But what is possible and what is essential here?

Music is acting by other means.

You can see this in the example of the 'Lullaby'. The theme of Ivan is introduced on the word 'black'. This is not bound to happen because of the actual lullaby, but because Serafima Germanovna Birman had to think that she was singing about Ivan when she reached the word 'black'. Without this, the lullaby would remain just a lullaby.

The music can be written when it has something to say – otherwise the music will have no dramatic progression. And you have to develop this feeling inside you.

You must know why you clothe someone in a red, blue or green shirt. What notions guide you when you clothe one person in dark fabrics and another in brighter tones. I am not saying that young people should wear red and older ones lilac. Lilac and silver give a sense of funereal splendour, while gold and blue create a more carnival mood. Again, I am not saying that if you need some festivity, then people should dress up in blue and gold. If you film a contemporary picture, and the hero is in the military, then he will be dressed in khaki and you cannot dress him in blue or show close-ups of his epaulettes.

Out of all the interesting colour combinations, you may find the one that in a specific case 'fastens on' to a specific theme.

The next point is very interesting too. When you make a film, you familiarise the viewer with a precise colour range that you use to convey a precise meaning. White cannot be termed the colour of a bad guy. Rather, white is associated with innocence. Yet, in *Alexander Nevsky*, the enemy is wearing white. If you recall the episode in Pskov showing the knights – in that episode their white clothing is associated with brutality, with annihilation, burning; that is, what might be termed a conditioned reflex is developed. People in white robes are juxtaposed with all kinds of repugnant actions. And then when you see a white cloak isolated from these details, it will still be associated with evil. You reach an agreement with the viewer and instil in him what you need to, precisely by associating a feeling with this colour. 'Educational work' of this nature – bringing the viewer to the necessary understanding – must be done during the prologue. This corresponds to the exposition of the characters provided in the first act.

From the floor When you were working with colour in *Ivan the Terrible*, did you ever find that you had somehow to link the colour resolution with the musical resolution on the same level? Suppose, for example, that in the colour

174

resolution there were highly contrasting spots of red, white and black, and they perhaps moved very jerkily. Did there have to be any sort of link with this in the musical resolution? Was the music also full of contrast, jerky and moving around a lot, or was it the reverse: very fluid, soft and understated music, by way of contrast?

Eisenstein I found this much less often. I personally think that our black-and-white cinema . . .[20] and so there is no special difference during the transition from the one to the other. There you work with a more limited palette, which forces you to move in extraordinarily precise . . .[21] They are harder to handle. With the transition to colour, the range of colours expands and the number of possibilities becomes much greater. With an abrupt, rhythmic drawing, when the music is really hammering it out, you can cut sections according to the rhythm of the music. They will coincide. In the film *October* there is the *lezginka* episode.[22] The 'Wild Division' is approaching Petrograd. They are met by workers' organisations, and they fraternise. The Petrograd lot do a Russian dance, and the 'Wild Division' respond with a *lezginka*. Two rhythms meet. There the accumulation of montage was driven by the rhythm of the *lezginka*. There was a precise coincidence. But it could have been done quite differently. You could cut a section for each musical accent, and add a new section with each beat. Or you could have a long section of conversation, accompanied by this chopped-up rhythm.

This also works with colour.

In the colour scene in *Ivan the Terrible*, the beginning of the dance was resolved with sections following musical accents; then comes a long section of conversation between Ivan the Terrible and Vladimir Andreyevich (the half-lyrical theme of the conversation) with the same music, which is then repeated. There you can separate the colour correspondence between the music and the coloration of the scene completely; and in the other part, you find almost pure, almost abstract spots. Each frame has been made almost black and white. You see the turn of gold brocade on the sleeve. The next turn is the red sleeve, the next is a hop. A splash of colour, a dance of spots.

Suppose it is a dance scene. At first all the colour themes are tied up in a knot. Then the red theme is gradually teased out, then the black, then the blue. What counts is that they are torn away from their original association with an object. Suppose that the red theme begins with a red sleeve; it is repeated with the red background of candles; when Vladimir Andreyevich goes to his death, the theme is picked up by the red carpet, which is cut up by the set and breaks off at the door. You need to distance yourself from the various red objects, take their overall redness and combine the objects according to their common feature. The Tsar's red shirt also works there in its hue in a certain section.

I wanted there to be red drops of blood in the black and white part, after the murder of Vladimir Andreyevich; but Fira Tobak would not have it, saying that would be Formalism.[23]

The theme of gold is associated with the crown of saints and Vladimir being dressed in golden robes.

The theme of black is the most interesting in this respect. It is here associated with death, appearing at first only in minor details, almost dividing the red from the gold. But what happens just before death steals up on Vladimir Andreyevich?

Here there is already a premonition of death. Before dawn, people go to pray at matins. They wear their ceremonial golden robes. Gradually monks' habits move towards the gold, and the gold is swallowed up by the black.

Vladimir Andreyevich is dressed in royal robes. Up to a certain point, the Tsar wears a red shirt; thereafter, a black fur coat. Then its colour changes, to a monk's habit. The next episode, filmed in black and white, continues the 'black theme' by means of the overall expressiveness. Black and red are interwoven. The gold vanishes, and the blue vault of the sky with gold appears, as a symbol of the purpose behind everything that is happening, as the decisive atmosphere that stands higher than what has to be done.

From the floor You said that the theme of black is the theme of death. What, then, does the red theme stand for?

Eisenstein The red supplies an ominous theme and acts as blood. There is a retort, mentioning blood: 'You and the Tsar are of the same blood: hold this sacred.' Old Basmanov is strongly opposed to Ivan's patronage of Vladimir Andreyevich, and allows himself to intervene in the Tsar's conversation with him. This earns him the Tsar's reproof. And an argument begins, in which Basmanov tells the Tsar that it was the Tsar himself who taught him how to 'uproot your own saplings', to which Ivan replies that Vladimir is the Tsar's blood, and that does not concern him: 'You and the Tsar are of the same blood: hold this sacred.' Blood acts as a sign of kinship. Basmanov replies, 'But are you and I not bound by the ... spilt ... blood of another?' At these words, there is a red glow and the faces shine red. This is the first time that red appears associated with the theme of spilt blood. Thus the theme has been activated in the necessary direction.

From the floor Can you say something about the theme of gold?

Eisenstein It is a festive, regal theme. Frescoes of saints with haloes, golden cloaks with hues of red and orange. The royal raiment, in which Vladimir is mockingly dressed – it is not the colour that provides the mockery, but the music. The theme of the argument proceeds utterly magnificently, like a war theme, an *oprichnik* theme. Then it undergoes an ironic change, that is, the musical imagery is repeated in a mocking resolution: the fourth couplet has no words and the Russian theme is resolved with three saxophones. Thus the gold is stripped off musically, not visually. The stress is placed on the area of expressiveness. Sometimes you can help with speech, and sometimes with music.

From the floor When Vladimir falls and Yevfrosinia explodes with a shout, what theme does she convey in colour?

Eisenstein Everything black.

From the floor And is the transition from black to colour essential?

Eisenstein It happens immediately, in an explosion. The tempi are reduced as much as is possible, reduced to a not very intense scene when Malyuta invites Vladimir to the feast. Then there is an explosion of colour. And, since there is music, there is a strong rhythmic impact. If there were no colour or music, we would still have shown the first episode in grey, and the second in black and white. There is no difference in principle as regards the rhythmic schema that was devised. You merely have a much greater potential for expressing it. In one case, you could supply this in a brief montage. Here you can do so through music. Instead of black and white, you have a chance to use different colours.

Ivan the Terrible: Evfrosinia Staritskaya cradles her son, the would-be tsar, Vladimir.

From the floor Are the colour sections the most important, the key moments in the general plan of the picture, or did you work using a different principle?

Eisenstein One episode, consisting of two parts, was not finished. And that led to the idea of doing it in colour. This scene could equally have been resolved in black and white. But the opportunity arose to resolve it in colour, and this motif lent itself to a richer and more detailed treatment.[24]

From the floor There are two themes in particular. Ivan's theme, which is resolved through his psychological condition – and there is a collision and combination of frames which are of varying coloration. How did that happen?

Eisenstein Do you know what a *leitmotif* is? When a sword is mentioned in Wagner's *Die Walküre*, the theme of the sword is played in the music.[25] There is a

177

part in Act One where a sword is struck into a tree, and this sword must be pulled out at the end. And just as the hero approaches the sword, the orchestra starts playing particular elements of the theme of the sword. And at the end, when he pulls this sword out, the theme is played in its entirety. There is also a leitmotif connected with the theme of Wotan and Siegmund. When Wotan grieves over his abandonment by his father, his theme begins. The music is 'affixed' to each element. Wagner does this magnificently, but in some cases this is taken to absurd lengths. This is the expressive, characteristic theme. For colour resolutions, it would be too primitive. Something along these lines was done in the Maly Theatre.[26] There the young Basmanov wore blue, or white; Malyuta red – that is, each had his own colour. This is a particularly primitive device.

What mattered to me was not that Ivan had a red or a black resolution but that at a particular moment in the drama's progression Ivan the Terrible should be seen in a corresponding colour resolution. At first he wears a red shirt. But by the time the drama has moved to the next stage, Ivan is in another colour – black. The moments on which the colour falls are important. At first Vladimir Andreyevich is in pink and gold. When the drama begins, he begins to cross over to gold. It is not the case that each has his own colour and so goes around in it: the idea is that colour is connected to theme, not character. When theme passes through a specific character, he appears in the correct colour resolution. This is the thematic line of the process.

And how does it all happen? Take the feast: how are we going to do it? Gold robes – fine; blue shirts – fine. A fiery moment. The Tsar is almost always resolved in black. On the occasion of a feast, he must wear an opulent brocade shirt. If there were no colour, this would have to be conveyed by texture. Here are a few considerations.

What else is possible? We know that there were saints on murals, and the saints could have gold haloes; and then there are the red flames of the candles. So, we have black, gold and red. You start by abstracting the routine details, deciding how to use colour to express the outlines of the characters. A fur coat will introduce an element of awe and the sense of a fatal moment. So, supplemented by the fur, the black element increases. The black needs further resolution. There are the *oprichniki* who will be dressed in black. The growth of black first turns into a black 'cloud' and then this 'cloud' becomes a group of *oprichniki*.

The same thing with red. A magnificent red shirt was made for the Tsar, from the trousers of the Emir of Bukhara. We were able to supply red through the red carpet, the candles and fire. There was one moment when we wanted to make the Tsar's shirt black and gold. This tradition survived from black-and-white photography. We even tried to film it. The results were wrong in terms of tonality, and so we switched to red.

So, there is the flame of the candle, the red shirt, the red carpet, and so on. Does red appear in this scene? Yes – the sense of blood. It grows further until red is understood as the menacing theme of murder.

We had to think what colour to make the frescoes, set and ceiling. First were the frescoes of Theophanes the Greek.[27] I travelled to Novgorod to see them. In one church there is an amazing blue vault, the saints painted in sepia against a background of absolutely pure sky-blue cobalt. This kind of light blue is at present beyond the reach of cinema. The potential for filters is very circumscribed. But we did achieve some kind of dark blue.

It is pretty successful, and is roughly what was wanted. This 'light blue option' has lodged in my memory. As soon as I added it to the overall composition, it harmonised splendidly like a pure tone. Apart from that, remember what I said about the crucial atmosphere of dark blue: it appears when the drama is reaching the end. Then a light blue background springs up.

That is how these things are 'assembled'. You have to look at this scene, bearing in mind how I conveyed the conception that I had pictured to myself. The conception is embodied in the material with maximum expressiveness. As I pictured it to myself, so too was it done. . . .

From the floor You said of the lullaby that music corresponds to the actor's action at a particular moment. You were talking about the audiovisual combination. In the sense of an ordinary combination, it corresponded because it was a lullaby.

Eisenstein No. The music corresponded to the moods, not to the actions; to the thoughts, not to the actions; to the subtext, not to the actions.

From the floor You said that music corresponds to the actions of the actor at a specific moment.

Eisenstein No. You have misunderstood: that is not what I said. The whole emphasis was on how the music worked at revealing the thoughts, and so on, at a different level – while having the outward appearance of a lullaby.

From the floor The second level was so that the actress's thoughts could be revealed through music, and in this sense there was a correspondence between music and action. A visual image came into being. You spoke of music that handles visual associations. At a specific moment we saw Staritskaya singing a lullaby to her son. We experience the visual images that are projected on to this portrayal. We picture the music which has been composed in a way that absolutely contradicts the emotional aims of this scene in their purely visual expression: for example there is the scene of the murder, and the background music for this action is easy and lyrical. We picture this theoretically. This music brings visual images to our minds. These are projected on to the screen images and begin to fight them. Can musical images be so strong as to displace the images that exist on the screen, and stop us from following the action happening on screen and start to think in music? Are there examples of this?

Eisenstein You film a man who is sleeping, and the music supplies everything that he is dreaming about at that time, in the way that Pimen dreamed of the clash of war: the old man is asleep, and there is the rumble of war. He is asleep, and you can hear the fall of Kazan. In *The Tale of the Invisible City of Kitezh*, there is a battle at Kerzhenets, which only happens in the music – the curtain is lowered.[28] There is no action.

I can understand the Jesuitical side of your question. You ought not to picture visual sensations too primitively. For example, if Staritskaya starts thinking about Ivan during the song about the beaver, that does not mean that at that moment she *sees* Ivan. If I had to have her see Ivan in front of her at that moment, I would have used a dissolve: here is Ivan, actually present. And then I would not use music, which somehow masks the visual images, but would resort to visible images.

179

There are three stages: the first is when a person is materially present; the second, when the presence is achieved by a dissolve, vaguely outlined; and the third, when the presence is indicated in the music. The first version of *Ivan the Terrible* had a scene in which Kurbsky was writing a letter. I built it around Ivan's genius driving Kurbsky mad. A typical psychological feature of the 'second stage'. In one of my earliest attempts he had a complete breakdown and began to imagine Ivan. His ghost appeared and Kurbsky threw himself at it with his sword. There, I needed Ivan's real presence in the form of a ghost. [*On the board he draws Ivan's ghost appearing to Kurbsky.*] These things should be handled through montage, using several shots to convey this sense. This could equally well have been done with a well-chosen camera angle. What mattered was that the actor saw, with his own eyes. . . . But what about the beaver song? At one particular moment, a shadow should fall on it. Music can convey this moment of an imperfect concreteness as well.

From the floor In discussions about *Alexander Nevsky* and the intonation and structure of the music, the music matched the composition of the shots, the dramatic action and the emotional content too. But, if the music conflicts with the events on screen, should the musical structure and the compositional structure also be in conflict?

Eisenstein In *Alexander Nevsky* there was an outline like this. [*Draws outline*] The link between the music and the depiction had to be taken into account in the composition. [*Draws an outline*] What makes *Alexander Nevsky* remarkable is that it contains the first correspondences, which it should be more complex to find. [*Draws an outline*][29]

From the floor What makes that sort of correspondence more complex?

Eisenstein It rarely happens. A full unison in an orchestra almost never happens; only at very powerful or very specific moments. It is akin to symmetrical compositions, or when the speaker addresses the viewer directly. It should happen at a moment that is divorced from the rest of the situation.

If you understand the transition of motif into line, your work with music and visual representation will be the same as, for example, your work with visual representation alone. [*Draws an outline*] Here is a person – purely representational. The music is here supplied graphically, as context. You take these motifs already present in the person and you develop a structure, and the result is a motif that corresponds harmoniously with the figure – albeit a motif without a subject. [*Draws an outline*] Now this was an environment without a subject, something like dust, or a cloud. But this environment could have been shown differently – for example, by a conventionally resolved outline of a horse. [*Draws an outline*] Further, the line goes all the way round the figure – in this case it is conveyed by the outline of an awesome horse. The repetition of the motif of the figure occurs at the top; there it goes laterally. Representative movement is also repeated in the musical movement. At the most crucial points, you need a congruence, so that all the means of expression work in unison. If the means of expression replicate one another, then the typicality will be lost, just as the expressiveness of the profile will be lost by encasing it with parallel lines. It is as though you are playing on just one string.

But, if the outline of the depiction is repeated in the musical movement, but worked out in a complex way, as it is in Prokofiev's orchestral works, it is as well to adhere to this outline closely. The treatment then can be as complex as you like – it cannot fail to sit correctly. The basic movement has been strictly defined, leaving you free to go wherever you please in the musical treatment. But, if the basic movement fails to coincide with a complex treatment, confusion will be the result.

From the floor Music extends through time. Can you speak of music as having a beginning and an end?

Eisenstein This device was used in *October*. First, a statue was taken to pieces. Then it flew back together again. The music for the film had been written, and the orchestral score was completed. It was also done backwards: that is, there was music for the statue being taken apart, and the same musical phrases were played backwards as it flew back together.[30]

From the floor But the composition of the shots – can we look at it from any direction? Basically we have a drawing that reads from left to right. But what happens if we start looking at it not from this side, but from the right? . . .

Eisenstein Read my article on *Alexander Nevsky*.[31] That deals with it, and it gives a precise explanation of how and why your eye moves.

The question is, whether musical movement has a determinate direction in time, and whether you can state that the eye, as it perceives the composition of a shot, also moves in a determinate direction – e.g. from left to right? Anyone care to answer?

From the floor The eye is generally accustomed to move from left to right.

From the floor I will attempt an answer, but I am not sure that my judgment is correct. You *can* make someone look from right to left.

Eisenstein That is precisely the point, exactly as I explained in some detail in my article. The point being that a more or less normal person follows the elements as they attract him in a shot. If you follow this sequence of shots in *Alexander Nevsky*, the stress always falls on the left-hand side, except the shot of Raven Rock where Alexander Nevsky stands in his cloak gazing in the opposite direction. There is the outline of threatening clouds and that marks the edge of the frame. Not many sane people would start at the other side. Some are bound to, but ninety per cent would be drawn first to the dark figure against the skyline. In all the other shots, the calculations were based on left/right movement. This 'educates' the eye.

Equally, you can make the eye read shots from top to bottom. For example, a descent down a mineshaft. You have to educate the eye to read downwards. This is done graphically. If you have marked out someone's gaze, you would probably show a person looking down in profile.

From the floor Each work always has two camps. Each will have a defining colour. The whole film needs to be constructed in two key tones as far as colour is concerned. If there are minor themes present, can they be done in the key tones, but using a weaker colour?

Eisenstein You mean that the bulk of dramatic works are based on conflict, and conflict is commonly expressed as two forces in opposition. This is not always obligatory and does not always take place, but works of the average sort are like that. And you say that this division in the conflict must be coloured differently: one side white, the other black.

From the floor Must there be a conflict of colours where one colour beats the other?

Eisenstein That will happen very crudely, and in colour film too.... But the point is that it is not only expressed in the colour scheme.

To take an example from real life. The Whites' camp began to break down into factions. (Suppose this was a picture from the Civil War period.) One part of the group has a tendency to join the Reds. And in the Reds' camp lurk enemies in disguise. After the Civil War, as you know, the struggle went much deeper. Compare the conflict in *The Little Red Devils*, where this was shown almost in outline; and the complex conflict in *A Great Citizen*.[32]

What is vital is that you do not colour the characters a definite hue, and then play them off against each other. The cases where themes are in conflict and convey a colour resolution as they move through the different characters are especially interesting.

From the floor Dealing with colour, we should also deal with the colouring. Creating the colouring for one shot is clear-cut. But, since cinema is not a single frame, but many taken in combination, obviously it is possible to give the whole film a general colour resolution. In a construction where one colour emerges the victor, it becomes very difficult to achieve an overall colouring in the whole because the principal approach is different. From what you have said so far, the work as a whole has no colouring. Once the blue theme has come into being, it will continue to develop, and so on, and that is its colour resolution: how is all this to be linked together in a whole?

Eisenstein A golden line is swallowed up by a black one. Parallel to this, a red line expands and a blue one starts somewhere. This is a typical polyphony, with many voices. As regards the colour tonality of individual frames, each time it is connected to the principle of a chord. Take shot 76 [in *Ivan*], for example: the gold has been practically devoured; the black has grown, and the blue has only just started and the frame must be balanced internally.

From the floor I am talking about a purely pictorial colouring. There can be no colouring with a polyphonic resolution. How does the colouring of a film as a whole come about? From one colour's triumph over another?

Eisenstein You will not get anywhere using mechanical terms – try instead more musical terminology, because everything here is linked to movement.[33] But we agreed that a mechanical film or an individual frame is essentially also not a fixed, but a temporal structure. Then what happens?

If we take *Christ Appearing to the Multitude*, by Ivanov, the construction there is a spiral, as you know.[34] So the movement of the eyes across the canvas is established. The arrangement of tones is also a given. Ivanov has resolved the departure into the distance not only graphically but in colour too. Combinations of a different order are also possible: inward graphic movement, with the movement in colour going the opposite way. Graphic movement does not take always account of colouring.

For example, Surikov is a great artist, but from the point of view of colouring, and colour schemes, he is extraordinarily ill-disciplined and haphazard. Think of *Boyarina Morozova*.[35] The harmony is magnificent in an ordinary reproduction, and the penetration inwards is wonderfully expressed. But look at it in colour. The first thing to hit you is the terrible brightness and the scattered spots of colour.

182

Surikov's spots of colour are not calculated, in the way that the plastic drawing is calculated; and the colour does not assist in the inward impetus; this is achieved partly by a trick of the perspective, in defiance of the colour. It is all extraordinarily bright and haphazard. If you recall the young boyar ladies and the beggars, they are almost all treated as independent portraits, thrown together at random, judging by the colour.

What happens with Ivanov's *Christ Appearing to the Multitude*? Consider the graphic movement as a montage movement. Each flourish is a separate segment. Here, the people are in the foreground and the middle distance; then in the distance is Christ and a large strip of scenery. And this is developed the same way in colour; they begin saturated and then fade.

The overall colouring of the work is built up from separate parts in the same way as the overall colouring of a scene. Details are built up in colour. And the actual episode must be resolved in the same way as each section within it is resolved. How is this done?

Have you read my article about *Potemkin* with the assembly of segments of montage – the meeting of the skiffs and the public at the Odessa Steps? The article is called 'Eh!'[36] Twelve shots, showing the meeting between the battleship and the skiffs, were dissected.[37] I wrote about how the foreground motif interacted with the background motif and how the two succeeded each other.

In the first shot, the whole field of vision is filled with the skiffs moving towards the battleship. That is the first subject. The second subject appears in the next shot: the frame is bisected by a colonnade. Then the verticals of the columns are repeated in the figures of people standing on the steps and the arch, marked out by the columns, turns into the arrangement of the group – people standing in a circle. The arch turns into the outline of a parasol, and the movement of skiffs seems to be continued in the movements of eyes and heads. Then the parasol vanishes, the circle vanishes, and the motif works in reverse. The boat is in the foreground, and the balustrade is in the distance. The line of the boat's hull is echoed in the lower part of the frame in the line of the balustrade. The sail – the chief compositional vertical – is repeated in the figure of the lady in white seated in the boat. Then the light tones of the sky and the building fade into the tones of the grey hull of the ship and the brilliant white water, and the verticals of the sails, which fill the entire depth of the shot, are repeated in the vertical figures of the sailors in the foreground.

That is how one shot turns into another. The same motifs are altered and rearranged, in terms of both line and tone.

Absolutely the same thing happens when you work in colour.

Colour is too mobile in film. You obtain a general sense of colour, but it is extraordinarily difficult to determine it unambiguously. It would be profoundly wrong to determine the colour resolution of a film with one colour. You cannot sustain a pale blue for the entire film. There is bound to be the same division as there is in music: andante, which you resolve in pale blue, say; and allegro, in red and black. I can tell you how I planned to make a film about Pushkin, where the whole thing was constructed on the shift in colour.[38]

Have you understood the principle of the separation of colour from object? In order to understand and express any principle, you have to take an extreme case.

Then the law becomes clear. You know the theory of limits? It is well known that you can find a consistent formula for a whole range of quantities, if you pick an extreme case. The same principle also obtains in the resolution of our problems.

If you use a Gillette razor, you know the rule: 'Tighten it as far as you can, then release it a half-turn'. That is roughly what we have to do too: take it to the limit, and then step back a little....

But to continue the discussion of colour. What can the 'tightening up' be demonstrated on? How should we work in colour, so that the principle be taken to its limits? Where can you do the craziest things in colour? In what sort of pictures?

Cartoons. To take the problem to its extreme, you have to make a cartoon. When I began considering what had been done with colour in cartoons, I thought that to resolve it correctly, you could find the very nature of the principle there.

In my dacha I have got some Vyatka dolls.[39] They are on a shelf upstairs. I lie and think: If I am to pursue work in cartoons, I would of course avoid the mice and pigs of Disney and follow Russian folklore. The models of folklore construction – Vyatka dolls. I began to look at them closely: what could be done with the colour? The first thing I thought was: you have a horse with little red and green circles on it; in the cartoon, the spots would come away from the horse and begin to lead a life of their own.

The second doll is a nurse. And now these red and green spots transfer themselves to the nurse, and the performance begins. The check on her skirt seems to exist purely for this. Then it goes further. The spots come away and run off. A spring landscape. An old man sitting beneath a bare tree. Red apples suddenly appear on its branches. Then these green circles become red, the apples ripen. The circles then fall off at a crossroads, on to a traffic light. A red light shines where there should be a green one – the red spots jumped up there, and all hell breaks loose.

Or this would not be a bad idea: a girl and a young man sit on a bench. She suddenly turns green, then he leaves and she turns red.

When I thought about all this, I observed one thing: what basic idea lies at the root of this invention? First, that colour has been differentiated from its object and, second, that colour has started to acquire different meanings, from the simplest abstract jumping spots to a traffic light, the expression of a face, and the colour of apples.

The principle has been correctly grasped here. That is how a razor is 'tightened and then released'.

From the very first attempt at defining how this should be done in an extreme case, it appeared that the key thing is to isolate, to take hold of this element. The key principle consists in separating colour from what necessarily lies beneath it, to draw it out into a general feeling and make this general feeling become a subject again.

What I tried to tell you when I began these lectures was essentially derived from this principle.

As regards Disney's treatment of colour, those pictures of his that I have seen remain only at the threshold of colour cinema.

Disney's most interesting – most valuable – contribution has been his skill at superimposing the 'drawing' of a melody on top of a graphic drawing. In live-action cinema, what is difficult is teasing out the line of the composition from the real material. On one occasion we were only able by chance to film the cloud we needed. We tried forty times before that, but it was always wrong. Only once was the cloud right. We unpacked again in a hurry and managed to film it. But that cloud might never have come along.

But Disney is lucky. He can just draw the outline he wants. He has an incomparable feel for an intonational gesture in music, and he can weave this gesture into the outline of his figures. Disney is a genius at doing this. No one can do this, apart from him.

He is an unsurpassed master of outline, but to date his colour work has been unremarkable. The colour in *Snow White and the Seven Dwarfs* [USA, 1937] is terribly saccharine. In *Bambi* the drawing is wrong. In *Bambi* the shading is done the same way as it is in the Mickey Mouse films. But, for a lyrical theme, rather than an ironic one, this work with a hatching pen is too harsh and bald.

I have seen sketches for *Bambi* which were done not with harsh outlines, but using a slightly wet brush and spots. This was much more pleasing than the film. It was done in the same gentle style as the Russian artist, Lebedev, who illustrated Marshak's books.[40]

If you have seen examples of Chinese painting, how they do birds and in particular monkeys, you will understand what I am talking about. They convey the thickness of the monkey's fur very well. To make *Bambi* completely lyrical, that sort of cartoon would have been better. Bambi itself has been perfectly executed, as far as the drawing is concerned. But in terms of the melody, it has been played on the wrong instruments. The melody is right, the timbre wrong.

Disney uses the 'Barcarolle' from *The Tales of Hoffmann*.[41] A peacock appears near a lake. A lake, a peacock and its tail. And all the movements are repeated. The complex musical passage has been remarkably caught in the splaying tail, which turns and is reflected in the water below. Disney's inventiveness for such things is inexhaustible. But it is less good when he turns to tonal resolutions. The pictorial form is always very poor. The figures are very good, but the landscape is poor – always poor. But with the transition to colour, the tone *per se* is always very well chosen. You have seen the grasshopper catching fish. You remember the amazing part where he skates across the water? How well the water and the fish are done, in terms of the body of colour. In themselves, these colours are very attractive, because they have the pallor of celluloid. But Disney's work in colour has been uneven so far. It is no more than his cartoon work, coloured in. There has been no sign in his technique of any new contribution, arising from his discovery of colour. He has not progressed to the next stage.

When you have been working in silent film and then progress to sound, there is some movement in your devices and constructions. I do not mean that this movement is always an advance. But style is always changing and developing. With Disney, however, everything has remained almost unchanged, except that it is now in colour. In *Bambi* there are a number of attempts at introducing a correspondence between colour and sound, but they are unsuccessful. Nevertheless, his way of making the movement of a line coincide with that of a sound is as remarkable as ever! The melody moves forward, and all the different twists in the line repeat the melody, whether corresponding or not, whereas in cartoons a corre-spondence between melody and drawing is almost obligatory. But when Disney is working with colour, there is no correspondence between the oscillations and changes in the colour and the melodic outline. He cannot synchronise the colour and the music . . .

Notes

Throughout these notes Eisenstein is referred to as 'E'. The following are the abbreviations used for the most frequently cited sources in these notes.

ESW 1   R. Taylor (ed. and trans.), *S. M. Eisenstein. Selected Works: Vol. 1. Writings, 1922–34* (London: British Film Institute and Bloomington IN: Indiana University Press, 1988).

ESW 2   M. Glenny & R. Taylor (eds), *S. M. Eisenstein. Selected Works: Vol. 2. Towards a Theory of Montage* (trans. M. Glenny) (London: British Film Institute, 1991; paperback edn, 1994).

ESW 3   R. Taylor (ed.), *S. M. Eisenstein. Selected Works: Vol. 3. Writings, 1934–47* (trans. W. Powell) (London: British Film Institute, 1996).

ESW 4   R. Taylor (ed.), *S. M. Eisenstein. Selected Works: Vol. 4. Beyond the Stars. The Memoirs of Sergei Eisenstein* (trans. W. Powell) (London: British Film Institute and Calcutta: Seagull Books, 1994).

FF   R. Taylor & I. Christie (eds), *The Film Factory: Russian and Soviet Cinema in Documents* (trans. R. Taylor) (London: Routledge & Kegan Paul and Boston MA: Harvard University Press, 1988; paperback edn, London and New York: Routledge, 1994).

Film Form J. Leyda (ed. and trans.), *Film Form. Essays in Film Theory* (New York: Harcourt Brace Jovanovich, 1949, and London: Dennis Dobson, 1951).

IFF   R. Taylor and I. Christie (eds), *Inside the Film Factory. New Approaches to Russian and Soviet Cinema* (London and New York: Routledge, 1991; paperback edn, 1994).

IP   S. I. Yutkevich *et al.* (eds), *Izbrannye proizvedeniya v shesti tomakh* [Selected Works in Six Volumes] (Moscow: Iskusstvo, 1964–71).

IS   R. N. Yurenev (ed.), *Izbrannye stat'i* [Selected Articles] (Moscow: Iskusstvo, 1956).

The other principal editions of E's writings hitherto available in book form in English are:

Eisenstein, S., *Notes of a Film Director* (New York: Dover, 1970).
Leyda, J. (ed.), *Eisenstein 2: A Premature Celebration of Eisenstein's Centenary* (Calcutta: Seagull, 1985).
Leyda, J. (ed.), *Eisenstein on Disney* (Calcutta: Seagull, 1986).
Leyda, J. (ed.), *Film Essays and a Lecture* (London: Dennis Dobson, 1968; New York: Praeger, 1970).
Leyda, J. (ed. and trans.), *The Film Sense* (New York: Harcourt Brace Jovanovich, 1942; London: Faber & Faber, 1943).
Leyda, J., and Z. Voynow, *Eisenstein at Work* (New York: Pantheon, 1982; London: Methuen, 1985).
Marshall, H. (trans.), *Immoral Memories. An Autobiography by Sergei M. Eisenstein* (Boston MA: Houghton Mifflin; London: Peter Owen, 1985).
Marshall, H. (trans.), *Sergei Eisenstein. Nonindifferent Nature* (Cambridge: Cambridge University Press, 1987).

Upchurch, A. (trans.), *Sergei M. Eisenstein: On the Composition of the Short Fiction Scenario* (Calcutta: Seagull, 1984).

Upchurch, A. (ed. and trans.), *Sergei M. Eisenstein. The Psychology of Composition* (Calcutta: Seagull, 1987; London: Methuen, 1988).

The principal English-language studies of E's life and work in book form are:

Aumont, J. *Montage Eisenstein* (London: British Film Institute; Bloomington IN: Indiana University Press, 1987).

Barna, Y., *Eisenstein* (London: Secker & Warburg; Bloomington IN: Indiana University Press, 1973).

Bergan, R., *Eisenstein. A Life in Conflict* (London and New York: Little, Brown, 1997).

Bordwell, D., *The Cinema of Eisenstein* (Cambridge MA: Harvard University Press, 1993).

Christie. I. and D. Elliott (eds), *Eisenstein at Ninety* (Oxford: Museum of Modern Art and London: British Film Institute, 1988).

Christie, I. and R. Taylor (eds), *Eisenstein Rediscovered* (London and New York: Routledge, 1993).

Geduld, H. M. and R. Gottesman (eds), *Sergei Eisenstein and Upton Sinclair: The Making and Unmaking of Que Viva Mexico!* (Bloomington IN: Indiana University Press, 1970).

Goodwin, J. *Eisenstein, Cinema & History* (Urbana and Chicago IL: University of Illinois Press, 1993).

Karetnikova, I. and L. Steinmetz, *Mexico according to Eisenstein* (Albuquerque NM: University of New Mexico Press, 1991).

Kleberg L. and Lövgren H. (eds), *Eisenstein Revisited: A Collection of Essays* (Stockholm: Almqvist & Wiksell, 1987).

Lövgren, H., *Eisenstein's Labyrinth. Aspects of a Cinematic Synthesis of the Arts* (Stockholm: Almqvist & Wiksell, 1996).

Marshall, H. (ed.), *The Battleship Potemkin: The Greatest Film Ever Made* (New York: Avon, 1978).

Mayer, D., *Eisenstein's Potemkin: A Shot-by-Shot Presentation* (New York: Grossman, 1972).

Montagu, I., *With Eisenstein in Hollywood. A Chapter of Autobiography* (New York: International Publishers, 1967; Berlin GDR: Seven Seas, 1968).

Moussinac, L., *Sergei Eisenstein. An Investigation into His Films and Philosophy* (New York: Crown, 1970).

Nizhny, V., *Lessons with Eisenstein* (ed. and trans. I. Montagu) (London: Allen & Unwin; New York: Hill & Wang, 1962).

Seton, M., *Sergei M. Eisenstein. A Biography* (London: The Bodley Head, 1952; revised edn, London: Dennis Dobson, 1978).

Swallow, N., *Eisenstein: A Documentary Portrait* (London: Allen & Unwin, 1976; New York: Dutton, 1977).

Thompson, K., *Eisenstein's 'Ivan the Terrible': A Neoformalist Analysis* (Princeton NJ: Princeton University Press, 1981).

Notes to Eisenstein: A Soviet Artist

1. 'About Myself', *ESW 4*, p. 3.
2. See above.
3. See, for instance, Boris Shumyatsky's March 1937 *Pravda* article 'The Film *Bezhin Meadow*', translated in *FF*, pp. 378–81. E was also attacked by fellow film-makers at the January 1935 Film-makers' Conference: see *FF*, pp. 348–55. For E's speeches and reaction, see *ESW 3*, pp. 16–47.
4. E's principal persecutor in the United States was Major Frank Pease, who apparently regarded his visit as 'more dangerous even than a massed enemy landing': *ESW 4*, pp. 286, 420, 548; M. Seton, *Sergei M. Eisenstein. A Biography* (revised edn, London: 1978), pp. 167–8.
5. A. Tarkovsky, *Sculpting in Time. Reflections on the Cinema* (trans. K. Hunter-Blair), (London: 1986), pp. 118, 183.

6. The most exhaustive chronology of Eisenstein's life, although it does contain some inaccuracies, is W. Sudendorf, *Eisenstein. Materialien zu Leben und Werk* (Munich and Vienna: Hanser, 1975). There are shorter chronologies in English in J. Leyda & Z. Voynow, *Eisenstein at Work* (New York: Pantheon, 1982; London: Methuen, 1985); and I. Christie & D. Elliott (eds), *Eisenstein at Ninety* (Oxford: Museum of Modern Art and London: British Film Institute, 1988). There is a comprehensive bibliography of E's work in Russian, compiled by V. Zabrodin, in: *Kinovedcheskie zapiski*, no. 37/8. (Moscow, 1998), pp. 345–97.

7. See 'The Knot that Binds', *ESW 4*, pp. 97–101.

8. All three are mentioned in *ESW 4*, especially in '*Monsieur, madame et bébé*', pp. 487–506, while the Marquis de Sade has one of the longest chapters devoted to his inspiration: 'To the Illustrious Memory of the Marquis', pp. 510–66.

9. *ESW 4*, pp. 390ff.

10. See 'How I Learned to Draw', *ESW 4*, pp. 567–91.

11. Y. Barna, *Eisenstein* (London: 1973), p. 38.

12. *ESW 4*, p. 125; see also pp. 433–4.

13. 'Obedient Child' was the subtitle of 'The Boy from Riga', *ESW 4*, pp. 16–21.

14. In fact E enrolled on the day that his father died in his Berlin exile of a heart attack, although E only discovered this coincidence some three years later: *ESW 4*, p. 126.

15. There are numerous references to E's experience in the Civil War in *ESW 4*, but see especially pp. 78–83, 127–42, 398–408, 479–84. See also Barna, pp. 38–45.

16. Eisenstein papers, RGALI [Russian State Archive of Literature & Art], Moscow 1923/2.

17. His first published article, 'The Eighth Art. On Expressionism, America and, of course, Charlie Chaplin', written in collaboration with Sergei Yutkevich, is in the first document in *ESW 1*, pp. 29–32. There are varying accounts of the circumstances surrounding his death; see Barna, pp. 269–70; Seton (1978), pp. 475–6; N. Swallow, *Eisenstein. A Documentary Portrait* (New York: 1977), pp. 139–41; D. Bordwell, *The Cinema of Eisenstein* (Cambridge MA: 1993), p. 32; R. Bergan, *Eisenstein. A Life in Conflict* (London: 1997), pp. 349–50.

18. Barna, p. 47; Swallow, p. 32.

19. Barna, pp. 49–53; Swallow, pp. 34–5.

20. This period is described in 'The Teacher', *ESW 4*, pp. 264–70. The reference to Meyerhold as E's 'spiritual father' is in '*Wie sag ich's meinem Kinde?*', *ESW 4*, p. 446.

21. Kuleshov's first articles defining the specificity of cinema as opposed to theatre as lying in the sphere of montage were published in 1917 and 1918 and they are translated in *FF*, pp. 41–6. Fellow film-makers including Vsevolod Pudovkin later wrote, 'We make films but Kuleshov made cinema': *FF*, p. 270.

22. The 'Eccentric' in the title derives from *ekstsentrik*, one of the Russian words for 'clown'. Like E, the members of FEKS (Sergei Yutkevich, Leonid Trauberg and Grigori Kozintsev) progressed from theatre to cinema.

23. *FF*, p. 58.

24. *FF*, p. 62.

25. *ESW 1*, pp. 29–32.

26. Barna, pp. 64–9; Swallow, pp. 34–41; Bordwell, pp. 6–8; *ESW 4*, pp. 551-2, 586–7, 660–1.

27. *FF*, p. 59.

28. 'Eisenstein on Eisenstein, the Director of *Potemkin*', p. 64.

29. Barna, p. 70.

30. 'Theatre and Cinema', *ESW 3*, pp. 3–4.

31. *ESW 3*, p. 4.

32. The exchange of letters is translated in J. Leyda (ed.), *Eisenstein 2: A Premature Celebration of Eisenstein's Centenary* (Calcutta: Seagull, 1985), pp. 1–8.

33. Vertov's writings have been translated in A. Michelson (ed.), *Kino-Eye. The Writings of Dziga Vertov* (trans. K. O'Brien) (Berkeley CA: 1984). His early manifestos are in *FF*, pp. 69–72, 89–94.

34. There is a clear influence of Constructivism here but E's critique has something in

common with Viktor Shklovsky's remark, when commenting on Dziga Vertov's work, that 'Mussolini talking interests me. But a straightforward plump and bald-headed man who talks can go and talk off-screen. The whole sense of a newsreel is in the date, time and place. A newsreel like this is like a card catalogue in the gutter': *FF*, p. 152. E is also playing with the concept of 'photogeny' or 'the photogenic' elaborated in France by Louis Delluc in his *Photogénie* (Paris: 1920) and by Jean Epstein in his *Bonjour cinéma* (Paris: 1921).

35. For details of *Potemkin*'s reception in the West, see H. Marshall (ed.), *The Battleship Potemkin: The Greatest Film Ever Made* (New York: 1978), pp. 117–35. For its reception in Germany, where the ban was debated in the Reichstag before being overturned, see G. Kühn, K. Tümmler & W. Wimmer (eds), *Film und revolutionäre Arbeiterbewegung in Deutschland 1918—1932* (Berlin GDR: 1972), vol. 1, pp. 323–69.
36. See also: 'The German Cinema. A Traveller's Impressions', *ESW 1*, pp. 85–8.
37. R. Taylor, *The Politics of the Soviet Cinema* (Cambridge: 1979), pp. 95–6.
38. 'Statement on Sound', pp. 80–1; and 'The Fourth Dimension in Cinema', pp. 111–23, for instance.
39. The best account of the collaboration is unfortunately not available in English: W. Sudendorf (ed.), 'Der Stummfilmmusiker Edmund Meisel', *Kinematograph*, no. 1 (Frankfurt-am-Main; 1984).
40. E re-visited the question of the model actor, with specific reference to Kuleshov's part-ner Alexandra Khokhlova, in 'However Odd – Khokhlova!', *ESW 1*, pp. 71–3, and the relationship between theatre and cinema in 'The Two Skulls of Alexander the Great', *ESW 1*, pp. 82–4.
41. *ESW 1*, p. 84.
42. *ESW 1*, p. 93.
43. B. Groys, *The Total Art of Stalinism: Avant-Garde, Aesthetic Dictatorship, and Beyond* (Princeton NJ; 1992).
44. *Zhizn' iskusstva*, 27 September 1927.
45. For detailed analyses of the events of 1928 and their significance, see Taylor, Chapter 6, and D. J. Youngblood, *Soviet Cinema in the Silent Era 1918–1935* (Ann Arbor MI: 1985; Austin TX: 1991), Chapter 7.
46. *ESW 1*, p. 100.
47. *ESW 1*, pp. 107–12.
48. *ESW 1*, pp. 123–6.
49. Some of the elements of such a programme are to be found in the interview entitled 'The GTK Teaching and Research Workshop', *ESW 1*, pp. 127–9. A full teaching programme for direction, devised in 1936 when Eisenstein was already in charge of the Faculty of Direction at what by then had become VGIK, is to be found in *ESW 3*, pp. 74–97.
50. A. Walker, *The Shattered Silents. How the Talkies Came to Stay* (London: 1978).
51. 'An Unexpected Juncture', *ESW 1*, pp. 115–22; this quotation is from p. 116. In a foot-note on the same page he stated: 'It is my firm conviction that cinema is the *contemporary stage* of theatre. Theatre in its old form is dead and, if it exists, it is only through inertia.'
52. *ESW 1*, p. 117.
53. Shklovsky's 'Art as Technique' is translated in L. T. Lemon & J. J. Reis (trans.), *Russian Formalist Criticism. Four Essays* (Lincoln NB: 1965), pp. 3–24.
54. *FF*, pp. 92–3.
55. *ESW 1*, pp. 151–60. The quotation is from p. 158.
56. *ESW 1*, p. 158.
57. Interview with Otar Ioseliani, Paris, August 1983, cited by Bernard Eisenschitz, 'A Fickle Man, or Portrait of Boris Barnet as a Soviet Director', in *IFF*, p. 163.
58. *ESW 2*, pp. 379–99.
59. English translations are available of the first two: H. Marshall (trans.), *Sergei Eisenstein. Nonindifferent Nature* (Cambridge, 1987); and *ESW 2. Direction* [Rezhissura] has still to be published in Russian.
60. *ESW 4*, pp. 283–4, 336–40.

61. The Sorbonne visit is described in: *ESW 4*, pp. 185–96, but there are numerous other references to his time in Paris in that volume. The actual lecture and the question and answer session that followed are reproduced as 'The Principles of the New Russian Cinema' in *ESW 1*, pp. 195–202.
62. It was a view that prevailed in official circles until 1954, although it could be shown to restricted film society audiences, who were deemed to know better.
63. 'Rin-Tin-Tin Does His Tricks for Noted Russian Movie Man', *ESW 1*, pp. 203–5.
64. For E's experiences in Hollywood see Seton (1978), pp. 156–92; Barna, pp. 154–62; Swallow, pp. 83–100; Bergan, pp. 190–215; *ESW 4*, especially pp. 286–9, 328–33. For Mexico the best source is H. M. Geduld & R. Gottesman (eds), *Sergei Eisenstein and Upton Sinclair: The Making and Unmaking of Que Viva Mexico!* (Bloomington IN: 1970), but the sources already mentioned summarise the main events.
65. 'The Dynamic Square', *ESW 1*, pp. 206–18.
66. Shumyatsky's policies are examined in R. Taylor, 'Ideology as Mass Entertainment: Boris Shumyatsky and Soviet Cinema in the 1930s', in *IFF*, pp. 193–216.
67. Seton, pp. 247–8.
68. *ESW 1*, pp. 219–37.
69. In June 1933, in response to an attack on his position by fellow film directors Sergei Bartenev and Mikhail Kalatozov, E had written 'An Attack by Class Allies' in which he stated, 'At this particular stage we need plot. Just as at a different stage we managed without it'; *ESW 1*, pp. 261–75.
70. D. Vertov, 'On My Illness', translated in D. Vertov, *Kino-Eye. The Writings of Dziga Vertov* (ed. A. Michelson and trans. K. O'Brien) (Berkeley CA and London: 1984), pp. 188–95.
71. Taylor, 'Ideology', p. 207; I. Grashchenkova, *Abram Room* (Moscow: 1977), pp. 134–75; E. Margolit & V. Shmyrov, *Iz"iatoe kino)* (Moscow: 1995), pp. 53–6.
72. *FF*, p. 355.
73. Trauberg's speech is translated in *FF*, pp. 348–54.
74. Although Mikhail Chiaureli had directed the first Georgian sound film *The Last Masquerade* the previous year, it is tempting to conclude that he received the Order at this stage in his career for the nationality that he shared with Stalin, rather than for his film output. Or perhaps Stalin was being unusually prescient, because Chiaureli went on to direct the classic Stalin cult films *The Great Dawn* [1938], *The Vow* [1946], *The Fall of Berlin* [1949] and *The Unforgettable Year 1919* [1951]. In 1941 Eisenstein penned an article entitled 'Three Directors' devoted to Mikhail Romm, Chiaureli and Dovzhenko: *Iskusstvo kino*, 1941, no. 5, pp. 32–7. The hagiographical section on Chiaureli (pp. 34–5) was entitled 'The Uniqueness of a Master' and began, 'Above all we love Chiaureli'. It has never been anthologised or translated.
75. His career is the subject of I. Christie and J. Graffy (eds), *Protazanov and the Continuity of Russian Cinema* (London: 1993).
76. Both speeches are in *ESW 3*, pp. 16–17.
77. *ESW 3*, p. 47.
78. Barna, p. 196.
79. Shumyatsky's article is translated in *FF*, pp. 378–81.
80. The account that follows is taken from L. Maksimenkov, *Sumbur vmesto muzyki. Stalinskaia kul'turnaya revolyutsiya 1936–1938* (Moscow: 1997), pp. 241–53.
81. Maksimenkov, p. 244.
82. *FF*, pp. 387–9.
83. K. Rudnitskii, 'Krushenie teatra', in *Meyerkhol'dovskii sbornik. Vypusk pervyi* (Moscow: 1992), vol. 2, pp. 7–29. E's own heavily masked recollection, written in 1944, of this rescue operation is to be found in 'The Treasure', *ESW 4*, pp. 274–8.
84. *ESW 4*, p. 448.
85. *ESW 2*, pp. 379–99. See also *ESW 4*, especially pp. 751–86; Seton (1978), pp. 379–98; Barna, pp. 206–21; Swallow, pp. 122–6; Bergan, pp. 297–306. There are analyses of the film in R. Taylor, *Film Propaganda: Soviet Russia and Nazi Germany* (revised edn, London: 1998), Chapter 8; and Bordwell, pp. 210–23.

86. *ESW 3*, pp. 117–20.
87. N. Cherkasov, *Notes of a Soviet Actor* (Moscow: 1953), p. 103.
88. See 'The Incarnation of Myth', *ESW 3*, pp. 142–69.
89. Bergan, pp. 322–3.
90. Bergan, p. 317, despite citing the English historian Alexander Werth as the source, gives the Eisenstein papers in TsGALI as the reference.
91. See the account by Naum Kleiman, 'The History of Eisenstein's Memoirs', in *ESW 4*, pp. xi–xxi.
92. L. Kozlov, 'The Artist and the Shadow of Ivan', in R. Taylor and D. Spring (eds), *Stalinism and Soviet Cinema* (London and New York: 1993), pp. 109–30.
93. *ESW 3*, p. 297.
94. Kozlov, citing an interview between himself and Mikhail Bleiman, p. 129.
95. Kozlov, p. 129.
96. Quoted in R. Yurenev, 'Ya byl svetil'nikom', in *idem* (ed.), *Eizenshtein v vospominaniyakh sovremennikov* (Moscow, 1974), p. 283; partly cited in Kozlov, p. 129.
97. V. Yerenkov, 'Think the Unthinkable about the Unsinkable', *The Independent*, 9 January 1998.

Notes to 1923

1. Source: S. M. Eizenshtein, `Montazh attraktsionov', *Lef*, 1923, no. 3 (June/July), pp. 70–1, 74–5.
2. *Enough Simplicity for Every Wise Man* [*Na vsyakogo mudretsa dovol'no prostoty*], the comedy by Alexander N. Ostrovsky (1823–86), was re-worked by Sergei M. Tretyakov (1892–1939) for Proletkult in 1923.
3. Proletkult, the Proletarian Culture organisation, aimed to produce a specifically proletarian culture for post-Revolutionary Soviet audiences. The organisation's ideas were seen by Lenin and others as a challenge to the authority of the Party. E clearly also regarded the Proletkult's ideas as extreme: he left the organisation after a dispute over the authorship of the script for *The Strike* in the winter of 1924/5.
4. *The Dawns of Proletkult* [*Zori Proletkul'ta*] was a stage performance based on the works of various proletarian poets. It was staged as a response to the 1920 version by Vsevolod E. Meyerhold (1874–1940) of *The Dawns* [*Les Aubes*] by the Belgian dramatist Emile Verhaeren (1855–1916): see *ESW 4*, pp. 265–6, 832.
5. *Lena* was a play by Valerian F. Pletnyov (1886–1942), based on the events in the Lena goldfield in Siberia in 1912 and staged at the Moscow Proletkult Theatre in October 1921. When E and Proletkult parted company he and Pletnyov indulged in a vitriolic exchange of letters, translated by N. Lary in J. Leyda (ed.), *Eisenstein 2. A Premature Celebration of Eisenstein's Centenary* (Calcutta: Seagull Books, 1985), pp. 1–8.
6. Boris I. Arvatov (1896–1940), art critic, was a member of Proletkult and later also of LEF.
7. *The Mexican* [*Meksikanets*], a stage version of the story by the American author Jack London (1876–1916), was E's first theatrical production (with Smyshlyayev) in January–March 1921. E also designed the sets and costumes. See: *ESW 4*, p. 412.
8. Valentin S. Smyshlyayev (1891–1936), originally an actor and director with the Moscow Art Theatre, worked in the 1920s as a director with Proletkult. The work referred to later in this paragraph is properly entitled *Tekhnika obrabotki stsenicheskogo zrelishcha* [The Technique of Treatment for a Stage Show] and was published in booklet form in 1922.
9. Pletnyov's *On the Abyss* [*Nad obryvom*] was produced by Proletkult in 1922.
10. Alexander A. Ostuzhev (1874–1953) was a Russian classical actor.
11. Charles Dickens's *The Cricket on the Hearth* was produced at the Moscow Art Theatre in 1915.
12. During E's production of Sergei Tretyakov's *Can You Hear Me, Moscow?* [*Slyshish', Moskva?*] squibs were let off under the seats in the auditorium.

13. Georg Grosz (1893–1959), the leading German satirical draughtsman of the 20th century, known especially for his bitter satires on the bourgeoisie of Weimar Germany.
14. Alexander M. Rodchenko (1891–1956), Constructivist artist and photographer and one of the founders of photo-montage.
15. The Russian word *montazher* is now principally used to mean ʽeditor' but at that time could also indicate ʽproducer' or ʽdirector'.
16. The Russian word *ekstsentrik* means initially ʽclown' but was adopted by the Petrograd-based Factory of the Eccentric Actor (FEKS), led by Grigori M. Kozintsev (1905–73), Leonid Z. Trauberg (1901–90) and Sergei I. Yutkevich (1904–85), whose self-proclaimed models in both theatre and cinema included circus and music-hall techniques and American cinema.
17. A Georgian chant, using the name of a Christian monastery, the pun being in the sound ʽAllah'.
18. The New Economic Policy (NEP), introduced by Lenin at the end of the Civil War in spring 1921, marked a limited return to private enterprise and was designed to restore the Soviet economy to 1913 levels. The ʽNepman' and ʽNepwoman', the *nouveaux riches* who emerged in the following years, were a constant object of satire, as for instance in the works of the poet and playwright Vladimir V. Mayakovsky (1893–1930).
19. E's first film, the short *Glumov's Diary* [*Dnevnik Glumova*] was made for part of this production.
20. Alexander N. Vertinsky (1889–1957) was a popular singer of ʽcruel' romances and film actor who emigrated in 1919 but returned in 1943.
21. The *lezginka* is a Caucasian dance.

Notes to 1924

1. Source: 'Montazh kinoattraktsionov', a typescript dated October 1924 held in the Eisenstein archive, RGALI, Moscow, and first published in this form in English in *ESW 1*, pp. 39–58. A distorted version of this article was first published in Russian by Alexander Belenson under his own name in his *Kino segodnya. Ocherki sovetskogo kinoiskusstva (Kuleshov – Vertov – Eizenshtein)* [Cinema Today. Essays on Soviet Cinema (Kuleshov – Vertov – Eisenstein)] (Moscow, 1925). In this and subsequent documents E is somewhat inconsistent in his use of the Russian equivalents of 'effect' and 'affect'. The Editor was initially tempted to improve on the original by making the English translation more systematic but ultimately felt it fairer to both E and the reader to reproduce E's inconsistencies. Both *vozdeistvie* and *effekt* are therefore translated as 'effect', *deistvennost'* as 'effectiveness' (although 'effectivity' could sometimes be an alternative), and *vozdeistvuyushchii* as 'effective', while *affekt* and *affektivnyi* are rendered as 'affect' and 'affective' respectively. The reader should however constantly bear in mind the possibility of the alternative meaning. Similarly *sopostavlenie* has, according to the context, been translated as either 'comparison' or 'juxtaposition' but retains both meanings in Russian.
2. The Cine-Eyes (plural: *Kinoki*, singular: *Kinoglaz*) were the documentary film-makers grouped around Dziga Vertov (pseudonym of Denis A. Kaufman, 1896–1954). The group published two major, and numerous minor, attacks on fiction film and on the concept of 'art' as a manifestation of bourgeois culture to be torn down 'like the Tower of Babel': 'We. A Version of a Manifesto' (1922) and 'The Cine-Eyes. A Revolution' (1923), which appeared in the same issue of *Lef* as E's 'The Montage of Attractions'. Both articles are translated in *FF*, pp. 69–72 and 89–94; and in: A. Michelson (ed.), *Kino-Eye. The Writings of Dziga Vertov* (trans. K. O'Brien), (Berkeley CA, 1984 & London: University of California Press, 1985), pp. 5–9, 11–21.
3. See 'The Montage of Attractions'.
4. *Cine-Pravda* [*Kinopravda*] meaning 'Cine-Truth' and pointing the analogy with the name of the Communist Party newspaper *Pravda*, was the name of the newsreel produced by the Cine-Eye group in twenty-three issues between June 1922 and 1925.
5. See 1923, n. 12.

6. *Alogizm*: a neologism coined by E to denote an action or event that had no logical explanation in its particular context.

7. *The Extraordinary Adventures of Mr West in the Land of the Bolsheviks* [*Neobychainye priklyucheniya Mistera vesta v strane bol'shevikov*, USSR, 1924] was directed by Lev V. Kuleshov (1899–1970) and satirised Western stereotypes of the Bolsheviks. It was Kuleshov who first developed the notion of montage as the essence of cinema specificity. See *FF*, pp. 41–6.

8. *Intolerance* [USA, 1916] was made by D. W. Griffith (1875–1948).

9. *The Palace and the Fortress* [*Dvorets i krepost'*, USSR, 1923] was directed by Alexander V. Ivanovsky (1881–1968).

10. *Andrei Kozhukhov* [Russia, 1917] was directed by Yakov A. Protazanov (1881–1945) after the February Revolution and starred Ivan I. Mozzhukhin (also Mosjoukine, 1890–1939) as the revolutionary Populist hero. It was still in distribution in 1924. *Stepan Khalturin* [USSR, 1925] was made by Alexander Ivanovsky.

11. See 'The Montage of Attractions'.

12. Reference to the play *Nathan der Weise* by the German dramatist Gottfried Ephraim Lessing (1729–81). E returned to the subject of Lessing in *ESW 2*, pp. 153–62, 167–8.

13. *Naturshchik*: a 'model' or 'mannequin', the word used by E, Kuleshov and others to denote an actor trained to function as a mere tool of the director and who expressed his emotions through specific physical actions.

14. See 1923, n. 3

15. See 1923, n. 12.

16. Reference to Guillaume-Benjamin-Arnand Duchenne, called Duchenne de Boulogne (1806–75), the first edition of whose *Physiologie des mouvements démontrée à l'aide de l'expérimentation électrique et de l'observation clinique* [Physiology of Movements Demonstrated with the Aid of Electrical Experimentation and Clinical Observation] was published in Paris in 1867. I can find no trace of an 1885 edition. The work was translated into English as *Physiology of Motion* (ed. and trans. E. B. Kaplan) (Philadelphia, PA: 1949).

17. Literally: 'Isolated muscular action does not exist in nature.'

18. The original text has 'two' but this is clearly a mistake.

19. H. Nothnagel, *Topische Diagnostik der Gehirnkrankheiten* [The External Diagnosis of Brain Diseases] (Berlin: 1879).

20. In German in the original: the English translation is 'thalamus', where the optical nerve ends originate.

21. Sergei Tretyakov's *Gas Masks* [*Protivogazy*] was produced by E for the Proletkult theatre in 1923 at the Moscow gas plant.

22. Roscoe ('Fatty') Arbuckle (1887–1933) was one of the leading stars of early Hollywood slapstick comedies.

23. Russian: *prozodezhda*, a term frequently used by the Constructivists.

Notes to 1925

1. Source: 'K voprosu o materialisticheskom podkhode k forme', *Kinozhurnal ARK*, 1925, no. 4/5 (April/May), pp. 5–8.

2. The implication here is that the past has prepared the present like a factory process.

3. *The Strike* was originally intended as one episode in this larger cycle.

4. *Massovost'* meaning 'mass quality' or 'mass character', by analogy with *klassovost'* meaning 'class quality' or 'class character' and *partiinost'* or 'Partyness', all three elements officially required of Soviet art.

5. E is referring here to earlier debates about whether cinema could be considered an autonomous art form in its own right or whether it was more properly regarded as an adjunct of another art form, such as literature, painting or, particularly, theatre.

6. The reference is to *Novyi zritel'*, 1925, no. 5. For Pletnyov, see 1923, n. 5.

7. Mikhail Ye. Koltsov (né Fridland, 1898–1942), the journalist who was later to become

editor of *Ogonyok* and *Krokodil*, reviewed *The Strike* ('Stachka', *Pravda*, 14 March 1925, p. 8), describing it as 'the first revolutionary work that our screen has produced', but in the film journals it was criticised, among other things, for a 'discrepancy between ideology and form'.

8. See 1924, n. 2.

9. See 1924, n. 4.

10. *Cine-Eye* [*Kinoglaz*], a six-reel 'exploration of "life caught unawares"', directed by Vertov, was released on 13 October 1924.

11. Khrisanf N. Khersonsky (1897–1968), critic and scriptwriter, wrote a hostile review of *The Strike* and participated with E, Pletnyov, Abram M. Room (1894–1976) and others in a discussion of the film at the headquarters of the Association of Revolutionary Film-makers (ARK, later ARRK) in Moscow on 19 March 1925.

12. The Association of Artists of Revolutionary Russia (AKhRR), formed in 1922, consisted of artists who adhered to the traditions of nineteenth-century social realism exemplified by the Wanderers [*Peredvizhniki*], one of whose leading members was Ilya Ye. Repin (1844–1930): see *ESW 2*, pp. 93–105.

13. See 1924, n. 6.

14. *Cine-Pravda* no. 19, released in May 1924, was variously subtitled 'A Trip with a Movie Camera from Moscow to the Arctic Ocean' and 'On the Train Summer and Winter'.

Notes to 1926

1. Source: 'Konstantsa. (Kuda ukhodit *Bronenosets Potemkin*)', dated 1926 and first published in: N. I. Kleiman and K. B. Levina (eds), *Bronenosets Potemkin* (Moscow: 1968), pp. 290–2.

2. *The Thief of Bagdad* [USA, 1924], starred Douglas Fairbanks.

3. *The Station Master* [*Kollezhskii registrator*, USSR, 1926], directed by Yuri A. Zhelyabuzhskii (1888–1955), was based on a story by Alexander S. Pushkin (1799–1837).

4. *Subbotnik*, derived from the Russian word *subbota* meaning Saturday, was an unpaid extra day of labour for the state introduced originally to help rebuild the Soviet economy but maintained until the demise of the Soviet system in 1991.

5. Muir and Merrilees was an exclusive foreign-owned department store in Moscow before the Revolution, somewhat similar in style to Harrods in London. The site has more recently been occupied by the state-owned TsUM store.

6. E had studied the works of Vladimir M. Bekhterev (1857–1927), in particular *Ob obshchikh osnovakh refleksologii kak nauchnoi distsipliny* [The General Principles of Reflexology as a Scientific Discipline], 1917, and *Kollektivnaya refleksologiya* [Collective Reflexology], 1921.

7. Harold Lloyd (1893–1971), American film comedian, whose best-known films at that time were *Grandma's Boy* [USA, 1922] and *The Freshman* [USA, 1925].

8. Sergei Tretyakov's play *I Want a Child* [*Khochu rebenka*] was accepted by Meyerhold for a production with sets by El Lissitzky but for censorship reasons it was never produced.

9. Source: 'Sergej Eisenstein über Sergej Eisenstein, den *Potemkin*-Regisseur', *Berliner Tageblatt*, 7 June 1926. The interview was conducted at the beginning of that month during E's second visit to Berlin. Translated by Leyda and included as 'A Personal Statement' in *Film Essays*, pp. 13–17.

10. See 1923, nn. 3 and 4.

11. For Meyerhold, see 1923, n. 4; for Mayakovsky, 1923, n. 18.

12. Konstantin S. Stanislavsky (1863–1938) was co-founder in 1898 of the Moscow Art Theatre and the leading exponent of both the theory and practice of psychological realism and naturalism on stage: see also *ESW 2*, pp. 138–46. Alexander Ya. Tairov (1885–1950) founded the Moscow Kamerny [Chamber] Theatre in 1914. It stood for an Expressionist style of production and acting as opposed to the naturalism of Stanislavsky's theatre.

13. This error was made by the *Frankfurter Zeitung* and later repeated by the American press.
14. See 1923, n. 2.
15. See 1923, n. 12.
16. See 1924, n. 21.
17. The 'happy ending' [Russian: *kheppi-end*] became a shorthand way of criticising the faults of Hollywood in general.
18. Antaeos was a figure in Greek mythology who derived his strength from his contact with the earth.
19. *Faust* [Germany, 1926] was directed by F. W. Murnau and starred Emil Jannings. E and Eduard K. Tisse (1897–1961), who was the cameraman for all E's Soviet films from *The Strike* to *Ivan the Terrible*, became acquainted with both men during the shooting of the film in Germany in the spring of 1926. *Metropolis* [Germany, 1926] was directed by Fritz Lang: again E and Tisse visited the studio during the shooting.
20. The paragraph in square brackets did not appear in the published version.
21. Source: 'O pozitsii Bela Balasha', *Kino*, 20 July 1926, and 'Bela zabyvaet nozhnitsy', *Kino*, 10 August 1926. This article is a polemical response to the Russian publication of an article by the Hungarian author, scriptwriter and film theorist, Béla Balázs (1884–1949): 'O budushchem fil'my' [On the Future of Film], *Kino*, 6 July 1926, translated in *FF*, pp. 144–5. This article, an extract from a lecture delivered by Balázs to the German Cameramen's Club, first appeared in German as 'Filmtradition und Filmzukunft' [The Tradition of Film and the Future of Film], *Filmtechnik*, 12 June 1926.
22. This is E's paraphrase of Balázs's statement: 'As long as the cameraman comes last, cinema will be the last art. The sentence ought to be turned on its head.'
23. Ilya G. Ehrenburg (1891–1969) lived in Paris from 1908 to 1917 and again from 1921 to 1923.
24. Francis Picabia (1897–1949), one of the founders of the Dada movement, wrote the script for *Entr'acte* [France, 1924], directed by René Clair (né René Chomette, 1898–1981). The painter Fernand Léger (1881–1955) made the experimental short film *Le Ballet mécanique* in 1924. Henri Chomette (1896–1941), elder brother of René, made a number of abstract films including *Jeux des reflets et de la vitesse* [Play of Reflections and Speed, France, 1923] and *Cinque minutes de cinéma pur* [Five Minutes of Pure Cinema, France, 1925].
25. Novokhopyorsk is a district on the Khopyor River south-east of Voronezh.
26. Three mythical firebirds from Russian folklore.
27. *Filmtechnik* was not in fact the official organ of the club, but represented its interests. The co-editor was Guido Seeber, whose book *Der Trickfilm* (Berlin: 1927) was translated into Russian as *Tekhnika kinotryuka* [The Technique of the Film Stunt] (Moscow: 1929), for which E wrote the preface. *Variété* [Germany, 1925], set in a circus, was directed by E. A. Dupont and starred Emil Jannings.
28. Prometheus-Film was founded in December 1925 by three prominent members of the German Communist Party (KPD), including Willi Münzenberg, to market Soviet films in Germany and finance German–Soviet co-productions.
29. For Tisse, see 1926, n. 19.
30. UFA was the largest film production company in Germany in the 1920s: see: K. Kreimeier, *The Ufa Story. A History of Germany's Greatest Film Company, 1918–1945* (New York: Hill & Wang, 1996).
31. Günther Rittau (1893–1971) was joint cameraman on *The Nibelungs* [Germany, 1924] and *Metropolis*, both directed by Fritz Lang.
32. UFA was taken over in 1927 by Alfred Hugenberg, press baron, leader of the nationalist DNVP and strong supporter of Hitler. After the Nazis came to power in January 1933 UFA formed the backbone of Goebbels' propaganda effort in feature films.
33. The somewhat obscure implication of this statement is that the German censors should not have tried to ban the film as their ban was not only unnecessary but counterproductive.

34. Another neologism by E, this time derived from the English word 'star'. In the 1920s E worked largely without professional actors. Balázs, by contrast, insisted on the importance of great actors: see 'Nur Stars' [Only Stars], *Filmtechnik*, 1926, no. 7, p. 126.

35. The 'iron five' [*zheleznaya pyaterka*] were E's assistants: Grigori V. Alexandrov, (né Mormonenko, 1903–84), Maxim M. Strauch (also Shtraukh, 1900–74), Mikhail Gomorov, Alexander Levshin and Alexander P. Antonov (1898–1962), who wore striped sailors' shirts during the filming of *Potemkin* in Odessa. See H. Marshall (ed.), *The Battleship Potemkin* (New York: Avon Books, 1978), pp. 63–7.

36. See 1924, n. 1.

37. Quotation from Isaak Babel's 'The Death of Dolgushov', one of his *Red Cavalry* stories: I. Babel, *Collected Stories* (Harmondsworth: Penguin, 1961), p. 76. One of E's unrealised projects was a filmed version of some of these stories.

38. E analyses this sequence in 'Eh! On the Purity of Film Language', see below, pp. 128–31.

39. This phrase was used at that time by LEF and others to denote straightforward montage that clarified rather than obscured the meaning.

40. Valerian V. Osinsky (1887–1938), journalist, diplomat, Party functionary and one of the leading organisers of the October Revolution.

41. *The Ten Commandments* [USA, 1923] was directed by Cecil B. DeMille.

Notes to 1928

1. Source: 'Nash "Oktyabr". Po tu storonu igrovoi i neigrovoi', *Kino*, 13 and 20 March 1928. The original manuscript is dated 8 March 1928.

2. *Broken Blossoms* [USA, 1919] was directed by D. W. Griffith and starred Lillian Gish.

3. *Zaum* is usually translated as 'trans-sense', denoting the idea of a suprarational force.

4. *Kamernost'*: 'chamber quality', as opposed to the monumentally epic.

5. Both directed by Vsevolod I. Pudovkin (1893–1953) in 1926 and 1927 respectively.

6. *A Sixth Part of the World* [*Shestaya chast' mira*, USSR, 1926] was a feature-length documentary directed by Dziga Vertov.

7. *The Eleventh Year* [*Odinnadsatyi*, USSR, 1928], also directed by Vertov.

8. *The Diplomatic Bag* [*Sumka dipkur'era*, USSR, 1927] and *Zvenigora* [USSR, 1928] were both directed by the Ukrainian film-maker Alexander P. Dovzhenko (1894–1956).

9. A quotation from Griboyedov's play *Woe from Wit* [*Gore ot uma*].

10. See 1926, n. 27.

11. Runich and Khudoleyev were both actors in pre-Revolutionary Russian films.

12. Lavr G. Kornilov (1870–1918) was one of the leading generals on the White side during the Civil War of 1918–21.

13. Alexei V. Efimov was a Soviet historian.

14. This manifesto was first published in an authorised German translation as: 'Achtung! Goldgrube! Gedanken über die Zukunft des Hörfilms' [Watch Out! Goldmine! Thoughts on the Future of Sound Film] in *Lichtbildbühne* on 28 July 1928. The Russian original was first published as 'Zayavka' [A Demand] in *Zhizn' iskusstva*, 5 August 1928, pp. 6–9, from which this has been translated, and *Sovetskii ekran* on 7 August 1928. An English translation appeared under the title 'The Sound Film. A Statement from USSR' in *Close Up*, October 1928, pp. 10–13. Jay Leyda included his own version as 'A Statement' in *Film Form*, pp. 257–9. Alexandrov (see 1926, n. 35) was E's chief assistant from *The Strike* to the unfinished Mexican film and later became the leading exponent of the Soviet musical comedy genre. For Pudovkin, see 1928, n. 5.

Notes to 1929

1. Source: 'Za kadrom', written as a postscript to N. Kaufman, *Yaponskoe kino* [Japanese Cinema] (Moscow: 1929), pp. 72–92. Translated by Leyda as 'The Cinematographic Principle and the Ideogram' in *Film Form*, pp. 28–44.

2. Throughout this piece E uses the Russian *ieroglif* [hieroglyph] rather than *ideogramma* [ideogram].

3. Also known as *haiku*. Historically the *haiku* was the first line of a *tanka*, literally a 'short song'.

4. Toshushai Haraku, Japanese Noh actor and painter, produced 140 pictures of Kabuki (the popular offshoot of Noh) actors between May 1794 and February 1795. Little is known of him apart from this, except that he died in 1801.

5. Alexander R. Luria (1902–77) was a noted Russian psychologist and pioneer of modern neuropsychology, whose best-known works include *The Nature of Human Conflicts* and *The Mind of a Mnemonist*.

6. Quotation from 'Little Bricks' [*Kirpichiki*], a popular Russian song of the 1920s.

7. Kuleshov's theory of montage is expounded at length in his book *Iskusstvo kino* [The Art of Cinema] (Moscow: 1929). This extract is from p. 100. See also R. Levaco (ed. and trans.), *Kuleshov on Film. Writings by Lev Kuleshov* (Berkeley CA: University of California Press, 1974), pp. 41–123.

8. *The Happy Canary* [*Veselaya kanareika*, USSR, 1929] was directed by Kuleshov.

9. The Tretyakov Gallery is Moscow's principal museum of Russian art. The collection, assembled by Sergei Shchukin before 1917, became the First Museum of Modern Western Painting after the Revolution. In 1923 it was merged with the Second Museum of Modern Western Painting, based on the collection of the Morozov brothers, housed in the Morozov mansion and called the Shchukin State Museum of Modern Western Art. In 1948 the museum was closed and the collections shared between the Hermitage in Leningrad and the Pushkin Gallery in Moscow.

10. A magician was then performing at the Moscow Hermitage music-hall under the name of Dante.

11. The 'black men' in Kabuki theatre serve as prompters and stage-hands and derive their name, and their invisibility, from their black clothes.

12. *Narukami*, one of the most popular plays in the Kabuki repertoire, was written by Suuti Hantsuro. Itakawa Sadanji (1880–1940), director, actor and playwright, visited Moscow in 1928 with the Kabuki theatre.

13. I.e. *The General Line*.

14. *The Forty-Seven Samurai* is one of the most popular plays in the Kabuki repertoire, written in 1748 by Takedo Idsumo and performed during the 1928 visit to Moscow. The play was also the basis for the Mizoguchi film *The Loyal Forty-Seven Ronin* [Japan, 1941–2].

15. *The Thief of Bagdad* [USA, 1924] starred Douglas Fairbanks. *Zvenigora* [USSR, 1928] was directed by Alexander Dovzhenko.

16. *The Man with the Movie Camera* [*Chelovek s kinoapparatom*, USSR, 1929] was directed by Dziga Vertov.

17. *The Fall of the House of Usher* [*La Chute de la maison Usher*, France, 1928] was made by the Polish-born French director and theorist, Jean Epstein (1897–1953). Henri Langlois described the film as 'the cinematic equivalent of a Debussy creation'.

18. The reference is to 'An Unexpected Juncture', *ESW 1*, pp. 115–22.

19. This piece, written by E in German, exists in two typescripts, one dated Moscow, 29 April 1929 and the other dated Zurich, 29 November 1929. Leyda translated it as 'A Dialectic Approach to Film Form' (a change of title approved by E) in *Film Form*, pp. 45–63. It was also published in *Close Up*, September 1929. This translation has been made from H.–J. Schlegel (ed.), *Sergej M. Eisenstein. Schriften 3* (Munich: Carl Hanser, 1975) pp. 200–25, with some alterations established by François Albera, to whom I am extremely grateful.

20. Kazimir S. Malevich (1887–1935), Russian painter and founder of Suprematism. In an unpublished diary entry for 1929 E described Malevich's Suprematism as 'a mixture of mysticism and mystification'. Wilhelm von Kaulbach (1805–74), German painter and graphic artist, known for his neo-classical monumental paintings; court painter to King Ludwig I of Bavaria from 1837. Alexander Archipenko (also Arkhipenko, 1887–1964), Ukrainian-born American sculptor associated with Cubism and the revival of polychromy.

21. The following line was deleted by E from the original typescript at this point: 'The temporal form of this tension (the phases of tension) is rhythm.'

22. Ludwig Klages (1872–1956), German philosopher and founder of biocentric metaphysics, developed a methodology for a 'science of expression'. His major work, *Der Geist als Widersacher der Seele* [The Spirit as Antagonist to the Soul] was published in three volumes between 1929 and 1932.

23. G. Wallas, *The Great Society. A Psychological Analysis* (London: 1914), p. 101.

24. Here E is drawing on the ideas of the Formalist school of literary criticism and, above all, on Yu. Tynyanov, *Problema stikhotvornogo yazyka* [The Problem of Poetic Language] (Leningrad: 1924).

25. J. W. von Goethe, *Conversations of Goethe with Eckermann* (London: 1930), p. 303. The conversation took place on 23 March 1829: 'I have found a paper of mine among other things,' said Goethe today, 'in which I call architecture "petrified music".' A similar metaphor is employed by Schelling in his *Philosophie der Kunst* [The Philosophy of Art], where he refers to architecture as 'frozen music'.

26. Deleted from the original typescript at this point: 'just as we lay (unwrap) bricks'.

27. For Léger, see 1926, n. 24. For Suprematism, see 1929, n. 20.

28. Honoré Daumier (1808–79), French caricaturist and lithographer, known for his bitter social and political satire. Henri de Toulouse-Lautrec (1864–1901), French painter and graphic artist. 'Cissy Loftus', dating from 1894, depicts an eighteen-year-old Glasgow-born singer, Marie-Cecilia McCarthy, who played male parts on stage: see J. Adhémar, *Toulouse-Lautrec. His Complete Lithographs and Drypoints* (London: 1965), pl. 105.

29. This painting is by the Italian Giacomo Balla (1871–1958) who was closely associated with Italian Futurism.

30. See 1929, n. 4.

31. Cf. caption to Fig. 9.2 above.

32. A page of the original typescript is missing at this point.

33. *The Living Corpse* [*Zhivoi trup*, USSR/Germany, 1929] was a co-production based on the eponymous drama by Lev Tolstoy and directed by Fyodor A. Otsep (1895–1949).

34. I.e. *Lev Tolstoy and the Russia of Nicholas II* [*Rossiya Nikolaya II i Lev Tolstoi*, USSR, 1928].

35. *The Bay of Death* [*Bukhta smerti*, USSR, 1929].

36. In French in the original: literally, 'Let us return to our sheep' and metaphorically 'Let us get back to the point'. An old French catchphrase, used by Rabelais, from whom E probably took it.

37. A remark attributed to Lenin by the Commissar for Popular Enlightenment from 1917 to 1929, Anatoli V. Lunacharsky (1875–1933), translated in *FF*, pp. 56–7.

38. Only the first part of this essay, written in Moscow in August and September 1929, was published in Russian in E's lifetime as 'Kino chetyrekh izmerenii' [Four-Dimensional Cinema], *Kino*, 27 August 1929. This appeared in English as 'The Fourth Dimension in the Kino', *Close Up*, March 1930. The second part of the essay, written in London in November and December 1929, appeared for the first time in English as 'The Fourth Dimension in the Kino: II', *Close Up*, April 1930. Jay Leyda re-translated both as 'The Filmic Fourth Dimension' and 'Methods of Montage' respectively in *Film Form*, pp. 64–71 and 72–83. The complete piece was published in Russian for the first time only in 1964 in *IP*, vol. 2, pp. 45–59 as 'Chetvertoe izmerenie v kino' [The Fourth Dimension in Cinema], which is the title given to the present translation.

39. See *ESW 1*, p. 117.

40. The Russian word here is *kuski*, plural of *kusok*, which may also be translated as a 'fragment', 'piece' or 'strip'.

41. In English in the original.

42. E is using 'Left' here to denote avant-garde composers generally. Claude Debussy (1862–1918) was a French composer; Alexander N. Scriabin (also Skryabin, 1871–1915) was a Russian pianist and composer who tried to develop audio-visual techniques.

43. A. Einstein, *Relativity: The Special and the General Theory* (London: 1920), p. 65, the

opening sentence of Ch. XVII, 'Minkowski's Four-Dimensional Space'. This quotation does not appear in the published Russian text of this document.

44. See *ESW 1*, p. 119.
45. W. Stekel was a German psychologist and psychoanalyst of the Freudian school. See also *ESW 4*, p. 104. E's quotation is presumably from *Nervöse Angstzustände und ihre Behandlung* [Nervous Anxiety States and Their Treatment] (3rd edn, Berlin/Vienna: 1921).
46. See 1923, n. 21.
47. *Storm over Asia* was the overseas release title given to Vsevolod Pudovkin's film *Potomok Chingis-khana*, literally *The Heir to Genghis-Khan* [USSR, 1929].
48. In English in the original.
49. A play on words between the Russian *tok*, meaning a 'stream' and *potok*, meaning a 'current'.
50. See 1929, n. 20.
51. The quotation is from Lenin's 'Conspectus of Hegel's *Science of Logic*' and appears to be a paraphrase of the section reproduced in *Collected Works*, vol. 38 (Moscow: 1961), p. 132.
52. E is making a cross-reference here to 'Perspectives', *ESW 1*, pp. 151–60.

Notes to 1934

1. Source: ' "E!" O chistote kinoyazyka', *Sovetskoe kino*, 1934, no. 5 (May), pp. 25–31. Translated by Jay Leyda as 'Film Language' in *Film Form*, pp. 108–21. The article is a response to Gorky's observations 'O yazyke' [On Language], *Pravda*, 18 March 1934.
2. A reference to the behaviour of the characters Bobchinsky and Dobchinsky in Gogol's play *The Government Inspector*.
3. A jocular reference to acetone, which smells of pears and was used to splice film together in the early stages of editing at that time.
4. The administrative and political head of Soviet cinema from October 1930 until his dismissal and arrest in January 1938 and summary execution six months later, Boris Z. Shumyatsky (1886–1938), enjoined Soviet film-makers to 'master the classics', partly in order to overcome the shortage of acceptable scripts on contemporary themes.
5. The tail here referred to being that of theatre. 'Tailism' derives from the political debates in the late 1890s between Lenin and the so-called 'Economists' about the proper future path for Russian Social Democracy.
6. Anna K. Tarasova (1898–1973), Moscow Art Theatre actress who was to play leading roles in *The Storm* [*Groza*, USSR, 1934] and *Peter the First* [*Petr Pervyi*, USSR, 1937–9], both directed by Vladimir M. Petrov (1896–1966).
7. Omitted from the published version.
8. The Russian word here is *kinopis'mo*, which literally means 'cinema letter'.
9. Andrei Bely [né Boris N. Bugayev, 1880–1934], Russian writer and, in the pre-Revolutionary period, one of the leading figures in Russian Symbolism. Best known abroad for his novel *Petersburg*, he published an analytical study of *Gogol's Mastery* shortly before his death. See *ESW 2*, pp. 354–5; *ESW 4*, pp. 638–46. In 1933 E chaired a lecture given by Bely at the Polytechnic Museum in Moscow.
10. *Ivan* [USSR, 1932] was directed by Alexander Dovzhenko: see 1928, n. 8.
11. E. Zola, *Germinal* (Harmondsworth: Penguin, 1954), p. 353.
12. Théroigne de Méricourt (1762–1817) was a participant in the French Revolution. On 31 May 1793, after she had delivered a speech defending the Girondists, she was attacked by a group of Jacobin women and birched: she then went mad.
13. Marie-Thérèse-Louise de Lamballe (1755–92) was imprisoned with Marie-Antoinette, murdered and disembowelled. The quotation is from: S. Mercier, *Paris pendant la Révolution* ... (Paris: 1862), vol. 1, p. 88.
14. Germinal was the name given to the seventh month of the French Revolutionary calendar, covering the period from 21 March to 19 April.

15. By analogy with *mise-en-scène*.
16. The *commedia dell'arte* was a form of popular Italian comedy that reached its height in the 16th and 17th centuries. It was performed by specially trained troupes of actors who improvised on standard synopses involving a group of formalised and familiar characters (such as Harlequin, Columbine, Pierrot and Pulcinella) and a series of stock situations.
17. The German *Vorschlag* denotes musical 'forestroke', an auxiliary note that anticipates and merges in performance with the principal note.
18. Popular Russian writers at the end of the 19th century.

Notes to 1937

1. Source: 'Oshibki "Bezhina luga"' [The Mistakes of *Bezhin Meadow*], in the booklet *O fil'me 'Bezhin lug' S. Eizenshteina* [On S. Eisenstein's Film *Bezhin Meadow*] (Moscow: 1937), pp. 53–63, which was also reproduced, minus the references to Stalin, in *IS*, pp. 383–8. A slightly different version was published in *Sovetskoe iskusstvo*, no. 18, 17 April 1937, p. 3. This translation is from the booklet. The filming of *Bezhin Meadow* had been stopped on 17 March 1937 on official orders.
2. Here E uses the word 'tipichnost''. For 'tipazh', the idea developed by E in the 1920s, see *ESW 1*, pp. 198, 200–1.
3. GUK [Gosudarstvennoe upravlenie kinofotopromyshlennosti], the State Directorate for the Cinema and Photographic Industry, was the state body responsible for all aspects of Soviet cinema. It was headed until January 1938 by Boris Z. Shumyatsky: see his piece on *Bezhin Meadow*, 'O fil'me *Bezhin lug*' [The Film *Bezhin Meadow*], *Pravda*, 19 March 1937 (two days after filming was stopped), translated in *FF*, pp. 378–81. Mosfilm was the Moscow film studio for which E directed both *Alexander Nevsky* and *Ivan the Terrible*.
4. *ESW 3*, p. 366 n. 1.
5. The Central Committee meeting of 23 February to 5 March 1937 launched the period of the purges and show trials known as the 'Yezhovshchina' after the People's Commissar for Internal Affairs and General Commissar for State Security, Nikolai I. Yezhov (1895–1939). While the Committee was in session, two of the principal surviving Old Bolsheviks, Nikolai I. Bukharin (1888–1938) and Alexei I. Rykov (1881–1938), were arrested for 'anti–Soviet rightist Trotskyite' activity. They were tried and shot in March 1938. The Committee meeting listened to a lengthy denunciation by Stalin of 'spies and wreckers' in industry, the administration and the Party, which served as the spur for the 'Yezhovshchina'. Seventy per cent of those attending the meeting were subsequently arrested and shot, most of them within the following eighteen months. In June 1937 Marshal Tukhachevsky and a group of the highest generals in the Red Army were secretly tried for treason and shot. The process of 'criticism, self-criticism, examination and self-examination' was supposed to flush out remnants of the spies, saboteurs, wreckers and other alleged 'enemies of the people'.

Notes to 1938

1. Source: 'Aleksandr Nevskii i razgrom nemtsev', *Izvestiya*, 12 July 1938.
2. The Tatars' domination of Russia began with the establishment of Mongol rule under Genghis Khan over most of the country in 1219–25 and the Battle of Kalka in 1223 was the crucial turning-point, but the thin layer of the ruling class could not at that time effectively subjugate the Russians. The Golden Horde began that subjugation in 1236 under Genghis Khan's grandson, Batu, and their victories led to Russia's exploitation, cultural decay and isolation from the rest of Europe, lasting for over two centuries until the liberation of Moscow from Tatar rule by Ivan III in 1480 (although the decline in Mongol influence can be dated to their defeat at the Battle of Kulikovo Field in 1380). The Mongols defeated an army of German and Polish knights at the Battle of Liegnitz (now Legnica) in 1241 but drew back from Europe

partly to take part in the selection of a successor to Khan Ogedei, who had just died. On their way back to Russia the Mongol armies were savaged at the Battle of Olmütz (now Olomouc). Wenceslas [Vaclav] I Przemysl was King of Bohemia from 1230 to 1253.

3. The Teutonic Order of Knights was founded near Acre (also known as Ptolemais and now called Akko) in 1190 (and *not*, as E claims, in 1191 or at the beginning of the 12th century) as a fraternity to serve the sick and became a chivalric military order in 1198. The Order settled in Transylvania but was expelled in 1225 and settled in Prussia in 1230. In 1237 the order was united with the Livonian Order, founded in 1201. The Teutonic and Livonian Knights were defeated at the battle on the frozen surface of Lake Peipus in 1242. This battle scene lies at the heart of E's film.

4. The Brown House in Munich was the original headquarters of the National Socialist German Workers' Party.

5. Livonia covered the area from the Gulf of Riga to Lake Peipus between Riga, now capital of Latvia, and Dorpat, now Tartu in Estonia. The Zhmuds came from an area known as Samogitia in what is now the South-western part of Lithuania between Kaunas, Klaipeda and Šiauliai.

6. In the film *Alexander Nevsky* Tverdila Ivankevich represents the figure of the traitor, saboteur or wrecker, who featured so largely in the propaganda campaigns that accompanied the show trials and the purges of the 1930s.

7. In 1019 Prince Yaroslav I empowered the *veche*, or town assembly, of Novgorod to elect its own prince, mainly as a military commander. But, after 1270 the *veche* elected only a mayor and sovereignty resided in the town itself, which was then styled 'Lord Novgorod the Great' [Gospodin velikii Novgorod].

8. These 'people's volunteers' are also referred to as the 'peasant levy'.

9. In Russian the term for the military formation known in English as a cavalry wedge is '*svin'ya*' or 'pig'.

10. At the Battle of Cannae in 216 BC Hannibal defeated the Romans by trapping their army in a pincer movement. This is regarded as the first time that the tactic had been used.

11. See the postscript to the film, cited in 'My Subject is Patriotism', *ESW 3*, p. 120.

Notes to 1940

1. Translated from the minutes of a speech delivered by E at the Creative Conference on Problems of Historical and Historical-Revolutionary Film in 1940 (TsGALI 1923/1/1241), printed in *IP 5*, pp. 110–28. E wrote an article based on his speech: 'Sovetskii istoricheskii fil'm' [Soviet Historical Film], *Pravda*, 8 February 1940.

2. This film was directed by Olga I. Preobrazhenskaya (1881–1971) and Ivan K. Pravov (1899–1971) and released on 19 September 1939. Unusually for a film of that time, it received very mixed reviews: see, for instance, *Pravda*, 4, 7 and 17 September 1939; *Kino*, 5, 11 and 17 September; *Literaturnaya gazeta*, 20 September 1939.

3. *Lenin in 1918* [*Lenin v 1918 godu*, 1939; awarded the Stalin Prize, 1941], directed by Mikhail I. Romm (1901–71).

4. Reference to Dom kino [Cinema House], a centre for those involved in all aspects of cinema opened in Moscow in 1934. Similar establishments were opened in the other large cities of the USSR. They provided facilities such as conference rooms and viewing theatres, libraries and restaurants. Major films were previewed and discussed at Dom kino before being released.

5. William Shakespeare was born, and Michelangelo died, in 1564. Ivan the Terrible died however in 1584 when Shakespeare would have been twenty, and not thirty as E claims here. Giordano Bruno (1548–1600), a Dominican friar who came to favour the astronomical views of Copernicus, was burnt at the stake in 1600: *Twelfth Night* was written between 1599 and 1601 and first performed in 1601, while *Hamlet* was probably written in 1601–2 and probably first performed in 1602. *Lear* was written in 1605–6

and first performed on 6 December 1606 and *Macbeth* was written at the same time and first performed in 1611. Boris Godunov died in 1605.

The Three Musketeers, in the eponymous novel by the French writer, Alexandre Dumas (1802–70), were swashbuckling heroes from the France of the early seventeenth century.

Ivan Susanin (d. 1613) was a hero of the early seventeenth-century Russian war of liberation against the Poles who sacrificed his life to save that of the newly elected Tsar Mikhail Fyodorovich Romanov in 1613. His story provided the subject for the opera *A Life for the Tsar* by Mikhail I. Glinka (1804–57).

6. Johann Wolfgang von Goethe (1749–1832), German poet and dramatist. Alexander S. Griboyedov (1794–1829), Russian dramatist, founding father of Russian stage realism and therefore essentially a more 'modern' figure than Goethe.

7. The actual title of Goldschmidt's book is *Ascaris. Eine Einführung in die Wissenschaft vom Leben für jedermann* [Thread-Worm. An Introduction to the Science of Life for Everyman]. See *ESW 4*, pp. 611–13.

8. *Viva Villa!* [USA, 1934] was directed by Jack Conway for MGM and starred Wallace Beery as Villa.

9. Francisco 'Pancho' Villa (1878–1923) was a Mexican bandit and general, who in 1910 supported Madero against the dictator Porfirio Díaz (1830–1915), played a leading part in the ensuing Mexican Civil War and was assassinated in 1923. Emiliano Zapata (1883–1918), leader of the left wing of the revolutionary peasantry during the Mexican Civil War. His 'Plan de Ayala' proposed radical agrarian reform akin to later Soviet policies. He was known variously as the apostle of agrarian reform and, because of his brutality, as the Attila of the south. He was assassinated in 1919.

10. Díaz (see previous note) made the mistake of telling a journalist in 1908 that he personally favoured democracy for Mexico. Francisco Indalesio Madero (1873–1913), a millionaire ranch-owner, took him at his word and stood against him in the 1910 presidential election. Madero's imprisonment on the eve of the election led to widespread popular resentment, the resignation of Díaz in 1911 and seven years of revolution and civil war. Madero, a liberal, became president until his assassination two years later.

11. Possibly a paraphrase of the remark by the English historian E. A. Freeman (1823–92) that 'History is past politics, and politics is present history.'

12. *A Great Citizen* [*Velikii grazhdanin*] was directed by Fridrikh M. Ermler (1898–1967) for Lenfilm and released in February 1938. It was based on the life of Sergei M. Kirov (1886–1934), the Leningrad Party leader assassinated, probably on the orders of Stalin, in December 1934.

13. Buskins were high thick-soled boots worn in ancient times by tragic actors. The dressing-gown and night-cap are used here by E to represent the mundane and the everyday as in the Pushkin quotation below.

14. Samson was the executioner at the time of the French Revolution, cited by Pushkin as one example of the phenomenon of horror stories popular in France at the time.

15. A. S. Pushkin, 'O zapisakh Samsona' [On Samson's Notes], first published in *Literaturnaya gazeta*, 1830, no. 5; reprinted in *Polnoe sobranie sochinenii* [Complete Collected Works], vol. 7 (Moscow: 1964), p. 104.

16. E is here referring to the period of the Weimar Republic in Germany from 1918 until Hitler's accession in 1933. *Bismarck* was a relatively straightforward biographical documentary film about the German Chancellor, released in 1926. *Fridericus Rex*, which was based on the life of Frederick the Great, was unashamed propaganda for the restoration of the monarchy: it was directed for UFA by Arsen von Cserépy and released in 1922.

17. Charles Stewart Parnell (1846–91), leader of the Irish Home Rule movement who used parliamentary obstruction and encouraged the 'boycotting' of unpopular landlords to further his cause and eventually won over Gladstone to Home Rule. Parnell was cited in 1890 in the O'Sheas' divorce case and this brought about his political downfall and hastened his premature death.

18. Thomas Carlyle (1795–1881), Scottish historian and man of letters, who believed in the importance of the individual in history. He saw Cromwell as the greatest English

example of the heroic ideal and in 1845 edited *Oliver Cromwell's Letters and Speeches. With Elucidations.*

19. T. Carlyle, *Carlyle's Cromwell, Abridged and Newly Edited* (London, 1905), p. 368.

20. Because of his Calvinistic upbringing, Carlyle tended to place greater emphasis on the role and responsibility of the individual in history than subsequent generations of historians have done.

21. *Chapayev* [1934] was directed by the Vasiliev 'brothers', Sergei D. (1900–59) and Georgi N. (1899–1946), see *ESW 1*, pp. 299–300.

22. *Lenin in October* [*Lenin v oktyabre*, 1937], directed by Mikhail Romm (see 1940, n. 3).

23. The project for a film about the Civil War under the title *Perekop* dates from the spring of 1939, between *Alexander Nevsky* and the project for *Fergana Canal*. Mikhail V. Frunze (1885–1925) led the Red Army forces in the decisive battle at Perekop in the Crimea during the Civil War in 1920.

24. The references are to Pushkin's *Boris Godunov*, written in 1825 but not performed until 1870. 'I have attained the greatest power' are the opening words of Boris's monologue in Scene 7 in which he laments the loneliness and unhappiness of high office. 'The people is silent' [Narod bezmolvstvuyet] is the final stage direction of the play: some translators have chosen to render the direction as 'The people are speechless'.

25. *Peter the First* [*Petr Pervyi*] was directed in two parts by Vladimir M. Petrov (1896–1966) for Lenfilm: Part One was released on 31 August 1937 and Part Two on 7 March 1939.

26. *Minin and Pozharsky* [*Minin i Pozharskii*, 1939] was directed by Pudovkin (see 1928, n. 5) and Mikhail I. Doller (1889–1952) and is based on the tale of the prince and the peasant who united to defend Russia against the marauding Poles. Kuzma Minin (d. 1616), a butcher from Nizhny Novgorod, and Prince Dmitri M. Pozharsky (1578–1642) were joint leaders of the Russian resistance to the Polish and Swedish invasion.

27. *The Mother* [*Mat'*] was directed by Pudovkin in 1926.

28. *Juarez* [USA, 1939] was directed by William Dieterle (1893–1972).

29. The actual title of this film was *The Life of Emile Zola* [USA, 1937] and it was also directed by Dieterle. Both this film and *Juarez* were part of a series of biopics for Warners and starred Paul Muni (1895–1967) in the title roles.

30. According to the editors of the Russian edition of E's works, this is a reference to a film by James Cruze (1884–1942); it therefore seems probable that it is *Sutter's Gold* [USA, 1936], a film project that had originally been assigned to E.

31. *The Battleship Potemkin* was in fact originally conceived as one part of an epic film *The Year 1905*.

32. I.e. the 'Maxim trilogy': *The Youth of Maxim* [*Yunost' Maksima*, 1934], *The Return of Maxim* [*Vozvrashchenie Maksima*, 1937] and *The Vyborg Side* [*Vyborgskaya storona*, 1938], directed by Kozintsev and Trauberg (see 1923, n. 16).

33. In the original treatment of the plot the film was to have ended with Alexander Nevsky paying tribute to the Tatar Khan.

34. Sokolniki is a north–eastern suburb of Moscow with a large pleasure park, including an ice-rink.

35. Ilya Ye. Repin (1844–1930), Russian painter associated with the Wanderers, who organised travelling exhibitions of their Realist paintings in an attempt to broaden the appeal of art.

36. Nicolas Poussin (1594–1665), French landscape painter.

37. F. Engels, 'Wanderings in Lombardy', written in the spring of 1841 and published in *Athenäum*, no. 48, 4 December 1841. This translation is from K. Marx and F. Engels, *Collected Works. Vol. 2. Friedrich Engels: 1838–42* (Moscow and London: 1975), p. 173.

38. The words 'spirit of nature' are in English in Engels' original German. The spirit of nature, represented by the pantheistic figure of Pan, appears in Shelley's works, particularly in *Queen Mab*.

39. The Drachenfels, near Königswinter, and the Rochusberg, near Bingen, were two beauty spots famed in the 19th century for their spectacular views across the Rhine

Valley. See K. Baedeker, *The Rhine from Rotterdam to Constance* (10th edn, Leipzig, 1886), pp. 81–2 and 120.

40. F. Engels, 'Landscapes', was first published in *Telegraph für Deutschland*, no. 122, July 1840. This translation is from Marx and Engels, *Collected Works. Vol. 2*, pp. 95–6.

41 The Dordrecht Synod of 1618–19 condemned the nonconformist sectarian views of the Arminians and reasserted strict Calvinist dogma.

42. Marx and Engels, *Collected Works. Vol. 2*, p. 97.

43. Nikolai K. Roerich (1874–1947), Russian painter, graphic artist and set designer, who worked with Sergei P. Diaghilev (1872–1929) for the Ballets Russes. Roerich was inspired by Russian folk motifs and designed the sets for Diaghilev's productions of *The Polovtsian Dances*, based on the opera *Prince Igor* by Alexander P. Borodin (1833–87), in 1909 and for the first performance of *The Rite of Spring* by Igor F. Stravinsky (1882–1971) in 1913. Valentin A. Serov (1865–1911), Russian painter and member of the Wanderers group (see 1940, n. 35).

44. Vasili I. Surikov (1848–1916), Russian painter also associated with the Wanderers.

45. In May 1939 E drafted a project for a film about the proposed Fergana Canal irrigation scheme in Uzbekistan, to be called *The Great Fergana Canal* [*Bolshoi Ferganskii kanal*]. The project developed into a proposal for a trilogy, for which the script, written in collaboration with Pyotr A. Pavlenko (1899–1951) – who had also worked on the script for *Alexander Nevsky*, was completed by August. E spent the period from mid–August to the end of October shooting test takes in Uzbekistan. On 26 July 1939 he wrote to Prokofiev, asking him to compose the score for the film and enclosing a libretto. In his covering letter E explained that the main theme of the film was the struggle between sand and water, with victory for water being assured only by man's intervention.

46. Vincent Van Gogh (1853–90), Dutch painter, whose purest and most transparent paintings were in fact done after he had left the Netherlands and moved to the South of France.

47. 'Quattrocento': Italian for the 15th century.

48. *The Volochayev Days* [*Volochayevskie dni*, 1937] was directed by the Vasiliev 'brothers'; see 1940, n. 21. *Aerograd* [1935], set in the Soviet Far East, was directed for Mosfilm by Dovzhenko (see 1928, n. 8).

49. *Engineer Kochin's Mistake* [*Oshibka inzhenera Kochina*] was directed for Mosfilm by Alexander V. Macheret (b. 1896) and released in December 1939.

50. See *ESW 4*, pp. 751–71.

51. Jacques Callot (1592/3–1635), French etcher whose masterpiece, completed in 1633, was entitled '*Les grands misères de la guerre*' [The Great Miseries of War]. See *ESW 4*, p. 542.

52. *Peter the First*: see 1940 n. 25.

53. See *ESW 2*, especially pp. 209–23 and 316–21.

Notes to 1947

1. This account of the meeting on the night of 25 February 1947 was taken down immediately afterwards by E and Nikolai K. Cherkasov (1903–66, who had played the title roles in both *Alexander Nevsky* and *Ivan the Terrible*) and first published under the general heading 'Groznye teni 1947 goda' [The Terrible Shadows of 1947] in *Moskovskie Novosti*, 7 August 1988, pp. 8–9, from which this translation has been made.

2. Alexander N. Poskrebyshev (1891–1965) was Stalin's principal secretary until his arrest in 1952.

3. Vyacheslav M. Molotov (né Skryabin, 1890–1986), an Old Bolshevik and one of Stalin's closest advisers; Chairman of the Council of People's Commissars 1930–40; Commissar (from 1946 Minister) for Foreign Affairs 1939–49, 1953–6.

   Andrei A. Zhdanov (1896–1948), also an Old Bolshevik and close adviser to Stalin; Secretary of the Party Central Committee 1934–48, from 1944 in charge of ideological affairs, pursuing a hard–line cultural policy and dealing especially severely with any

205

signs of Western influence in the immediate post-War years, as is amply demonstrated by the tone of this document.

4. The Time of Troubles [*smutnoe vremya*] is the term used to describe the period of confusion after the death of Ivan the Terrible in 1584 and before the first Romanov, Mikhail Fyodorovich, ascended the throne in 1613, when Russia was dominated by feudal clans known as the boyars, whose power both Ivan the Terrible and, in his turn, Peter the Great, set out to destroy.

5. Demyan Bedny (pseudonym of Yefim A. Pridvorov, 1883–1945) wrote the libretto for an opera *The Knights* [*Bogatyri*], which was heavily criticised after its first performance in 1936.

6. See 1940, n. 26.

7. The part of Prince Andrei Kurbsky, who betrayed Ivan after losing his favour, was played by Mikhail M. Nazvanov (1914–64) and that of Vladimir Staritsky, Ivan's cousin, by Pavel P. Kadochnikov (1915–88), who had played his first screen role at the age of twenty.

8. Ivan G. Bolshakov (1902–80) was appointed chairman of the Committee for Cinema Affairs in 1939 and became the first Minister for Cinema in 1946.

9. Lyudmila V. Tselikovskaya (b. 1919) played the part of Ivan's wife, the Tsarina Anastasia Romanovna. She had been trained at the Shchukin Theatre Institute in Moscow and had worked in the Vakhtangov Theatre there from 1941. Stalin's remark that she was a ballerina is not therefore to be taken literally.

10. Mikhail I. Zharov (1899–1981) played the part of Malyuta Skuratov in the film after a long and distinguished film acting career in the 1920s and 1930s. He did not make another film until the 1960s.

11. I.e. 1.10 a.m. the following morning, 26 February 1947.

12. These extracts come from lectures delivered to the Faculty of Direction at VGIK on 12, 18 and 19 March 1947, kept in typewritten form in TsGALI 1923/2 and first published in *IP 3*, pp. 591–610.

13. This lavish production of *Masquerade* [*Maskerad*] by Mikhail Yu. Lermontov (1814–41), with music by Alexander Glazunov (1865–1936) was directed by Meyerhold (see 1923, n. 4) and had its première on 25 February 1917 in the midst of the February revolution.

14. Meyerhold directed Dumas' play at his own theatre in March 1934, with I. I. Leistikov as designer.

15. See *ESW 4*, pp. 264–70.

16. E is here referring to eurhythmics, developed by Emile Jaques-Dalcroze (1865–1950).

17. See *ESW 1*, pp. 183–94.

18. Walt Disney (1901–66), leading American cartoon film-maker, inventor of such characters as Mickey Mouse and Donald Duck. See J. Leyda (ed.), *Eisenstein on Disney* (Calcutta, 1986).

19. E was searching for a common denominator for audio-visual counterpoint in the later 1920s: see *ESW 1*, pp. 115–22, and above, pp. 82–92 and 115.

20. There is a gap in the manuscript at this point.

21. Ditto.

22. See above, 1923, n. 21.

23. Esfir V. Tobak (b. 1908) was assistant editor on *Bezhin Meadow*, *Alexander Nevsky* and *Ivan the Terrible*. Formalism began as an aesthetic movement in the 1920s but became during the purges of the 1930s an all-purpose term of abuse for artistic experimentation that allegedly represented 'art for art's sake'.

24. This 'opportunity arose' because of the Agfacolor film stock removed as war booty from German film studios and laboratories by the Red Army in 1945.

25. See 'The Incarnation of Myth', *ESW 3*, pp. 142–69.

26. E is here referring to the production at the Maly Theatre in 1944 of the play *Ivan the Terrible* by Alexei N. Tolstoi (1882–1945): see *ESW 4*, pp. 681–9 and 870–1.

27. Theophanes [Feofan] the Greek (*c.* 1330–*c.* 1415), whose origins were in Byzantium, was one of the leading icon painters in mediaeval Russia.

28. Opera, first performed in 1904, composed by Nikolai Rimsky-Korsakov (1844–1908).

29. Cf. the last section of 'Vertical Montage', *ESW 2*, pp. 371–99.

30. E is referring to the score by Edmund Meisel (1874–1930), composed for the German release of *October*. See *ESW 1*, p. 131.

31. *ESW 2*, pp. 371–99.

32. *The Little Red Devils* [*Krasnye d"yavolyata*, 1923], directed for the Georgian film studio by Ivan N. Perestiani (1870–1959), is generally seen as the starting point for the Civil War genre in Soviet cinema. For *A Great Citizen*, see 1940, n. 12.

33. For the link between movement and music see 'How I Learned to Draw (A Chapter about My Dancing Lessons)', *ESW 4*, pp. 567–91.

34. The painting by Alexander A. Ivanov (1806–58) is now in the Tretyakov Gallery, Moscow. See *ESW 2*, pp. 103, 155, 328 and especially 388, where E makes substantially the same point as he is making here.

35. This 1887 painting by Surikov (see 1940, n. 44) also hangs in the Tretyakov. See *ESW 2*, pp. 99–103.

36. See above, pp. 124–33.

37. E's memory is at fault – there were fourteen shots in the analysis: see above, p. 133.

38. In addition to a film version of *Boris Godunov*, planned in 1940, E worked on a projected film biography of Pushkin under the title *A Poet's Love (Pushkin)* between 1940 and 1944: cf. *ESW 4*, pp. 712–24, and see W. Sudendorf, *Sergej M. Eisenstein. Materialien zu Leben und Werk* (Munich, 1975), pp. 230–1.

39. Formerly Khlynov and latterly Kirov, Vyatka, as it was known between 1780 and 1934, became a railway and industrial centre but remained famous for its toys, especially those made of wood.

40. Vladimir V. Lebedev (1891–1967), St Petersburg painter, graphic artist and illustrator, best known for his illustrations for the works of Samuil Ya. Marshak (1887–1964).

41. 'Barcarolle' describes the rhythm of a Venetian boat song, ostensibly imitating the motion of a gondola. This rhythm was used most famously by Jacques Offenbach (1819–80) in his opera *The Tales of Hoffmann* [*Les Contes d'Hoffmann*], which Disney used for the soundtrack of his 'Silly Symphony', *Birds of a Feather* [USA, 1931], to which E is here referring.

Index

This Index covers the Introduction and the Documents but not the endnotes. Eisenstein is referred to as E. Film titles are followed by the name of the director.

actor, in cinema, 3, 6, 66, 135; model actor (*naturshchik*), 3, 6, 14, 43, 50–1
Admiral Nakhimov (Pudovkin), 162
Aerograd (Dovzhenko), 155
Alexander Nevsky (E film), 17, 24–5, 140–5, 150–2, 155, 157, 174, 180–1; 'battle on the ice', 143–4, 155–8; tale of the vixen and the hare, 158–9
Alexandrov, Grigori V., 10–11, 18, 20, 73, 80–1
American Tragedy, An (E film project), 19–20
Andrei Kozhukhov (Protazanov), 40
Arbuckle, Roscoe 'Fatty', 50
Arsenal, The (Dovzhenko), 107
Atasheva, Pera, 21
attraction, 4–5, 8, 29–52, 65; definition of, 4, 30, 35–6

Babel, Isaak E., 23
Balázs, Béla, 8–9, 67–72
Balzac, Honoré de, 84
Bambi (Disney), 171, 185
Barnet, Boris V., 15, 23
Battleship Potemkin, The, 1, 5, 7–9, 17–18, 24–5, 60–6, 68, 74, 77–8, 103, 118–20, 128–31, 133–5, 147–8, 151, 157; Odessa steps sequence, 62, 68–71, 100, 102, 117, 128, 151, 183
Bay of Death, The (Room), 107
Bedny, Demyan, 161
Beethoven, Ludwig van, 113
Belenson, Alexander, 69
Bely, Andrei, 126
Beyond the Stars (E memoirs), 26
Bezhin Meadow (E film project), 21, 23–5, 134–9
biomechanics, *see* Meyerhold
Birman, Serafima G., 26, 167–86
Birth of a Nation, The (Griffith), 72

Bode, Rudolph, 46, 52
Boris Godunov (Pushkin play), 150
Broken Blossoms (Griffith), 74

Callot, Jacques, 159
cameraman, role in cinema, 67–72
Can You Hear Me, Moscow? (E stage production), 36n., 45, 64
Capital (E film project), 11, 16, 79
Carlyle, Thomas, 149
Chapayev (Vasilievs), 21, 149, 151–2, 158
Chaplin, Charles, 3, 4, 30, 37
Cherkasov, Nikolai P., 26–7, 160–6
Chiaureli, Mikhail E., 22
Cine-Eyes, *see* Vertov, Dziga
Civil War, and E's career, 2; on film, 149–50; *see also* *Chapayev, Little Red Devils, The*
collision, *see* conflict
colour, 97, 167–86
common denominator, for sound and image, 12–14, 88–9, 97–8, 111–23, 167–86
conference, March 1928, *see* Party; January 1935, 22
conflict, as essence of art, 88–9, 93–123; *see also* counterpoint
counterpoint, 11–12, 80–1, 89, 97–9

Daumier, Honoré, 2, 84, 97
Debussy, Claude, 112–13, 115
Delluc, Louis, 51n.
dialectic, 6, 10–12, 14–15, 17, 54, 88, 93–110, 121–2
Diplomatic Bag, The (Dovzhenko), 75
Direction (E book project), 128
Disney, Walt, 171, 184–6
Dovzhenko, Alexander V., 22, 75, 92, 107, 126–7
Duchenne, G.-B., 45–6

Eccentrism, *see* FEKS
Ehrenburg, Ilya G., 67
Einstein, Albert, 114–15
Eleventh Year, The (Vertov), 75, 77, 116
End of St Petersburg, The (Pudovkin), 75, 106, 116–17
Engels, Friedrich, 153–4
Engineer Kochin's Mistake (Macheret), 156
Ermler, Friedrich M., 22–3, 148, 151, 187
Extraordinary Adventures of Mr West in the Land of the Bolsheviks, The (Kuleshov), 37

Fairbanks, Douglas, Sr, 7
Fall of the House of Usher, The (Epstein), 92
Fantasia (Disney), 171
Faust (Murnau), 66
FEKS (Factory of the Eccentric Actor), 3, 4, 55; *see also* Kozintsev; Trauberg
film institute (GIK, GTK, VGIK), 20, 22–3, 167–86
'films without film': *see* Kuleshov
form, and content, 6, 53, 93–110
Formalism, 19, 23, 53, 125, 175
Forty-Seven Samurai, The (Kabuki play), 91
Freund, Karl, 67n., 68

Gas Masks (E stage production), 4, 49, 64
General Line, The, 9, 16–19, 21, 24, 66, 79, 111–15, 119, 121
GIK, *see* film institute
Glumov's Diary (E short film), 3, 33
Goethe, Johann W., von, 95, 146
Gogh, Vincent van, 155
Gogol, Nikolai V., 126–7, 132
Gorky, Maxim, 124, 132
Great Citizen, A (Ermler), 148, 151, 182

Griffith, David Wark, 37, 40, 72
Grosz, George, 7, 30
GTK, *see* film institute

Happy Canary, The (Kuleshov), 87
happy endings, 63, 65
historical films, 145–60
homosexuality, and E, 19, 21–2

intellectual cinema, 10–11, 14, 16–17, 27, 93–110, 122–3
Intolerance (Griffith), 37
Ivan (Dovzhenko), 126–7
Ivan the Terrible (E film), 25–7, 160–86
Ivanov, Alexander A., 182–3
Ivanovsky, Alexander V., 37–8, 40

Japan, graphic art, 2, 84–6, 89–90; Kabuki theatre, 12, 14, 17, 86, 91–2, 111–23; poetry, 83–4; script (ideograms), 12–13, 82–92, 95–6
Jewishness, and E, 19, 26
Juarez (Dieterle), 151

Khersonsky, Khrisanf N., 56
Kino-Eyes, *see* Vertov, Dziga
Klages, Ludwig, 47, 51n., 94
Kozintsev, Grigori M., 3, 22
Kuleshov, Lev V., 3, 6, 13–16, 22–3, 37, 52, 87, 95, 117
Kurth, Julius, 85

LEF (Left Front of Arts), 64
Léger, Fernand, 67, 96
Lenin, Vladimir I., 6, 22, 110, 134
Lenin in 1918 (Romm), 145–6, 151
Lenin in October (Romm), 149, 151
Life of Emile Zola, The (Dieterle), 151
Little Red Devils, The (Perestiani), 182
Living Corpse, The (Otsep), 106
Lloyd, Harold, 62
Luria, Alexander R., 85

Malevich, Kazimir S., 120
Man with the Movie Camera, The (Vertov), 92
'Maxim trilogy' (Kozintsev & Trauberg), 151
Mayakovsky, Vladimir V., 27, 64, 132

Meisel, Edmund, 7–8
Metropolis (Lang), 66, 67n.
Mexican, The (E stage production), 3, 29
Mexico, 2, 19, 147, 156
Meyerhold, Vsevolod E., 3, 4, 14, 24, 64, 169–70
Mickey Mouse, 122, 185
Milton, John, *Paradise Lost*, 157
Minin and Pozharsky (Pudovkin), 150, 152, 155
Molotov, Vyacheslav M., 27, 160–6
montage, 3–18, 20, 27, 29–53, 62, 65, 70, 80–134, 167–86; metric, 17, 116–17, 120, 170; rhythmic, 17, 117, 120; overtonal, 17, 112–15, 120, 123; tonal, 17, 117–20; dominants, 111–23; *see also* shot
Moskvin, Andrei N., 26
Mother, The (Pudovkin), 75, 151
music, and cinema, 98–9, 167–86

Nathan the Wise (Lessing play), 41
non-played film, 10–13, 73–9; *see also* Vertov, Dziga

October (E film), 8–10, 12–13, 19, 73–9, 101–3, 106–10, 116, 128, 134, 149, 175, 181; cycle battalions, 106; images of gods, 16, 101–3, 109–10, 123; Kerensky, 107–8; Kornilov, 107, 110
Old and the New, The, see General Line, The
Oliver Twist (Dickens novel), 37
Otsep, Fyodor A., 106

Palace and the Fortress, The (Ivanovsky), 37–8, 40
Parnell, Charles Stewart, 148
Party, Conference on Cinema, March 1928, 10
Pavlenko, Pyotr A., 24
Peter the First (Petrov), 150–1, 159
photogeny, *see* Delluc, Louis
Picabia, Francis, 67
Pletnyov, Valerian F., 29, 55
plot, 20, 41–2, 55, 79, 132
Poussin, Nicholas, 152
Prokofiev, Sergei S., 17, 25–6, 167–86
Proletkult, 2–3, 5, 29, 31, 43, 53, 64

Protazanov, Yakov A., 22, 40
Pudovkin, Vsevolod I., 11, 15–16, 22, 75, 80–1, 87–8, 95, 106, 117, 162
Pushkin, Alexander S., 132, 148, 156–7, 159, 183

Que viva México! (E film project), 19

Rabelais, François, 126–7
Repin, Ilya Ye., 152, 164
Rin-Tin-Tin, 19
Rittau, Günther, 68
Rodchenko, Alexander M., 30
Roerich, Nikolai K., 154
Room, Abram M., 21, 107

Savchenko, Igor A., 23
Scriabin, Alexander N., 112–13, 115, 116
script, 5–6, 41, 151
Serov, Valentin A., 154
Shakespeare, William, 146, 156
Sharaku, Toshushai, 84–6, 97
Shchors (Dovzhenko), 149–51, 158
Shklovsky, Viktor B., 13
shot, relationship to montage sequence, 8, 12–16, 44–5, 69–72, 82–123
Shub, Esfir I., 23, 107
Shumyatsky, Boris Z., 19–20, 22–5
Sixth Part of the World, A (Vertov), 75, 77
slow motion, 88, 91–2
Smyshlyayev, Valentin S., 29
social command, 54
Socialist Realism, 22
sound, 11–12, 17, 80–1, 97–8, 115
Stalin, Joseph V., and E, 14–15, 134, 144, 160–6; Stalin Prize for E, 25–6
Stanislavsky, Konstantin S., 24, 64–5
Station Master, The (Zhelyabuzhsky & Moskvin), 61
Stepan Khalturin (Ivanovsky), 40
Stepan Razin (Preobrazhenskaya & Pravov), 145
Storm over Asia (Pudovkin), 117
Strike, The (E film), 5–8, 10, 17, 38–40, 42, 50, 53–9, 61–2, 65, 69, 78, 149; hosing sequence, 62; slaughter sequence, 38–9, 42, 105–6

210

Suprematism, 96
Surikov, Vasili I., 154, 182–3
Sutter's Gold (E film project),
  19, 151

Tairov, Alexander Ya., 64
Tales of Hoffmann, The
  (Offenbach operetta),
  barcarolle, 185
Tarkovsky, Andrey, 1, 4
Ten Days that Shook the World,
  see *October*
theatre, and cinema, 3–6, 9, 11,
  15–16, 29–52, 64–6, 80–1
Thief of Bagdad (Walsh), 6, 92
Tisse, Edmund K., 18, 26, 61,
  68, 73

Toulouse-Lautrec, Henri de, 97
Towards the Dictatorship
  (projected film series), 53,
  55
Trauberg, Leonid Z., 22–3
Tretyakov, Sergei M., 4, 63

Variété (Dupont), 67n., 77
Vasiliev 'brothers', 22–3
Vertov, Dziga, 5, 7, 8, 11, 14,
  21–2, 35–7, 41, 56, 57n.,
  58n., 59, 75, 116
VGIK, *see* film institute
Vishnevsky, Vsevolod V., 24
Viva Villa! (Conway), 147
Volochayev Days, The
  (Vasilievs), 155

Walküre, Die (E staging), 26,
  177–8
War and Peace (Tolstoy novel),
  88, 157–8
We, the Russian People (E film
  project), 24
Wise Man, The (E stage
  production), 3–4, 29–34, 64

Yutkevich, Sergei I., 3, 22

zaum, 74
Zharov, Mikhail I., 164
Zhdanov, Andrei A., 27, 160–6
Zola, Emile, 2, 127–8; *see also*
  Life of Emile Zola, The
Zvenigora (Dovzhenko), 75, 92